Play by Play

PHOENIX AND BUILDING THE HERBERGER THEATER

Play by Play

PHOENIX AND BUILDING THE HERBERGER THEATER

ELIZABETH B. MURFEE
JACK L. AUGUST JR.

Foreword by Terry Goddard

Texas Christian University Press
Fort Worth

Library of Congress Cataloging-in-Publication Data

Murfee, Elizabeth
Play by play: Phoenix and building the Herberger Theater / Elizabeth B. Murfee and Jack L. August Jr.—1st ed.
p. cm.
Includes bibliographical references and index.
ISBN 978-0-87565-410-2 (cloth : alk. paper)
1. Herberger Theater Center (Phoenix, Ariz.)—History. I. August, Jack L. II. Title.
PN1588.P55M75 2010
792.09791'73—dc22
2009033450

TCU Press
P.O. Box 298300
Fort Worth, Texas 76129
817.257.7822
http://www.prs.tcu.edu

To order books: 800.826.8911

Front and back cover images courtesy of Bob Rink Photography

Design: fusion29, Fort Worth, Texas

In Memory of Bob and Kax Herberger

...to prevent the traces of human events from being erased by time, and to preserve the fame of important and remarkable achievements.

HERODOTUS, *The Histories*

Contents

Acknowledgments

My roster of gratitude starts with my publisher, Texas Christian University Press, and the special staff they engaged to bring this book to the public. Everyone at the press demonstrated an uncommonly high degree of commitment and care in producing a top-notch publication, regardless of the tremendous economic pressures faced by their industry today. Excellence matters as much to them as it does to me. My thanks go to June Koelker, interim director; Judy Alter, former director; Melinda Esco, production manager; Susan Petty, editor; Louise Slominsky, researcher, copy editor, and proofreader; Bill Brammer, text and cover designer; and Elisabeth Wolfe, indexer.

I also thank Jack August Jr., my coauthor, who provided a level of scholarship and historical analysis that could not have been achieved without his invaluable involvement. In addition, I extend my thanks to Arizonans for Cultural Development who received the grant from a fund at the Arizona Community Foundation to enable me to start my research quite a few years ago—far more many years than I would like to admit!

To the fifty individuals I interviewed who gave unstintingly of their time, recalling detail after detail of their experience with this project, my sincere thanks. Quite a few of them opened their personal files, diaries, and scrapbooks to me, including a most gracious Kax Herberger. Her reminiscences and meticulous scrapbooks revealed that the Herberger Theater was no ordinary undertaking for Kax and her family, but something they held near and dear to their hearts. Bob Herberger proudly showed me the gold shovel given to him at the groundbreaking and insisted that I hold it in my hands. Although each person I interviewed gave me valuable information and insights, one interview stands out as a piece of theater in itself, that of Everett King's. A former actor turned businessman, King's interview was more like performance art, fueled by his phenomenal passion for theater. Sometimes I replay it just to enjoy his mesmerizing personality.

My thanks also to my personal editor, Tuckie Begley, who taught me the value of Anglo-Saxon words, to see the miracle that writing can be, and to respect the validity of my vision. Her belief in me was an important reason that I completed this book.

Thanks also go to my sister, Faye Hubele, who opened her Paradise Valley home to me, letting it become my own private McDowell Colony, as she took care of my everyday needs and kept almost everyone at bay so that I could focus entirely on the demands of this book.

Although writing takes long days, weeks, months, and years of being alone with the material and the empty page, no writer can do his or her work without the support of a surprisingly large number of people, as is witnessed by the many pages of acknowledgments that accompany most books. Of necessity, it seems the writer's family gives the most support and, in turn, makes the most sacrifices. So, to my son, Keith Murfee-DeConcini, and to my husband, Dino DeConcini, I thank you for understanding why I thought this story was important to tell, why it was worthy of your sacrifice and support, and for reminding me of this when my own dedication would start to flag. From the bottom of my heart, *grazie e baci!*

—Elizabeth B. Murfee

Many thanks to the archival staff of the Arizona Historical Society in Tucson for their professionalism in the context of severe budgetary constraints. They located several remarkable historical images that add grace and elegance to the narrative. Donna Carlotta and the staff at the *Arizona Republic* archives located several indispensible images for this book. Mark Mettes, of the Herberger Theater, also located and provided several outstanding images from the theater's growing collection.

This book was the result of a complex collaboration that included philanthropic organizations, individuals, and the professional editorial team at TCU Press. The encouragement and support of the Arizona Community Foundation, Flinn Foundation, Herberger Theater, Metro Phoenix Partnership for Arts and Culture, Dino DeConcini, Gary and Jeanne Herberger, Richard Mallery, Elizabeth Murfee, and Elizabeth Rosenzweig, along with the input of scholars, artists, and public servants, contributed to the completion of this work. I thank them all.

—Jack L. August Jr.

Foreword

Downtown Phoenix in the early 1980s may not have been the cultural wasteland of America, but someone could easily see it from there. In those days I was part of a small group, desperate for any kind of life after five o'clock, who plotted to enliven a derelict alley between Central Avenue and First Street by promoting a few bars, restaurants, and galleries with a lot of banners and fresh paint. At that moment, Richard Mallery was tackling the same problem with much greater vision and audacity. All that came later to enliven and refresh downtown Phoenix—theaters, museums, sports arenas, bars, restaurants, and galleries—sprang from the inspiration and the example of the Herberger Theater Center.

That the job was difficult goes without saying. There was little consensus then about *where* downtown Phoenix should be, and definitely none that it was a future arts center. That Mallery and his conspirators aspired not just to create an adequate performing arts venue, but one to rank among the finest in the country, is testament to far more than pluck and stamina, but also to an inspiring refusal to accept anything but the best for their city, whatever the obstacles.

The story of the Herberger Theater is a blueprint for how to conceive, design, and build a performing arts center. What was done in Phoenix in the 1980s can be produced in many less forbidding environments using the same formula. From Richard Mallery's original dream, to the opening night curtain, Elizabeth Murfee and Jack August Jr. detail exactly how the job got done. From the strategic use of experts, to unprecedented partnerships with the city and the community to raise the money, to select an architect, and to oversee construction, they follow every step. Mallery and company visited theaters in other major cities to learn what worked and what did not. They brought the arts community to the table at the earliest stages of the design and won their approval.

Perhaps most important, their vision captivated the Herberger family and gained not only an unprecedented private contribution, but engaged that amazing clan in every step. I had the privilege to get to know Bob and Kax and Gary and Jeanne Herberger and to see firsthand their love for Arizona and their willingness to support a host of cultural and social causes. Our state was blessed that the Herbergers, who hailed from Minnesota, discovered Arizona while on vacation in 1947 and liked it so much that they stayed. They were always surprised and a bit mystified when other wealthy citizens were not right there with them in civic commitment, but it never slowed them down.

The founders of the Herberger Theater built a quality performing arts center at a time when Arizona faced its toughest financial challenges to date. The path definitely was not easy or smooth, as the authors show us. When most thought of Phoenix as little more than a place to play golf in the winter, Richard Mallery, Gary Herberger, and company were breaking new ground, not just for a theater, but for their city. They believed that the capital of Arizona should be held to a higher standard. Thankfully, they had the wisdom to insist that a vibrant cultural life for Phoenix should match its phenomenal growth. Like a Colorado River pilot navigating through treacherous rapids, they stayed the course with creativity and courage. Had anyone tried to convince the city council, the Civic Plaza Building Corporation board, or the business leaders of Phoenix at the beginning of this escapade that they were about to embark on the design, construction, and financing of a two-theater complex covering a square block and costing over $20 million, they would have fled in horror. But, like Meredith Wilson's *Music Man,* Richard Mallery had to vary the tune a time or two to fit the audience and circumstances and change the program when needed to keep up momentum, but he never lost sight of his goal—a theater center of the highest quality.

The success of the Herberger Theater is attributable, no doubt, to Mallery's singular creativity, persistence, and fiscal ingenuity, in addition to his gambler's instinct. But the Herberger Theater would never have been possible without a remarkable group of titans who saw Phoenix as far more than what it was and never stopped trying to reach the next level. Unfortunately, many are no longer here to enjoy what they created. This book is, in significant measure, a testament to them. To Edward "Bud" Jacobson, Keith Turley, and A. J. "Jack" Pfister, to Barry Starr, Denny Maus, and Everett King, along with Bob and Kax Herberger, *muchas gracias por las bendigas.*

Today, we hear and read a lot about "creative cities" and the "rise of the creative class." The National Governor's Association recently published a comprehensive guide on how arts and culture can energize a state's economy. Sadly, Arizona still barely receives a mention in that detailed, fascinating guide.

Now that the Herberger Theater has reached its twentieth anniversary, we should definitely celebrate, but this is also a time to take stock of its founders' dreams and set the stage to finish and enlarge the production to benefit all of Arizona. Our state needs more Herbergers and more Richard Mallerys. Who will step forward? It is beyond dispute that, in today's economy, the competitive edge and the creative edge go hand in hand. Arizona is rich in creative and artistic talent. In the spirit of the Herberger Theater, let's nurture that native genius so that we enjoy the benefits for generations!

—Terry Goddard

Prologue

As Gertrude Stein wrote, "...there is no there there."[1] Although she had never visited Phoenix, Arizona, that line was an apt description of this southwestern city in 1980. A sprawling metropolis, the ninth largest in the United States at the time, Phoenix possessed no core; it was a city without a center. One big suburbia, Phoenix thrived on the automobile and on cheap land. Many residents never even ventured downtown, such as it was. Nevertheless, the desert metropolis possessed the heady air of a boomtown that had experienced unprecedented growth since the end of World War II. Comparatively, this urban oasis was affordable like few others. People arrived by the thousands, searching for and finding the good life. Nearly 60 percent of the state's population lived in the "Valley of the Sun," a moniker coined in 1934 by a local ad agency searching for a more enticing name than Salt River Valley.[2]

The name stuck. "You know, next to water, air, food, and sex, Americans want sunshine the most," Eugene Pulliam, the future publisher of the *Arizona Republic,* noted in a front page article in the early 1940s.[3] Its ever-present sun, clouded over by only seven inches of rain a year, became one of the city's strongest attractions, that is, at least once air-conditioning became universally affordable in the 1950s. Phoenix transformed into the most air-conditioned city on earth, thus making it possible to blunt its sweltering desert summers.[4]

During the 1950s, however, Phoenix also witnessed the decline of its central business district, and the city's vitality retreated to the periphery. By the late 1960s, every major department store and dozens of other businesses had abandoned the downtown area. One of the culprits of this decline was the automobile, which provided the city's residents with the means to drive en masse from the city's center to newly developed, air-conditioned suburban malls. By the 1960s Phoenix's physical dimensions encouraged a car culture, especially because political and civic leaders provided next to nothing in the way of public transportation.[5] Even freeways virtually were nonexistent.

Eugene Pulliam playing golf at Paradise Valley Country Club, Scottsdale, Arizona, in 1957. "You know, next to water, air, food and sex, Americans want sunshine the most," he said.
Arizona Republic, January 24, 1957. Used with permission.

The city and its people had been quick to accept the automobile. The first car arrived in the Valley as far back as the summer of 1900, twelve years before Arizona attained statehood.[6] By 1908 Henry Ford's inexpensive Model T became popular in the Valley; by 1913 Phoenix could boast that it had ten automobile dealers and a good number of paved streets in a valley once covered in mesquite thickets and paloverde trees. From 1913 onward, the car was king.[7]

Growth became queen, fabled, as Phoenix outpaced every other city in the country, breaking records every year. The *Saturday Evening Post,* dazzled by the city's economic and demographic explosion, hyped Phoenix in a 1960 article as a place where "new millionaires breed like forced hothouse flowers."[8] Well, maybe. Yet the city arising below hauntingly beautiful mountain peaks—using an irrigation system that followed the design created by the Hohokam Indians (the people who went away) 500 years earlier—was less than the sum of its parts. A heavily individualistic lifestyle predominated, with little more than lip service paid to the old-fashioned, eastern notion of giving back to the community. Phoenix was as low on the philanthropic and cultural totem pole as it was on taxes.

Among residents, there were exceptions, of course, who for the most part were transplants from the Midwest or the East, among them Dwight and Maie Heard who had moved from Chicago to Arizona for health reasons in 1895. The only real jewel in Phoenix's cultural crown stemmed not only from their generosity, but also from their insight into the value of the town's heritage. The Heards donated the land, the building, and their magnificent collection of Indian artifacts to create the Heard Museum, which opened in 1929. They also donated land that Phoenix later would use to construct a modern library, a little theater, and the

Phoenix Art Museum in the late 1950s. It is of little wonder that people hailed Dwight Heard as "Arizona's greatest citizen" and recognized Maie Heard as "the single most generous philanthropist Phoenix has ever known."[9]

During the 1930s, several outstanding artists arrived in Phoenix, Philip Curtis and Lou Davis among them. Frank Lloyd Wright made the Valley his winter abode, and in 1937 he began constructing Taliesin West, a western branch of his architectural school.[10] The performing arts received a boost from Mrs. Archer (Jessie) Linde who, like the Heards, moved to Arizona from Chicago for her health. Drawing upon her strong musical background, she became somewhat of an impresario and worked tirelessly to bring a high-arts culture to Phoenix. It was through her efforts that the likes of Vladimir Horowitz, Jascha Heifetz, Victor Borge, Anna Pavlova, Van Cliburn, Duke Ellington, and Leonard Bernstein graced Valley stages beginning in 1947. Phoenix Union High School usually hosted these stellar performances, but the space was painfully inadequate. There were other embarrassments, too. When Metropolitan Opera singer Marian Anderson arrived for her concert, the city was so segregated that not one hotel would rent her a room. Anderson ended up staying in Jessie Linde's home.[11]

Lewis Ruskin, who also hailed from Chicago, turned his attention and support to the Phoenix Chamber Music Society, of which he and Louise Kerr were cofounders, and to the Phoenix Symphony, becoming the most influential patron of both. Department store magnate G. Robert Herberger and his wife Katherine, who became avid symphony supporters soon after their arrival from Minnesota in 1949, joined Ruskin. Before long, the Herberger name could be found on every arts contributors list.

Most efforts to promote the arts in Phoenix, however, were motivated by the desire to create a positive image for the city, as well as to increase its ability to attract capital investment. The city built the Phoenix Civic Plaza convention center downtown in 1972, which included Symphony Hall in the building plans, thereby finally providing a home for the city's orchestra. Civic and political leaders could now refer to Phoenix Civic Plaza as a civic and *cultural* center and point with pride to the new 2,575-seat concert hall filled with chandeliers and big-city elegance. No one mentioned the acres of empty concrete that surrounded the hall, making it as inviting as a stroll on an airport tarmac. In an unrelenting drive to create a first-class city in the desert Southwest, civic and political leaders appeared oblivious to two essential elements that mark a great city, namely the arts and a vibrant downtown. They just were beginning to understand that cities without a vibrant downtown were lacking in an intangible, but essential quality. In 1980 Phoenix needed to take a closer look at what it had missed and to consider how the arts and a revitalized city center could be mutually reinforcing, even transformative.

1

The Leader

Richard Mallery looked down from the top floor of the Valley National Bank building onto the parking lot at Monroe and Second Streets in downtown Phoenix. He did not see merely an empty block of asphalt just beginning to fill with the cars of early morning arrivals. Instead, he envisioned the barren plot of land dissolving into an inviting square, with an elegant building in the center surrounded by lush desert trees and people rushing inside—not to escape the raw Arizona sun, but to witness what was inside—the performance of a play. He almost could sense the air of excitement, the anticipation.

Mallery was neither an actor nor a stage director, but he was a player. As a senior partner at Snell & Wilmer, the largest and one of the most influential law firms in the American Southwest, Mallery acted on a different stage, but with gestures that could be just as bold, just as riveting. He was not the type of man who sought the limelight.[1] That was not what drove him; it was something more complicated that he kept to himself. Mallery wanted to make things happen, to transform Phoenix into a great city, not just a big city. He knew how to play the game, but he refused to play by the old rules. Mallery wanted to do something new and audacious, even galvanizing. Building a theater for Phoenix seemed to be the perfect expression of his vision, which was why he devoted every moment of his free time to finding a way to build a performing arts theater befitting an emerging desert metropolis and its people.[2]

Mallery frequently lunched on the top floor of the forty-story Valley National Bank building, the tallest building in the entire state, always choosing a table that overlooked this particular plot of vacant land. He relaxed by imagining the land's transformation into a showplace for the performing arts. Indeed, Mallery saw what others did not; he would act deftly in the ensuing years, turning the invisible into the visible and convincing others that it was their own vision, not his.

A view of downtown Phoenix in 1980. By the end of the decade, a new theater would be built on the parking lot to the right of the building with the round top, the Hyatt Regency Hotel.
Herberger Theater Archives. Used with permission.

Mallery almost did not return to Phoenix after completing his law degree at Stanford University in 1963. He found San Francisco appealing and had received a good job offer; but something about the desert city's harsh, yet glorious environment had a hold on him. After revisiting the city where he had spent his teenage years and breathing in the intoxicating scent of the orange blossoms, he knew that he must return to Phoenix and make it his permanent home.

Mallery had lived in Phoenix since high school, when his mother and former opera-singer stepfather (who had retired from the Metropolitan Opera), finally settled down after moving the family to different areas of Florida, then to Hawaii, and then to Houston for a brief six months. Those were hardscrabble years, unlike his first seven years spent in Akron, Ohio, where his father had owned the largest billboard and neon sign company in the state. After his father died, Ohio became a distant memory of a time when it seemed that young Mallery had everything.

Richard Mallery, Snell & Wilmer attorney, at his desk in April 1975. Mallery wanted to make things happen, to transform Phoenix into a great city, not just a big city.
Richard Mallery Papers, Snell & Wilmer, Phoenix, Arizona. Photograph by Markow Photography.

Mallery's many childhood interests included music. He sang, his young voice a beautiful soprano that had been rigorously trained by his stepfather, and he went into show business professionally with his younger sister, Patti. For four years, they performed at Florida resorts and conventions several nights a week. Mallery sang Hawaiian songs, playing the ukulele, while Patti danced. On weekends, he had a radio show and was the lead soloist at major churches in St. Petersburg. He demonstrated a precocious business acumen, too. While in the fourth grade, Mallery started his first business, cleaning up coconuts in peoples' yards, which he then sold to a distributor. Two years later, while still in elementary school, Mallery opened a toy store, which he had purchased from a wholesaler. Later, he had a fishing business, ran a marina, and went shrimping; in apt rehearsal for his future as a deal-making attorney, he fished for sharks.[3]

There was a philosophical and theological side to young Mallery. For several years, he considered the ministry and had served as a youth minister at a Methodist Church in Indiana during his college years, but somehow pastoring seemed too limiting for someone with his ambitions and wide-ranging interests. After completing his undergraduate degree at DePauw University, as well as a Woodrow Wilson Fellowship to Cornell University and a Fulbright Scholarship to Oxford University in England, Mallery obtained a Master's in English Literature from Cornell University and gave serious thought to becoming an English teacher or professor. As with the ministry, however, he found academia too limiting. Mallery finally settled on the law, which he viewed as a type of *applied* ministry, and attended Stanford Law School. After clerking on the Arizona Supreme Court, he joined Snell & Wilmer in 1964 where, among many other influences, he watched and worked closely with Frank Snell, the firm's cofounder and one of the most influential political, legal, and business power brokers in Phoenix.[4]

Richard Mallery as a young boy of eleven years recording his radio show Voice of Hawaii *for a St. Petersburg, Florida, radio station in 1948. Besides singing Hawaiian songs, Mallery sprinkled his Sunday morning patter with Hawaiian phrases delivered with a perfect accent. After the show, Mallery would perform in area churches, singing decidedly different melodies.*
Richard Mallery Papers, Snell & Wilmer, Phoenix, Arizona.

A close-up view of the parking lot that would become the site of the future Herberger Theater in downtown Phoenix. Symphony Hall is seen behind the parking lot; the Hyatt Regency Hotel, with its circular restaurant on top, is to the right.
Phoenix Gazette, October 11, 1985. Photograph by D. Kevin Elliott. Used with permission.

Snell and two other business titans, Eugene Pulliam and Walter Bimson, virtually shaped Phoenix's economic environment from the 1940s through the 1970s. They became known as the "Big Three," and virtually nothing significant happened that did not have their handprints, or at least their imprimatur. Snell had the deepest roots in Arizona, having come to Globe, Arizona, as a young man in 1924 to represent the copper-mining interests of Phelps Dodge. Besides consolidating several utilities around the state into what then became the state's largest utility, Arizona Public Service, Snell became known as Arizona's most facile "rainmaker" and political persuader.[5] Pulliam, an influential Indiana newspaper publisher, had owned the state's largest and most powerful newspapers, the *Arizona Republic* and the *Phoenix Gazette*, since 1946 under the corporate name Phoenix Newspapers, Incorporated.[6] The third member of the so-called Big Three was Walter Bimson, who had left Chicago in 1933 to start what would become Arizona's largest bank, Valley National Bank.[7] For decades, Snell, Pulliam, and Bimson had shepherded the growth and development of Phoenix in ways that they deemed were good for the state, good for business, and, of course, good for themselves.[8]

Frank Snell, cofounder of Snell & Wilmer and a major Phoenix leader during the postwar years.
Arizona Republic, December 7, 1984. Photograph by Earl McCartney. Used with permission.

Walter Bimson, the retired board chair of Valley National Bank, receiving an award from the American Bankers Association for his economic and civic contributions to Arizona. The award, presented at the bankers convention held at the Arizona Biltmore, highlighted his support for the arts.
Arizona Republic, November 11, 1972. Used with permission.

By 1974, however, these three men had grown old. Snell, the youngest of the three, was 75; Pulliam, a staunch conservative, was 85; and Bimson, a close friend of President Franklin Delano Roosevelt, was 82. Clearly, the three leaders must have known it was time to pass the torch to the next generation. They soon would receive the impetus to do just that.

In December 1974 Mallery and his friend, William Shover, who served as director of public affairs for Phoenix Newspapers, met for lunch. They frequently lunched together at the University Club on East Monte Vista Road in downtown Phoenix, where they discussed their bosses, Snell and Pulliam, and pondered their respective futures; however, during this particular luncheon, they decided to take action. Mallery and Shover scheduled a meeting with Pulliam at his home on Palo Christi Road in Paradise Valley; with the brashness of young men who envisioned a bigger role for themselves, they attempted to convince the aging publisher that younger leaders needed to start actively shaping the future of Phoenix.

Phoenix had an image problem, they told Pulliam. Crooked land speculators, such as Ned Warren Sr., coupled with the gangland-type slaying of Ed Lazar, a witness who had been scheduled to appear before a county grand jury, suggested that organized crime honchos viewed Arizona as an area of promise for their nefarious activity. As a way to address this negative situation, Mallery and Shover cited an organization, Goals for Dallas, which consisted of a group of business leaders in that growing city who were committed to developing a positive civic image after the assassination of President John F. Kennedy. Mallery and Shover argued persuasively and convinced not only Pulliam, but also Snell and Bimson, that younger leaders were needed and that their time had arrived.[9]

Mallery and Shover's successful maneuver was aided by the long and trusting relationship that had formed between Mallery and Pulliam. The two had met when Mallery began attending Central Methodist Church during his high school years after becoming disenchanted with the Catholic Church. Over the years, Mallery grew to admire the public service philosophy of John Wesley and, besides becoming a Methodist, he also became a junior minister.[10] He preached throughout Phoenix and devoted time to some of the poorer churches in the southern part of the city. Pulliam noticed the devout youngster at Central Methodist, and he nurtured and encouraged Mallery's desire to become a full-fledged minister.

The publishing magnate and the self-disciplined high school student eventually formed a type of mentor–student bond. In fact, Mallery held Pulliam in such regard that he took the older man's advice to turn down a full scholarship to Harvard. "They will corrupt you at Harvard," Pulliam counseled.[11] Mallery took Pulliam's advice to heart and enrolled at the Methodist-affiliated DePauw University, which had been Pulliam's alma mater. Pulliam had become more than a mentor; he became a father figure to young Mallery.

Based on their long and mutually beneficial history together, and taking into consideration the younger man's increasingly mature counsel, Pulliam accepted the notion of a changing of the guard in Phoenix's civic stewardship. On February 4, 1975, just four months before his death, Pulliam invited a group of men to lunch at the Adobe Room of the Arizona Biltmore. The composition of the group told a revealing story about Phoenix leadership; they were all white males, mainly businessmen and Republican, plus a few religious leaders. Pulliam's letter of invitation opened with, "This is probably one of the most important letters you have ever received because the immediate future of Phoenix may depend on your response to this challenge."[12] Every individual accepted Pulliam's invitation. This elite, self-appointed group became known as the Phoenix 40.[13] Mallery, not surprisingly, emerged as one of its most active and influential members. Several years later, he would turn to this group often in his quest to build a theater for Phoenix.

Mallery remembered the precise moment he had decided to accept the challenge of building the theater.[14] His good friend Dino DeConcini called together a group of influential Phoenix businessmen shortly after DeConcini's appointment as chair of the Arizona Commission on the Arts by Governor Bruce Babbitt in 1979.[15] From a prominent Tucson political family, attorney DeConcini served as chief of staff for Governor Raul Castro from 1975 through 1977, where he became friends with Mallery. After DeConcini lost the race for attorney general of Arizona, Babbitt appointed him to the state arts agency post. As only the second person to lead the fledgling agency, he determined that he would transform it from a mere conduit for funding from the National Endowment for the Arts into a much more comprehensive institution. With his political

Dino DeConcini, attorney and chair of Arizona Commission on the Arts. With his political connections, knowledge of Arizona history and culture, and his access to corporate and community leaders, DeConcini intended to ratchet-up the cultural sophistication of the entire state. *Arizona Republic,* July 26, 1982. Photograph by Charles Krejcsi. Used with permission.

connections, his knowledge of Arizona history and culture, and his access to corporate and community leaders, he intended to ratchet-up the cultural sophistication of the entire state.

In his role as the Arizona chair, DeConcini emulated the administration of Nancy Hanks, the much-beloved chair of the National Endowment for the Arts in Washington, D.C., who headed that newly created independent federal agency from 1969 through 1977.[16] At the endowment, Hanks maintained an informal kitchen cabinet, a brain trust that played a major role in her success.[17] Hanks was only the second person to lead the national arts agency, just as was DeConcini in Arizona with the state arts agency. Indeed, since the creation of the National Endowment for the Arts in 1965, a virtual renaissance in the arts was occurring in many areas of the country. In Arizona, however, the arts remained in the background of public discussion. If not a cultural desert, Arizona, and its capital city of Phoenix, were certainly not a cultural oasis.

DeConcini embarked on his mission to convince the state legislature to increase its minuscule annual appropriation of $60,000 to the Arizona Commission on the Arts. In doing so, he broke the promise that Lewis Ruskin, who served as the first chair of the commission, had made to the legislature in his efforts to convince them to create the state arts agency in the mid-1960s. In a story that had become a bit of Arizona folklore, Ruskin, often dubbed "Mr. Arts" because of his strong personal support, was chosen to make the case for the state arts agency to the state legislature. He went before both state houses, with tin cup in hand, and promised that if they created a state arts agency, it would never come to them for a penny more than administrative money.[18] That was about to change. By the time DeConcini left the Arizona Commission on the Arts in 1985, state support for the arts had become commonplace and, just as critically, funding had increased tenfold to $632,200.[19]

One way that DeConcini succeeded in increasing the funding was to convene 250 Arizona leaders for "The Future of the Arts in Arizona" conference held in October 1980 at the Arizona Biltmore. The meeting spurred the group to pass a resolution calling for the formation of a permanent arts-advocacy organization and to seek increased private and public funding for the arts in Arizona. In February 1981 DeConcini harnessed the momentum spurred by the October conference and created the state's first arts-advocacy organization, called Arizonans for Cultural Development; Sam Campana skillfully led the organization in the ensuing years.[20] During this time, Jeanne Herberger, director of civic and governmental affairs for Diamonds department store (owned by Dayton-Hudson) and a civic activist, came to DeConcini with the idea of establishing annual awards to be given by the governor in recognition of outstanding artists, arts organizations, and arts contributors. DeConcini immediately arranged for Jeanne Herberger to meet with Governor Babbitt to sell her idea, which she did. Thus, the Governor's Arts Awards were established. Held at the Arizona Biltmore, the first gala awards dinner featured nationally known keynote speakers Livingston Biddle, chair of the National Endowment for the Arts, and Ken Dayton, chair of Dayton-Hudson department stores.[21] The Governor's Arts Awards ultimately became coveted and raised the visibility of the arts among state legislators; in addition, the proceeds from the awards dinners provided funding for Arizonans for Cultural Development.[22]

DeConcini, like Hanks at the endowment, selected an informal cabinet to advise him on arts issues. He chose this group of men not only for their interest in the arts, but also because of their community clout. DeConcini called this group together every month for an early morning breakfast. Sitting around the table almost unfailingly, besides Mallery and DeConcini, were attorney Edward "Bud" Jacobson, businessman Keith Turley, banker Don Tostenrud, and publisher Darrow "Duke" Tully.[23]

Jacobson, a partner at Snell & Wilmer, had a long history of civic and cultural activism. Widely respected for his devotion to the arts, particularly to creative photography, his contributions were incalculable to DeConcini. Turley, the long-time president, chief executive officer, and board chair of the state's largest utility, Arizona Public Service, led the Phoenix 40 when DeConcini worked for Governor Raul Castro. Tostenrud, rumored to be Phoenix's highest paid businessman as chief executive officer and board chair of Arizona Bank, was an accomplished photographer in his own right, and his bank was known for its outstanding collection of western paintings. Tully, who had succeeded Pulliam as publisher of the *Arizona Republic* and the *Phoenix Gazette*, contributed substantial energy to the discussions. Tully was, in his own modest assessment, the most powerful man in Arizona.

DeConcini and Turley were the only native Arizonans, although Mallery, a graduate of West Phoenix High School, came close. Community activism and a love of the arts bonded these leaders. DeConcini, a soft-spoken intellectual, knew that seeking the counsel of these individuals would help him achieve his goal of elevating the arts in Arizona. The members of his informal cabinet previously had formed the corps of the Combined Metropolitan Phoenix Arts and Sciences (known as COMPAS), an arts fund-raising vehicle that had become the most significant source of private dollars for the arts in Phoenix.[24]

DeConcini's cabinet met either in Tully's dark and windowless private dining room at Phoenix Newspapers or in Tostenrud's bright and open private dining room on the top floor of the Arizona Bank building. They ate early, around 7:00 A.M., and elaborately. DeConcini relished his cultural leadership role; he was in his element. Although he had established the Phoenix office of his family's Tucson law firm after helping his brother Dennis win election to the United States senate, the arts were his greatest passion.

At one particular meeting early in his tenure, DeConcini's energy was palpable and infectious, and the group's talk turned lively. He argued that a pressing need existed for a theater in Phoenix, one designed specifically for plays—for the spoken word—that would be a credit to the capital city's status. The lack of such a theater had been a problem for years. The problem had become acute now that the Tucson-based Arizona Theatre Company—the state's only professional theater company—had begun performing in Phoenix in 1978, although never in a suitable venue. Supporters of Arizona Theatre Company had approached Phoenix civic leaders and urged them to take action, and DeConcini responded to their request with zeal. In fact, DeConcini told his informal cabinet, just days before the staff of the Arizona Commission on the Arts had notified him of the announcement of a new program in Design Arts at the National Endowment for the Arts. This new endowment program awarded feasibility study grants to cities that were considering building new arts facilities. "Maybe, if we can get this feasibility grant..." he mused aloud, letting the thought hang in the air.[25]

DeConcini knew that the challenges of building a theater in Phoenix would be immense. A previous experience in Tucson had provided a sobering education about the innumerable obstacles that could occur. Interior decorator and theater aficionado Sandy Rosenthal had recruited DeConcini and about twenty other individuals—including attorney Marvin Cohen, realtor Martin Ginsburg, and arts patrons Carol DuVal and Hope Silvestri—in 1966 to help found the Arizona Theatre Company in Tucson. The theater company lacked a decent place to perform, so DeConcini had raised the funds and then supervised the construction of its second home in the old Santa Rita Hotel building in Tucson. Raising funds for that comparatively small effort had proved daunting. From his experience in Tucson, DeConcini learned well that money for the arts did not flow freely in Arizona. In fact, securing large donations for arts and cultural initiatives nearly was impossible.

As the discussion continued that morning, the group coalesced in its discussions of a new theater for Phoenix, and they prepared to move on the problem. Someone was needed, however, to spearhead the effort. DeConcini knew that Richard Mallery was the one. Based on his instincts and experience, DeConcini recognized that if the project were to succeed, he would need a leader who not only was politically savvy, but also personally devoted. He knew that Mallery's mother-in-law, Forest Burgess, loved the theater and had often complained to Mallery of the "crying need for a decent theater building."[26] For all of Mallery's high-powered ambitions and record of accomplishment, DeConcini also knew that what truly motivated the well-known attorney and civic leader was his fealty to family.

Even beyond fealty, DeConcini had witnessed Mallery use his increasing influence in the community in myriad ways, whether aggressively courting stakeholders in a cause or subtly convincing others on a particular project through moral persuasion. DeConcini believed that those skills, when utilized selectively and appropriately, ensured that Mallery would be effective in seeking the generosity of some of the wealthiest people in Phoenix society. He knew that Mallery cared deeply about Arizona, that he saw himself as its present and future advocate, and that he cared even more about Forest Burgess and what she wanted.

Mallery sensed that he was expected to step forward. Believing in the vital role the arts play in any developing and dynamic society, he pondered his next move. For fourteen years he had raised money as board chair for Combined Metropolitan Phoenix Arts and Sciences, so his leap into the unknown was not entirely blind. "OK, I will do this," he proclaimed to DeConcini and the other members of the group, all of who immediately embraced his leadership. Mallery could not foresee, however, that Phoenix would undergo its greatest rate of population growth in its history, that the local arts community would pose challenges of enormous proportions, and that the economic disruptions of the late 1980s would create obstacles that nearly derailed the entire effort. His assignment would prove exceedingly more difficult than in his wildest imaginings; however, during 1979 and 1980, the seeds of a civic drama had been planted.

2

The Patron

Richard Mallery began developing a strategy for a theater in Phoenix almost immediately after his meeting with Dino DeConcini. As he deliberated, he considered not only the role that a new theater could play in unifying downtown development, but also that it could infuse a much needed artistic elegance to the area. His musings led him to focus on G. Robert "Bob" Herberger. In recent years, Herberger had played a major role in shaping modern Phoenix. For nearly three decades, he had selectively and brilliantly acquired valuable land holdings in the Valley and, with his increasing wealth and influence, Herberger had contributed to the community through public service and philanthropy.

Herberger began his career not as a savvy real estate mogul, but rather as a highly successful and innovative owner of retail stores in the Upper Midwest. Mallery knew Herberger's background as a business leader and philanthropist fit well within his emerging conceptualization of a theater for downtown Phoenix. Robust and handsome, with a shock of white, slightly wavy hair, Herberger projected the image of an outspoken and charismatic leader, although he remained an enigma to many.

The Herberger family hailed from small-town Minnesota. Bob's grandfather, Conrad Herberger, had emigrated from Germany in 1856 and arrived in the bucolic environs of St. Cloud, sixty miles northwest of Minneapolis–St. Paul. Conrad quickly established a blacksmith shop there; the following year, he married Catherine Schurmann. The couple eventually had twelve children.[1] After one of their children tragically drowned in 1876, the Herbergers sold their business in St. Cloud and bought a farm four miles south of Osakis.[2] They quickly developed a healthy land base—within one decade, he owned more than 900 acres—and sold cattle and horses. In 1888 Conrad purchased a flour mill, where his sons George and Frank ran the operation. Two years later, the two brothers bought the stock of the bankrupt Frye and Cash store in Osakis; however, Frank soon succumbed to the opportunities emerging on the West Coast, and he sold his interests to brother, George.[3]

In time, George married Emily Curry, and the couple had three children. The youngest, George Robert (G. Robert) Herberger—quickly called Bob—was born in Osakis, population 1,200, on September 12, 1904. Bob's father expanded his store in Osakis and eventually owned twenty small-town stores. He also acquired a significant amount of land. At one point in his career, George Herberger owned more land than any other individual in Minnesota. The bulk of these holdings were farms, most of which he rented to others. The senior Herberger, whose real estate acumen was prodigious, thrived on his inherent ability to buy and sell land until he was eighty-five years of age.

Bob Herberger at his home in Paradise Valley, Arizona. For nearly three decades, he had selectively and brilliantly acquired valuable land holdings in the Valley and, with his increasing wealth and influence, Herberger had contributed to the community through public service and philanthropy.
Arizona Business Gazette, June 30, 1989. Photograph by Dana Leonard. Used with permission.

As a young child, Bob Herberger suffered bouts of rheumatic fever. The family doctor had warned his mother of the necessity of diminishing the impact of Minnesota winters on her illness-prone son. She decided that they would spend winters in Hollywood, California, which soon would serve as the incubator for the nascent film industry. She rented a house in California during the school year for Bob and her two other children; her husband visited when possible, at least twice during the winter months, coming by train. The intrepid Emily returned to Minnesota with her children only in the summers to protect the health of her youngest son. By his high school years, Bob was strong enough to withstand the cold Minnesota winters.

Music played a significant role in Bob Herberger's early life, just as it had for Mallery. In California, eight-year-old Herberger began piano lessons, and the piano soon became a consuming passion. As a teenager, he played background music for silent movies, formed a dance band, and explored other musical genres. After high school, Herberger enrolled in the Minnesota School of Music, and the path of his career seemed charted. After only one year at the school, however, he arrived at a pragmatic conclusion, "In classical music, only the people at the very, very top make money. The rest of them starve. It's a rough life."[4] At this juncture, he abandoned the notion of a musical career.

Herberger changed course quickly, enrolling first at Hibbing Junior College and then at the University of Minnesota. He studied business and, recalling his experience working in his father's stores as a young teenager, he realized that he should pursue a career in the retail industry. Herberger subsequently left the university after one year, having decided, "You don't need a degree to work in retail. You just have to love it. And be willing to work your butt off."[5]

Evidently, Herberger had merchandising in his blood, a seemingly genetic predisposition. He maintained his uncanny instinct about what would sell, the sign of a true merchant. "It's a God-given talent, like music," he asserted.[6] Herberger purchased a bankrupt store in 1927, sold off the merchandise, and then opened his own store in the same building. The business realized a profit that first year, and his direction was clear. Following his father George's blueprint, Herberger opened additional stores in small- and medium-sized towns. What became Herberger Incorporated cut a high profile throughout the Upper Midwest.

Herberger was ahead of his time in his promotion of women to management positions. Decades later, he could still recall the name of his first female manager, Margaret Bush, who worked in South Dakota, adding, "She did one hell of a job. I always had women store mangers, long years ago. I couldn't figure out why you had to have men."[7]

Herberger's meteoric rise and sustaining successes—even during the Great Depression—attracted the attention of Butler Brothers of Chicago, which at the time was the largest U.S. wholesale-merchandising company. In 1947 the company's board of directors needed someone to overcome an approximate $1 million monthly loss and return the company to solvency. The board persuaded Herberger to accept the position of president. He initiated the necessary changes that triggered the company's recovery. Within one year, Butler Brothers realized a $3 million profit. Throughout Herberger's three years at Butler Brothers, he retained ownership of his midwestern stores, as well as his title as board chair of Herberger Incorporated. He clearly demonstrated his ability to operate two major business enterprises not only simultaneously, but also profitably.

Meanwhile, Bob met his future wife Katherine in early 1934, and they were married four months later on August 25, 1934. They eventually had three children. In the course of raising a young family in St. Cloud, Kax (Katherine's nickname bestowed on her by her father and adopted by everyone) and the three children began spending their Thanksgiving and Easter holidays at the Camelback Inn in Scottsdale. They discovered the Arizona town after a trip to Texas had turned cold, and they wandered west in search of the sun. The family enjoyed the desert, mountains, and vistas so much that they moved to Scottsdale in 1949. Bob, who maintained his relationship with Butler Brothers as a member of the board of directors, commuted to Chicago every other week. The family continued to spend their summers in Minnesota, where Bob oversaw the expansion of Herberger Incorporated to thirty-four stores in seven states.

During the late 1940s and early 1950s, Herberger began to acquire huge, inexpensive parcels of Arizona desert land. According to Mallery, Herberger scouted the land in a jeep, or sometimes on horseback, because paved roads were infrequent, if not nonexistent.[8] Herberger eventually bought thousands of acres of land throughout five Arizona counties.

Herberger was able to imagine what others could not, namely growth and development miles from the emerging metropolis of Phoenix and its smaller satellite city of Scottsdale. He foresaw housing subdivisions, shopping centers, and recreational opportunities. Timing was everything, and Herberger had an uncanny sense of timing. While others viewed such speculation on future growth as an enormous gamble, with hands-on experience of expanding Herberger Incorporated in the Upper Midwest, Herberger asserted his well-honed instincts. He was not taking chances.[9] For example, one parcel of land that Herberger purchased in 1950 for $32,000 sold for $6.4 million in 1980; a 20,000 percent return on investment. At another time, Herberger sold a one-half acre parcel of land at the corner of Scottsdale and Shea Streets for nearly the same price as he had paid for the entire eighty acres of the parcel he purchased in the late 1950s. The Herberger real estate portfolio teemed with the results of his foresight.[10]

How did a merchant switch to land acquisition and succeed? "They are directly opposed," Herberger stated. "With land, the longer you hold, the more money you make. In merchandising, you need turnover, fast. You don't think, you move."[11] In Arizona, Herberger bought, and he waited until urban sprawl caught up with him. That type of agile mind moving effortlessly in either direction as needed was a skill Mallery greatly admired.

There was more to Herberger, however, than money and business. As Mallery grew closer to Herberger, he recalled that Bob would laugh and say, "Well, I can't help but be excited about making money. But I don't look at making money just to grab a lot. I like to make it to be able to *do* things with it or to give it away to important things."[12]

Bob and Kax had always been philanthropic, and Mallery learned of their legendary largesse in Minnesota. When Herberger accepted the Butler Brothers job and the couple prepared to leave for Chicago, St. Cloud honored them with a huge confetti-filled parade and banquet. The Herbergers continued their charitable and civic activities in Chicago, as well as in Phoenix.

Not only were the Herbergers patrons of the arts, but Bob was a classically trained pianist, and Kax was an amateur painter and sculptor who shared her husband's love of music. Kax had joined the symphony guild, later served on its board, and then served on the national board of the American Symphony Orchestra League for seven years. Bob helped Lewis Ruskin found the Phoenix Chamber Music Society in 1960. To celebrate the fiftieth anniversary of Arizona statehood in 1962, the Herbergers commissioned a symphony competition, which Paul Nelson won, and the Phoenix Symphony premiered his new work. They became major patrons of Arizona artists such as Philip Curtis, Lou Davis, and John Henry Waddell. They supported many other causes that were not related to the arts, including the Salvation Army, the Arizona Crippled Children's Hospital, and Planned Parenthood. Bob played a key role in the establishment and expansion of the Valley Presbyterian Church, and Kax regularly assisted at the Salvation Army's Thanksgiving and Christmas dinners. They gave money, raised money, served on numerous boards and committees, and encouraged others to join them in their public stewardship. They found it difficult to understand others who did not do the same.

Mallery knew that Herberger had curtailed his activities in recent years. He had ceased his record-shattering fund-raising activities for the Republican Party, saying, "Time to let the younger fellow do this."[13] His son Gary recently had assumed the role of president of Herberger Enterprises, Bob's land acquisition and development company, although Bob remained as board chair, saying, "Without work, I don't know what a person would do. If someone could tell me a better way to live and have fun, I'd like to hear about it."[14] Bob sold his Midwest stores to his key employees, and he actually helped them put together the financing to do it; even so, he continued to visit every store at least once during the summer months.[15] Perhaps most telling, he recently had a pacemaker implanted.[16]

Bob and Kax Herberger at their home in Paradise Valley, Arizona. Their multimillion dollar gift helped to make the Herberger Theater a reality, and it signaled a new era in public–private partnerships in Phoenix.
Phoenix Gazette, October 6, 1989. Photograph by Mike Rynearson. Used with permission.

Mallery witnessed how the Herbergers steered their lives and surmised that he could interest Bob in a substantial project like this new theater. Herberger clearly was devoting more time to philanthropy. Maybe Mallery could convince him to become involved in something lasting. Both men shared a longtime devotion to the state; although Herberger maintained ties to Minnesota, Mallery had often heard him say, "There's no place like Arizona in my book."[17]

Mallery knew "the ask" must be made at the right time. He also knew that he needed a clear, forthright plan, as Herberger preferred uncluttered and uncomplicated communication; he never allowed a letter exceeding one page to leave his desk. Mallery needed to synthesize all of the details in advance, including a comprehensive financial package. A genius at math, Herberger added faster in his head than most calculators at the time. Still, Mallery sensed that Herberger had begun casting about for his legacy. The theater, perhaps, could cement the Herbergers' presence in Arizona. As Mallery analyzed his potential patron, Bob Herberger, he also considered the political dimensions of his efforts on the city of Phoenix and on Mayor Margaret Taylor Hance.

3

The City

Margaret Taylor Hance, first elected mayor in 1975, thought she had the best job in the country. She attracted national attention by making Phoenix the largest city in the United States to elect a female mayor. By 1980 the classy, witty, and popular Hance was just beginning her third, two-year term and enjoyed shaping public policy in one of the fastest growing cities in the country.[1] The daughter of a local banker and the widow of the vice president of one of Arizona's largest insurance companies, Hance cut her political teeth on a Junior League fight to save Camelback Mountain from development. Once that battle was won, she was at the forefront of campaigns as a member of the Phoenix City Council to pass bond issues to preserve Phoenix's mountains, which allowed the city to purchase Camelback Mountain, Squaw Peak, and South and North Mountains to create the Phoenix Mountain Preserve. Hance became known as "Maggie, Mother of the Mountains." She had won her seat on the city council in 1971, where she served two terms before her successful run for mayor.[2]

Hance knew that her city needed a more vibrant downtown. Along with several prominent business leaders, she spearheaded the Central Phoenix Redevelopment Plan created several years earlier at her behest. Among other things, the plan called for the expansion of Phoenix Civic Plaza to include a theater on the plaza opposite Symphony Hall, a fact that had not escaped Richard Mallery.[3] Hance could not mobilize Phoenix's business leaders, however, and little downtown redevelopment occurred.

The Phoenix economy was booming, and Mallery knew the time was ripe to approach C. A. Howlett, Mayor Hance's chief of staff. Howlett was set to exit city government after working for the previous mayor.[4] Hance enticed Howlett to stay, however, by offering him the top position as her chief of staff, as well as by giving him downtown revitalization as his primary portfolio. Moreover, Howlett shared Hance's commitment to downtown, giving Mallery a touchstone with the city of Phoenix.[5]

Mallery and Howlett lamented the lack of progress in downtown Phoenix. "During my time in city government," Howlett recalled, "I have witnessed several fledgling attempts to 'save' downtown. In 1972 Valley National Bank built its forty-story headquarters, the tallest in the region. First Interstate built their tower, too. Then the completion of the civic center with Symphony Hall that same year prompted the new twenty–six-story Hyatt Regency to be constructed in 1976, along with a rebuilt Hotel Adams, although they are both still money losers. Arizona Bank built their building on First Street in 1976, but that's about it. We are still casting about for a mechanism to spark some sustained energy about downtown."[6] Mallery convinced Howlett that the new theater idea dovetailed with this need and that it had enough merit to interest the mayor. After a thorough briefing from Howlett, Hance readily agreed to meet with Mallery and Howlett on June 16, 1980.[7]

Getting straight to the point, Mallery began, "Mayor Hance, will there be support from the city of Phoenix for building a major theater?" She responded without hesitation, "Absolutely!...Well, in theory," she added.[8] At the time, Hance was trying to keep another cultural institution, the Arizona Historical Society, downtown. Although she sensed that the society's leaders were going to relocate their facilities elsewhere in the Valley, perhaps this project might influence them to stay put.

Classy, witty, and popular, Margaret Hance was mayor of Phoenix from 1976 through 1986. She supported the building of the theater, but insisted that it be downtown.
Arizona Republic, November 16, 1979. Photograph by Kevin Scofield. Used with permission.

In addition, the Phoenix City Planning Commission had adopted an urban village concept in 1979, called the Phoenix Concept Plan 2000, which divided the city into nine village units. Each "village" was to be self-contained, offering the neighborhood residents everything they needed within their village's parameters, including jobs, stores, and educational and recreational facilities. Admirers of the plan called it the urban form of the future. Exactly what distinguishing feature the downtown Phoenix village would offer, however, concerned Hance. She told Mallery, "A central arts district makes sense to me. You just cannot have great theater in every neighborhood or great symphonies and museums in every community. It won't work to anyone's benefit that way. But if all or most of the arts activity is downtown, or close to downtown, at least in the central corridor, then you can make things happen. Why, we might even be able to bring back the trolleys to downtown."[9] They discussed the possibility of putting the theater on Phoenix Civic Plaza. "There is great demand, too much in fact, for use of Symphony Hall, and not just by arts groups," Howlett pointed out. "Corporations also are putting the pressure on to use Symphony Hall for meetings that could last up to eight weeks. Another quality venue is definitely needed."[10]

Hance asked Mallery about the logistics and the financing of the proposed theater. Without skipping a beat, Mallery outlined a detailed public- and private-sector partnership plan that he had developed just days before. "The city of Phoenix will be needed in a prominent role, but they won't be alone by any means. The private sector would be involved in a big way, as full-fledged partners with the city, in fact as a majority partner," he emphasized.[11] Hance pressed for further elaboration on the city's role. "Spending tax dollars to build a theater is out of the question, no doubt," Mallery said. "It just will not happen, not in Phoenix." Mallery, however, had figured out a way around that. "The Civic Plaza Building Corporation could use its bonding capacity to finance roughly half of the project. The theater would have to be part of the civic center, but that might be OK. In fact, if that were to happen," Mallery paused, "the theater might become a catalyst for a revived city center."[12]

Hance listened carefully as Mallery continued, "Raising the other half of the money from the business community will not happen easily either; although we have lots of big-name electronic and aerospace companies here—Motorola, General Electric, Goodyear, Sperry, Honeywell, Intel, Digital—these are branches, not headquarters, without access to top-level officials or major corporate funds. The only major corporations headquartered in town are Greyhound and Phelps Dodge, which isn't enough. So, realistically," and Mallery paused as if to say *you know I am a realist,* "the business community can be counted on for only about 25 to 26 percent of the funds. That means a major patron would have to be found for the final quarter."[13] Even though Mallery did not mention Bob Herberger by name—or anyone else for that matter—Hance concluded he was not merely speculating about a mystery private donor. She knew Mallery had access to some of the wealthiest people in the Valley, and she imagined that he already had someone specifically in mind.

Mallery finished his discussion with Hance and Howlett, saying, "Taking all of this into consideration, the city, through the civic plaza board perhaps, would pay 49 percent; the private sector would pay 51 percent, with a major donor providing approximately one-half of that share."[14] Hance embraced the notion of the city being responsible for less than the private sector, and she appreciated the upside of a public–private partnership. "Just one thing more," Mallery interjected. "For their 49 percent, the city can own the theater, the land, and the

A view of downtown Phoenix, showing the block of the future Herberger Theater, with a grid overlay.
Herberger Theater Archives. Used with permission.

building, just like they own the Phoenix Art Museum. Like the museum, the 'price' of this ownership will be to provide the maintenance, utilities, insurance, and security for the theater. That will lighten the burden on the arts groups, allowing them to focus on what goes on the stage."[15]

Mallery viewed the framework as beneficial for all parties. "The city will get a building paid for 51 percent by the private sector and won't have to manage it. The arts groups will get a state-of-the-art facility, which will be subsidized so that rents can be low. The business community will get credit for building a cultural amenity that will help revitalize downtown at the same time. Why, the major donor might even get his name on the building."[16] Mallery did not reveal his reason for seeking this private-sector majority stake. If the city held a minority interest and the private sector held a majority, the theater would be protected from the vagaries of public control and political meddling, such as those that beset the Scottsdale Center for the Arts. He intended to insulate the arts groups from politics. This point was nonnegotiable.[17]

Mallery's enthusiasm and conceptual framework for the theater impressed the mayor; yet, Hance still hesitated. "Tell the mayor how you see the idea getting from here to there," prompted Howlett. "Tell her about the study."[18] Mallery described his earlier meeting with Dino DeConcini and the possibility of obtaining a National Endowment for the Arts feasibility study grant. "DeConcini and the arts commission staff are applying for that grant right now," he informed Hance, "and the credibility gained through such a study will go a long way toward answering the inevitable naysayers." Howlett added that the study "provided a way for the city to get involved without getting in too deep at the start, in case enough support is not forthcoming."[19] Mallery realized that winning the endowment grant could tip the balance of support and convince Hance to place her political capital behind the project. She wanted Mallery to understand unequivocally that she would do anything to help "provided the theater is downtown."

Mallery met again with Hance when the National Endowment for the Arts grant request proved successful, and he later made a presentation to the Phoenix City Council. On November 24, 1980, the city council created the Central Phoenix Theater Study Committee. Members of the committee included Mallery; Arthur "Jim" Baumann, head of Dayton-Hudson in Arizona; attorney Harriet "Hattie" Babbitt, wife of then-Governor Bruce Babbitt; Patricia Tully, wife of publisher Duke Tully; and C. A. Howlett in an ex officio capacity.[20] Mallery savored the progress and grew excited at moving that much closer to turning downtown Phoenix into a dynamic, lively gathering place.

4

The Arts

Richard Mallery turned his considerable energies from the world of public and private finance to the raison d'être for a new theater in the first place, namely, the art of theater itself, and of Arizona Theatre Company in particular. The theater company had pressed the need for a professional performing arts facility to Phoenix community leaders, and the promise of the Tucson-based company presenting high-quality performances in Phoenix provided the initial impetus for the project. David Hawkanson, the enterprising managing director of Arizona Theatre Company, had started the ball rolling for the new theater almost from the moment he arrived in Arizona in 1975 after leaving the renowned Guthrie Theater in Minneapolis, where he had been associate manager. It had taken nearly five years of meetings and persuasion to move the idea to this point, but Mallery hoped that this earlier groundwork would pay off in future support from a key group of Phoenix citizens.

Indeed, Arizona performing arts groups considered Hawkanson's acceptance of the managing director's position an arts coup because of the recognition he had received as an up-and-coming star in regional theater.[1] Hawkanson was passionate about theater, and he quickly realized that he would need greater resources than theatrically sophisticated Tucson could provide, given its small size, to realize his dream for the company to operate on a par with the best theaters in the country.[2] He knew that Phoenix did not have a professional theater company and that the city had made several failed attempts to start one over the years.[3] Hawkanson saw an opportunity in this, and he began to explore the expansion of Arizona Theatre Company's performances to Phoenix.

It was a startling idea, with no model to follow, but Hawkanson believed a two-city operation would provide some economies of scale, enlarge the audience, and give him the means to tap the larger Phoenix population for contributions. Mallery hosted several meetings in his living room with others who shared an interest in the idea, such as his good friend William Shover, director of public affairs for Phoenix Newspapers; Kim Sterling, assistant to the board chair of Phelps Dodge; Henry Sargent, chief financial officer of Arizona Public Service; and his mother-in-law, Forest Burgess. Subsequently, in 1978 Arizona Theatre Company produced *Equus*, directed by Mark Lamos, at the Scottsdale Center for the Arts to widespread critical acclaim.[4,5] The company then performed several plays each season in Phoenix at different small theaters, including Phoenix Little Theatre, which further underscored the pressing need for a permanent home for Arizona Theatre Company in the capital city.

To build a new theater from the ground up, Mallery knew that the feasibility study would be critical, so he turned to Dino DeConcini and the Arizona Commission on the Arts for further guidance. They decided to ask Michael Pittas, the director of the Design Arts program at the National Endowment for the Arts in Washington, D.C., to come to Phoenix to discuss their plans further. DeConcini arranged for Pittas to meet with Mayor Hance, along with Mallery, C. A. Howlett, and Deborah Whitehurst, who served as museum and special projects director on the arts commission's staff. The youthful, confident Whitehurst represented the arts commission's interest in the theater project, and her work subsequently would result in a $15,000 National Endowment for the Arts award for the Central Phoenix Theater Study Committee's feasibility study.[6]

"Before you begin a building, first you should ask some fundamental questions," Pittas advised the group. "You should start with the *need*. My advice would be to see what the local arts organizations need, and then build a facility based on those needs." Whitehurst chimed in, "Sure, Arizona Theatre Company needs a place to perform, but so might a lot of other arts groups in Phoenix. The feasibility study should start from that point. What are the needs? That should be addressed first."[7] Mallery, Hance, and Howlett agreed with Pittas and Whitehurst's reasoning. If the feasibility study demonstrated a strong demand for a theater from a broad range of groups, including Arizona Theatre Company, the case for a new theater would be further strengthened.[8] The project now made an important shift from creating a home solely for Arizona Theatre Company to creating a venue that could accommodate many arts groups.

Pittas and Whitehurst based their arguments on the national concern over "spaces and places" for the arts. An increase in federal funding for the arts had triggered similar support from many city and state governments, which motivated the private sector to contribute more money as well. Because of this convergence, hundreds of arts groups throughout the country sprang into existence. Many cities found themselves long on talent, but short on facilities.

To address this shortage, cities responded by hastily building theaters and performing arts centers, which led to glaring mistakes. Stages were built without fly space or adequate wings. The dressing rooms were cramped or inaccessible, and acoustics were given scant attention. Unwilling to appear ungrateful, performers were nevertheless dismayed by the poorly designed facilities. Generic, multipurpose facilities were often the worst. City bureaucrats did not realize that the technical needs for concert halls were vastly different than the technical needs for dramatic theater or dance. Too often, these multipurpose halls ended up not serving any purpose very well.

Professionals with the endowment realized the necessity of involving theater experts from the onset of the design phase of performing arts venues; they provided knowledgeable consultants armed with guidelines on how best to build high-quality arts venues. The endowment wisely set aside federal funds for feasibility study grants, one of which enabled the theater study committee to address its challenges in an informed manner. Mallery and DeConcini wanted the best consultants; within a few weeks, the Arizona Commission on the Arts staff targeted Bradley Morison, president of Arts Development Associates in Minneapolis, as lead consultant. William Fleissig, William Morrish, and Peter VanDine of CityWest, an architectural and urban design firm based in San Francisco, were selected to assist Morison. After a flurry of phone calls and letters, the Central Phoenix Theater Study Committee, through the Arizona Commission on the Arts, engaged Morison and Fleissig's group in January 1981.[9]

Hawkanson was optimistic about the newly created theater study committee, and he grew even more so as several other developments in Phoenix demonstrated strong support for Arizona Theatre Company further extending its presence into the capital city. The recent opening of an Arizona Theatre Company office in Phoenix, as well as the addition of seven Phoenix-based board members, signaled new levels of leadership commitment to the theater company, while the company's performances at the Phoenix Little Theatre attracted unprecedented large audiences.

Learning that Bradley Morison had accepted the lead consulting position also pleased Hawkanson. He knew that Morison championed regional theater and its unique vision and mission. The philosophy of regional theaters captured the imagination of many in the arts community when they initially began to sprout up across the United States during the late 1960s.[10] Unlike commercial theaters in New York City, regional theaters embraced their nonprofit status with passion; art trumped profits. In the twentieth century, regional theaters thrived when they developed a close relationship with their community, city, and region. Hawkanson had explained the mission of regional theaters to Mallery, although he remained unsure whether the Snell & Wilmer law firm partner and civic steward grasped all the implications of this fresh approach to creating the

A scene from As You Like It, *performed by Arizona Theatre Company in Phoenix during their 1981–1982 season.* Arizona Theatre Company Archives. Photograph by Tim Fuller. Used with permission.

art of theater. On the other hand, attorneys Marvin Cohen and Dino DeConcini, who were founding board members of Arizona Theatre Company, had a clear understanding of the vitality of regional theater.[11] Cohen tried to explain the singularity of regional theater to other colleagues, beginning with Jonathan Marshall, publisher of the *Scottsdale Progress*. Marshall had been working to bring the Globe Theater from San Diego to the Valley for an annual winter season. "Jon, the Globe Theater comes through and then it is gone," explained Cohen. "With Arizona Theatre Company, we are talking about something that is *here, that stays here;* and it is *ours*, part of our community." In time, Marshall, like many others, supported bringing Arizona Theatre Company to the Valley.[12]

Morison had served as a foot soldier in the regional theater movement. In the early 1960s, he participated in the creation of the celebrated Guthrie Theater in Minneapolis, which caught the nation's attention and put the concept of regional theater on the map. Lavishly funded from the region's plethora of Fortune 500 companies, and buttressed with a progressive government and philanthropy-minded citizens, the Guthrie Theater set a high standard for other communities. The Guthrie sprang to life with a debt-free, new state-of-the-art building, which gave it the luxury to devote its energy to creating not only a brilliant resident company of artists, but also to building a committed audience. In his role as the theater's first public relations director, Morison helped build this audience. He then coauthored a book based on that experience, which quickly became a classic in the field of audience development.[13]

Although Hawkanson understood that the precedent achieved by the Guthrie Theater in Minneapolis could not be duplicated in Phoenix, he knew that Morison's extensive theater background could provide expert guidance to the Central Phoenix Theater Study Committee in a way that would be of value to Arizona Theatre Company. By the time Morison and Fleissig arrived in Phoenix in March 1981, however, their mandate had expanded well beyond merely how to build a theater for Arizona Theatre Company; they instead would assess the needs of all arts groups in Phoenix for performance space. In a signal that something important was afoot, stories of Morison and Fleissig's arrival appeared in the local newspapers. They assured the public that they were "not committed to any preconceived plan" for a new theater building, a renovated one, or even to the necessity of any facility at all.[14] "Everyone should realize," Morison told the press, "that we may say there is not enough reason to go any further toward developing a theater."

Even though Morison conducted feasibility studies in more than fifty cities, he never had visited Arizona. He first interviewed local artists, having discovered over the years that they often held the inspired answers for a city's cultural growth. Morison determined that there were 121 performing arts groups in the Valley. Further analysis revealed that approximately one-half of the arts organizations were incorporated as nonprofit, tax-exempt organizations. He expressed his disappointment when he discovered that less than one-third of these organizations paid their performers or maintained a paid staff. To the surprise of some of the smaller groups, Morison devoted as much attention to them as he did to the more established organizations, as he sought to fully understand the arts environment in Phoenix.

The sketchy financial landscape and overall fiscal weakness of the collective arts community would prove to be a serious challenge, Morison suspected, but its surprising diversity nevertheless impressed him. The survey identified more ethnic and folk dance groups than any other arts discipline, with the largest ethnic group being Hispanic; however, as he pointed out in the report, "There is an exciting array of other cultures represented, including Scandinavian, Irish, Serbian, Vietnamese, Ukrainian, Chinese, and Scottish. The number and diversity of these organizations is certainly one of the cultural assets of the Valley."[15] He also suspected that these organizations probably were an unnoticed and undervalued asset.

Morison noted that the performing arts groups generally operated on a small scale and that Phoenix had fewer mature, professional institutions compared with cities of similar size. He expressed chagrin that only sixteen of these organizations had budgets of more than $50,000.[16] The size of an arts organization's budget often indicated the level of community involvement, and the small budgets of these organizations signaled potential problems in raising private funds for a new theater; yet, these groups fostered a substantial amount of performance activity altogether, nearly 1,000 performances each year. Morison sensed that a few organizations were on the verge of evolving from small, struggling organizations into more stable entities capable of real artistic accomplishment.[17]

The Central Phoenix Theater Study Committee members, and Mallery in particular, especially were interested in Morison's analysis of arts audiences. The committee sought data on the public's impression of traveling to downtown Phoenix for cultural events. Several skeptics pointed to the Camelback corridor as a more suitable site, believing that the downtown area lacked appeal. Morison decided that the audiences of the seven largest arts groups could provide critical insight into this question. His survey results surprised many. The majority of audience members responded that traveling downtown was not a deterrent; in fact, it actually was preferable. Even considering that Phoenix did not possess the freeways that link the various Valley communities together today, audience members who responded to the survey in 1981 informed Morison that downtown was ideally positioned for the proposed cultural venue.[18] Downtown served as a crossroads in the center of burgeoning Maricopa County.

Phoenix city officials, the theater study committee, and community leaders listened to the preliminary conclusions carefully. Morison outlined how the Guthrie Theater altered Minneapolis's cultural, social, and economic landscape, with each aspect illuminating the other. He forecasted that cultural growth could spur Phoenix's downtown redevelopment. Morison also provided specific examples beyond Minneapolis and the Guthrie Theater. He asserted that the construction of an arts facility was not an indulgence or an extravagance; it was a catalyst for local economic development.[19]

Concerning the specific needs of Arizona Theatre Company, Morison had to find common ground. Hawkanson and his board of directors reaffirmed their commitment to Phoenix; however, the theater study committee now had a more comprehensive focus. Although not mutually exclusive, the two agendas differed in fundamental ways. Building a performing arts center was a different prospect than providing a home for a regional theater company. Morison looked for ways to finesse this issue or, better yet, to develop a plan that met both agendas. The feasibility study made it clear, however, that the lack of a theater of appropriate size, technical capability, and availability severely restricted Arizona Theatre Company's efforts to serve the Valley.[20]

On November 17, 1981, Morison presented the conclusions of the feasibility study to the Phoenix City Council. He recommended building *two* theaters, not merely one. The first theater would seat 800, with a second, smaller venue seating 300, both of which could be housed in one building. Two theaters were necessary, he said, because Phoenix had too many performances for only one theater. He envisioned the new theater as a "coming together" of the many cultures and arts groups in the Valley, placed in downtown Phoenix at the "crossroads in the heart of the center of the city."[21] Hence, he suggested naming the new building the Crossroads Theater Center. The study identified three possible downtown sites, including the north end of Phoenix Civic Plaza, opposite Symphony Hall. Fleissig's team, which focused on fiscal and design issues, estimated building costs at between $11 million to $14.6 million.[22]

Morison went further still, suggesting the need to renovate Phoenix Little Theatre at Central Avenue and East McDowell Road, as well as converting a state-owned former Baptist church at Moreland and Third Street into yet *another* 800-seat theater, which could be called Valley Playhouse.[23] At an estimated price tag of *merely* $2.5 million, he urged that these two projects be undertaken as soon as possible to forestall "stagnation and possibly the withering" of existing Valley arts groups who did not have adequate performance space.[24]

For idealists, it was clear that Morison's suggestions could transform Phoenix into a thriving cultural mecca. For others, like Mallery, who signed on to build one theater, the thrust of the report seemed overly optimistic, if not totally unrealistic. After the Phoenix City Council listened to and digested the heady recommendations, they instructed Morison, Morrish, and Fleissig to proceed with the second part of the study. This second portion of the study required fiscal recommendations and a comprehensive financial package, as well as an additional analysis of the site recommendations. Mayor Hance called the final report "a significant milestone in achieving another anchor project in what hopefully will become a central Phoenix cultural district."[25] Mallery commented publicly, "Now we are into the 'how do we pay for it' stage."[26] He was well aware of the monumental challenges that lay ahead; however, he could not foresee the savings and loan and real estate crisis that in the late 1980s dramatically altered the economic boom in the desert and rocked the financial world in the rest of the country for the better part of a decade. Now, however, Mallery clearly could imagine a new theater rising in downtown Phoenix that would bring new energy to the performing arts and to his beloved city.

5

Ninety Days

One year had passed since Bradley Morison presented the results of the feasibility study to the Phoenix City Council, but Richard Mallery had not been idle. He had devoted countless hours to analyzing complex site-selection issues, to cultivating a relationship with members of the Civic Plaza Building Corporation, to strategizing preliminary financing through a consortium of banks led by Valley National Bank, and to laying the groundwork to convince a major donor to support the cause. In December 1982 Mallery faced a crucial ninety-day test in which he needed to bring all parties together to start building the theater.

Mallery, as chair of the Central Phoenix Theater Study Committee, entered into a conditional purchase agreement with Monroe-Second Associates for the southern half of a block of land located directly north of Phoenix Civic Plaza on Monroe Street, between Second and Third Streets. Once he signed the document, he had only ninety days to secure financing. The trouble was that each of the various stakeholders—the city of Phoenix, the Civic Plaza Building Corporation, the banks, and the major donor—was waiting for one of the other stakeholders to make the first move before signing on to the project. To Mallery, it was the moment of truth.[1]

Much had transpired during the past year. Besides the many issues being addressed by Mallery, there were tantalizing meetings with Rouse Corporation, which was considering the prospect of developing a nine-block area downtown, referred to as the Superblock by city planners.[2] They could envision the Rouse Corporation creating something that would transform downtown Phoenix, much as Faneuil Hall Marketplace had reenergized Boston. One all-day, retreat-like meeting held at apartment magnate William Schulz's home on Camelback Road near Fifty-sixth Street, brought together some of Arizona's best business minds. The meeting attendees were not only members of the Phoenix 40 and company executives, they also were Mallery's friends. The group included Keith Turley of Arizona Public Service, Roger Lyon of Valley National Bank, A. J. "Jack" Pfister of Salt River Project, Gary Driggs of Western Savings and Loan, and Gene Rice of First Federal Savings and Loan. C. A. Howlett, Mayor Hance's chief of staff, who was representing the city of Phoenix, and Jerry Smalley, board chair of the Rouse Corporation, joined them. They assessed the Superblock idea with Smalley, who was deeply impressed with their concept for a downtown theater.[3]

Nevertheless, Smalley wanted assurances that the theater actually would be built and that it was not merely a good idea that might not be realized. Mallery understood that Smalley fixed the theater in his mind as a symbol of whether downtown could regenerate.[4] Smalley also gauged the city's progress in completing the Papago Freeway, as well as the then-called Squaw Peak Parkway, both of which would make the downtown area more easily accessible.[5] Smalley believed that the theater and the transportation projects needed to be on the boards before he could commit his company to the Superblock project. Howlett left the Schulz meeting with redoubled resolve to speed up additional funding for both freeways. The following year, Howlett was instrumental in the passage of a complicated gas-tax bill by the legislature, which supplied the money for these major thoroughfares.[6]

Meanwhile, the site-selection process had proven to be an enormous challenge for Mallery and the Central Phoenix Theater Study Committee. Of the three sites recommended in the feasibility study, Morison favored the Superblock; however, it was risky. Would the city be able to find a tenacious developer and to find that developer soon? Morison saw great promise in placing the theater in an enlivened urban environment that was meant to draw people there to work, eat, shop, and enjoy the arts. The arts groups, however, were skeptical. They believed that linking the theater to the Superblock development could further delay construction. Because Rouse Corporation had not yet made a commitment to develop the area, and then when another prospective developer, Gerald Hines, retreated from his interest in the Superblock site, Mallery settled on Morison's second site recommendation, namely, the north end of Phoenix Civic Plaza.[7]

Mallery appreciated the strategic placement of New York City's Lincoln Center complex, and with the theater on the plaza directly across from Symphony Hall, Phoenix would have the beginnings of a similar layout. The design also would free up funds from the Civic Plaza Building Corporation, which was part of Mallery's initial strategy. Others on his committee agreed that the site was appealing. Phoenix residents already viewed civic plaza as a cultural destination because the Phoenix Symphony performed there, and it had the advantage of existing abundant parking. Mallery and the theater study committee moved forward on securing the site. However, the underground parking below the plaza posed insurmountable problems. City engineers had cited structural incompatibilities that precluded construction of a theater on that section of the plaza. Hope turned to disappointment.

Mallery, undaunted by this setback, focused his attention on the open parking lot across the street from Symphony Hall. Five separate entities owned the northern half of the block, which complicated any action on that portion. The southern half of the block, with only one owner, looked promising, and it appeared large enough for a theater. Mallery started his negotiations with Bertram French, a partner with Monroe-Second Associates, whom he had worked with in the past. Because there were no new downtown developments or building projects underway, he was able to convince French to sign the conditional purchase agreement for zero down.[8] At this juncture, Mallery brought the Civic Plaza Building Corporation into the negotiations. The corporation's board of directors, composed of nine private citizens, issued bonds to support, maintain, and expand Phoenix Civic Plaza as a prime convention site. The funding for this venture came from a variety of special taxes on building and construction, as well as on hotels, restaurants, bars, and other related business enterprises. This allowed the city to keep its public commitment of using general revenue solely for essential needs. Newton Rosenzweig, president of the Civic Plaza Building Corporation, was the dominant force on Phoenix Civic Plaza matters. Mallery knew that Rosenzweig opposed any use of these taxpayer funds other than for retiring the civic plaza debt.[9]

Rosenzweig, one of three children of Austrian Jewish immigrants Isaac and Rosa (Gross) Rosenzweig, had transformed his family's second-hand store and pawnshop into one of the finest jewelry stores in the state. As the eldest son, Newton was completely dedicated to the family business and excelled in its management.[10] When the family sold the store to a national firm in 1973, Rosenzweig, in keeping with his dedication to the family business, stayed on as a consultant for only a few months. Unlike his flamboyant brother Harry, who was a close friend and confidante to Senator Barry Goldwater and had served as the Republican Party state chair, Newton was a proud, formal, and introverted man known as being fastidious and methodical.[11] He lived with his wife in the family home on East Monte Vista, near downtown.

Rosenzweig channeled his energy into civic causes. He supported groups that aided the underprivileged and, as he described, "organizations which dealt with the quality of the day-to-day life of the people."[12] Rosenzweig helped form the reformist Charter Government Committee in Phoenix in the late 1940s; he also served one term on the Phoenix City Council. Less known was that he was a cultured man who enjoyed the arts, an affection Mallery had noted in meetings of the Phoenix 40. Although his fiscal conservatism could pose problems for Mallery, he nevertheless hoped to bring Rosenzweig into the fold.[13]

Henry Sargent, another board member of the Civic Plaza Building Corporation, strongly supported the theater initiative, and he could counter Rosenzweig's possible opposition somewhat. Chief financial officer of Arizona Public Service, Sargent was an avid theatergoer and arts patron. He previously had worked with Mallery to bring Arizona Theatre Company to Phoenix, and he eventually accepted an appointment to Arizona Theatre Company's board of directors. Sargent, a natural ally on the Civic Plaza Building Corporation board, agreed to help with the new theater project when it came before the board.[14]

Denny Maus, director of Phoenix Civic Plaza, emerged as Mallery's ally in generating consensus. An outgoing, athletic, and devoted city employee, with a streak of show business in his persona, Maus knew each member of the Civic Plaza Building Corporation's board well.[15] Mallery relied on his deftness in working effectively with the varied personalities on the board. Maus successfully neutralized the obstructionists and convinced others that the theater was worth the energy and the expense. In a brilliant move, Maus uncovered the original plans for Phoenix Civic Plaza and found that they indeed had included a theater, but the theater had been cut as a budget-saving measure.[16]

Denny Maus, director of Phoenix Civic Plaza, emerged as Mallery's ally in generating consensus from the Civic Plaza Building Corporation to support the new theater. He uncovered the original plans for Phoenix Civic Plaza and found that they indeed had included a theater, but the theater had been cut as a budget-saving measure.
Arizona Republic, April 12, 1985. Photograph by Suzanne Starr. Used with permission.

With Maus working the internal board politics effectively, Mallery advanced his cause and argued that the project was fiscally feasible. Sargent confirmed what Mallery had already deduced; he would need to demonstrate financial strength, which meant securing a private donor's multimillion-dollar commitment. Meanwhile, Mallery sounded out various banks for preliminary financing. The largest and preferred choice, Valley National Bank, had a long history in Arizona; Walter Bimson, the bank's board chair, was proud to have established it as a workingman's bank, one that was friendly to Arizonans with ideas and vision, but who were short on credit. Although Bimson died in April 1980 at the age of eighty-eight, his influence persisted; Mallery believed that he would receive a fair hearing.[17]

Roger Lyon, president of Valley National Bank, was cut of the same cloth as Bimson, and Lyon was an ardent supporter of downtown development. He stated, "It takes just one evening newscast to see what can happen to a city that ignores its downtown area. It quickly becomes a slum and spreads like cancer through a healthy body."[18] Nevertheless, when Mallery petitioned Lyon about the theater, he suggested a consortium of banks, or at least one additional bank, to work in partnership with Valley National Bank. Mallery believed that Don Tostenrud, board chair and chief executive officer of Arizona Bank, was his best bet. Tostenrud was well versed in the theater idea from its birth, having attended the breakfast meeting when DeConcini first broached the subject with his informal cabinet. Tostenrud agreed to work with Lyon; however, both bankers insisted that Mallery should have some money in hand before they would commit. Once again, the project hinged on a major private donor. Mallery telephoned Bob Herberger and requested a lunch date.

Mallery had approached Herberger during lunch months before, on a hot July day, outlining his clear plan for financing the new theater. He appealed to Herberger's pride in Arizona, pointing out that "we are the only city of our size in the United States that does not have a performing arts theater."[19] Herberger raised tough questions. Would the city come through with its share? What assurance was there that the business community would ante up? Is downtown Phoenix truly viable as an economic and cultural center? Is a new theater really needed? How did he fit into the equation?

Mallery responded to all of his questions with detailed answers; he could tell that Herberger had read Morison's study thoroughly. Mallery left the meeting without asking for a donation. Instead, he sent a letter formally asking Herberger to donate $3 million for the construction of the theater and another $1 million for an endowment. He posited that another $3 million could be raised from other private sources and that these sums would prompt an investment of $7 million from the city of Phoenix through the Civic Plaza Building Corporation. Herberger considered Mallery's proposal without committing or rejecting it outright. He suggested that Mallery contact his son, Gary, who was amenable to looking over the plans. Gary Herberger and Mallery met twice, first on September 12, 1982, and then again on September 28, 1982.[20] They quickly developed an easy rapport as they discussed the details of the theater project.

Mallery remained in close contact with Bob Herberger, keeping him apprised of the ongoing discussions, as Herberger warmed to the idea that the new theater could spur downtown development. Mallery knew that Herberger had given

$1,000 to 100 former and long-time present employees who had worked at his stores for twenty years or more, excluding executives. The personal letters that accompanied the checks opened with, "When I review my own personal accomplishments, growth, and success over the years, I fully realize that a tremendous amount of credit has to be given to people such as yourself."[21] It was the gesture of a man who not only valued his merchandising past and the people who helped make him a success, but also a sign of a man paying attention to his legacy.

Bob Herberger agreed to Mallery's invitation to a second lunch, this one at the Golden Eagle, on the top floor of the Valley National Bank building. Mallery asked Hattie Babbitt, wife of Governor Bruce Babbitt, to join them; he ensured that they were seated at a table overlooking Phoenix Civic Plaza and the parking lot on Monroe Street.[22] True to form, Mallery had completed all of his preluncheon preparations, including briefings with Gary Herberger and his wife Jeanne, an executive with Dayton-Hudson's Arizona stores, as well as a cultural leader. Mallery also had spent a lot of time with Kax Herberger. Although Bob Herberger clearly was the ironclad decision maker of the family, Mallery knew that the family's support was crucial.

St. Mary's twin towers appear behind the parking lot. Symphony Hall is to the far right, with shade awnings sprinkled on the plaza in front. The photographer took the photo from the top of Valley National Bank's parking garage. *Arizona Republic,* July 23, 1987. Photograph by Pete Peters. Used with permission.

After pleasantries, Mallery reviewed the high points of the theater project and segued gracefully into its potential to be a hallmark of Herberger's legacy in Arizona. He mentioned the land held in escrow, and he highlighted the key role that a major gift from Herberger would play in obtaining final support from the banks and from the Civic Plaza Building Corporation board. After a few thoughtful moments, Herberger smiled broadly, looked out the window at the parking lot, and, with a laugh, extended his hand across the table to Mallery, saying, "Yes, I will be the donor." The fact that Herberger said he would give $2 million, instead of the $4 million Mallery had requested, detracted little from the subsequent celebration.[23]

Now that he had the major donor's commitment, Mallery's proposal to the Civic Plaza Building Corporation drew unanimous approval on February 7, 1983. Shortly thereafter, Arizona Bank agreed to finance the purchase of the land while Mallery arranged permanent financing for the rest of the project. The ninety-day deadline had been met, with little time to spare. The land for the theater had been secured, and Richard Mallery savored the moment. The new theater was in play, moving toward becoming a tangible reality.

6

A New Entity

"This announcement is one of the most exciting that I have had the opportunity to make in my term as mayor," stated Margaret Hance on May 12, 1983, in a press release announcing the $2 million grant from Bob Herberger and his family.[1] Hance foresaw that the Herbergers' generosity signaled a new era in public–private partnerships in Phoenix, and she was elated that it happened on her watch.[2] The entire Herberger family, not just the patriarch, issued the donation in the form of a challenge grant that had to be matched by other private sources before the end of 1985. A provision in the grant agreement stated that the 800-seat theater would be named after its patron, that the theater would be designed with the intention of later adding a 300-seat venue when the funds became available, and that the total anticipated cost of the theater, including the land, would be in the vicinity of $11 million.[3]

The press release tellingly omitted important relevant information; for example, it did not mention one arts group. When *Arizona Republic* reporter Michael Maza quizzed David Hawkanson, he responded obliquely that "he knew an announcement was pending." When pressed further, Hawkanson said that Arizona Theatre Company's use of the new theater "had not been discussed."[4] Although a passing comment in Maza's story, it suggested that indeed something had changed since the days of the DeConcini breakfast meetings when Arizona Theatre Company was a central piece in the discussions about a theater.

Even so, Arizona Theatre Company continued to develop closer ties to Phoenix. By now, the company performed most of its plays in Phoenix, including some that opened first in Phoenix before subsequently moving to Tucson. Prior to Mayor Hance's announcement, Arizona Theatre Company had moved out of Phoenix Little Theatre's building, not only because of scheduling conflicts, but also because of the more troubling problem that audiences were confusing them with the amateur group that usually performed there. Phoenix College stepped forward to offer the use of its theater, a new facility that was one of the best equipped in the metropolitan area. Although the theater was small and inconveniently located away from the city center, Phoenix College gave Arizona Theatre Company complete freedom by making its theater available on a flexible schedule based solely on the company's rehearsal and performance requirements, including any inevitable last minute changes.

In addition to these developments, the Phoenix Friends of Arizona Theatre Company, chaired by Linda Whitney, was growing in membership and contributions, an indication of the company's expanding strength in Phoenix.[5] Plans for the upcoming season were ambitious, with the company performing its entire production of six plays in both Phoenix and Tucson. With this expansion, Arizona Theatre Company became the only theater company in the country to perform regularly in more than one major city. In 1983 Arizona Theatre Company received a presidential citation for this unique endeavor, bringing national notice and accolades to the company.[6] "We are trying to develop a new model based on the fact that we are a two-city operation," said Gary Gisselman, artistic director.[7] Clearly, Arizona Theatre Company was making Phoenix its second home, with or without a suitable performing space of its own.

A scene from A Funny Thing Happened on the Way to the Forum, *performed by Arizona Theatre Company during their 1982–1983 season.* Arizona Theatre Company Archives. Photograph by Tim Fuller. Used with permission.

Meanwhile, a growing and discernable rift had opened between Mallery and Hawkanson, one that in many ways mirrored the long-standing rivalry that existed between the cities of Phoenix and Tucson. The seemingly irrational civic competition between the two cities began with the founding of Phoenix in 1868 by John W. "Jack" Swilling, a former confederate soldier turned Arizona prospector and speculator. According to most historians, the respective histories of the two cities set them apart politically, culturally, socially, and economically. During the territorial period, from 1863 to 1912, Tucson and Phoenix entered into a fierce competition for the state capital to be moved from Prescott to their respective cities. Tucson previously had been the state capital for ten years, from 1867 to 1877, and Tucsonans believed that the designation should rightfully be theirs again in 1889. When the upstart smaller town of Phoenix, which already had developed a reputation for being greedy and acquisitive, won the state capital title and then retained its state capital status when Arizona became a state, Tucson never forgave Phoenix for stealing the designation away. The resultant power, prestige, and prosperity that accrue to a capital city became the hallmark of Phoenix; by 1920 the city could boast that it had twice the population of Tucson, forever leaving the older historic city in its dust.[8]

The rivalry that seethed just below the surface for more than 100 years was kept alive because of the strikingly divergent character of the two cities. Tucson, established as a presidio and settled by the Spanish in the 1600s, had a long, gracious history and retained its ties to Mexico.[9] Phoenix, whose origins were rooted in the westward movement of American pioneers after the Civil War, reflected a very different culture and attracted a more acquisitive, restless group of Anglo-Americans who were determined to carve out an existence in what arguably was a very inhospitable environment.

Phoenix was crass, rapacious, and self-centered—at least from Tucson's point of view. Tucson was intellectual, cultured, and authentic; it looked askance at its younger, yet more economically vigorous sister community to the north. The more culturally mature city of Tucson spawned theater, ballet, and opera companies that eventually served the entire state. Indeed, in the late 1970s, Tucson was the smallest city in the United States to boast a professional theater company, a professional ballet company, a professional opera company, and a professional symphony. Phoenix had only a symphony and a basketball team, the Phoenix Suns.[10]

Centered within 500,000 acres of irrigated farmland, Phoenix repudiated the desert, ignored it, or erased it. Tucson embraced the desert and respected it; the city easily had more environmentalists per square mile than any other Arizona city. Compared to Phoenix, Tucson was more politically conscious, the home of influential political families, such as the Udalls and DeConcinis, and the birthplace of the sanctuary movement for Central American refugees.[11] Despite Tucson's progressive political and environmental credentials, Phoenix continued its meteoric growth and became an economic juggernaut compared to the Old Pueblo, a beloved moniker for Tucson.

Mallery avoided the Phoenix–Tucson rivalry, except when it interfered with his goal of making Phoenix into a great city. He was acutely aware of the rivalry's effect in the Valley, however, having confronted it often in the course of business. Arizona Theatre Company was a *Tucson* organization, and Mallery anticipated the challenges of raising money in Phoenix for a theater designated primarily for a Tucson group. He already had detected percolations of discontent, as well as a few bitter complaints, from smaller Phoenix-based arts groups who claimed he favored Arizona Theatre Company.[12] Mallery reasoned that it was better to defer this point of contention until he had achieved the primary goal of raising the money for the new theater.

Coupled with this disconcerting rivalry issue were Mallery and Hawkanson's dissonant approaches to the theater and its operations. As Hawkanson described his theater company's needs in terms of the actual use of the prospective building and how a professional theater season required big blocks of time reserved for rehearsals and performances to produce high-quality art, Mallery determined that Hawkanson wanted total control of the building, which could be detrimental to the other arts groups. Mallery maintained a more systematic approach than Hawkanson, and he focused on the next phase of the project rather than jumping ahead to usage policies. Mallery wanted to complete the acquisition of the Monroe-Second Associates property, and the best course, according to Bradley Morison's study, was to create a nonprofit organization that would acquire the property, raise the money, commission the design and construction, and later operate the building.[13] On May 20, 1983, the Phoenix Performing Arts Center six-member board of directors, which included Mallery as president, Patricia Tully as vice president, Dino DeConcini as

A scene from A Streetcar Named Desire, *performed by Arizona Theatre Company during their 1983–1984 season.*
Arizona Theatre Company Archives. Photograph by Tim Fuller. Used with permission.

A second scene from A Streetcar Named Desire, *performed by Arizona Theatre Company during their 1983–1984 season.* Arizona Theatre Company Archives. Photograph by Tim Fuller. Used with permission.

secretary and treasurer, Keith Turley as fund-raising committee chair, as well as Gary Herberger and Hattie Babbitt, announced their existence and intentions.[14] By June 6, 1983, through the financial backing of Valley National Bank and Arizona Bank, the new organization owned the Monroe-Second Associates property.[15]

As Mallery pressed forward with Turley on fund-raising, Mayor Hance made a surprising announcement; she would not seek another term as mayor. Hance disagreed with Proposition 200, a voter initiative approved the previous December to divide the city into districts for city council representation, instead of the at-large system in place since the late 1940s. A young activist attorney, Terry Goddard, led the drive for the change.[16] Goddard's Committee for District Representation aroused much interest among Phoenix voters. The mayor; existing city council members, except one; the chamber of commerce; and Phoenix 40 members all opposed the initiative. In a blatant attempt to decrease voter turnout, the city council scheduled the vote for an odd Wednesday, just one month after a general election. Goddard and the reformers nevertheless prevailed. Citizens approved Proposition 200 by a vote of 39,591 to 37,821, thereby recalibrating the Phoenix power structure. Phoenix became the last city of its size in the nation to drop at-large elections. Mallery maintained a cordial working relationship with Goddard, even though he opposed the reform, and he publicly praised Goddard for his "pragmatic idealism."[17]

With Mayor Hance retiring, Mallery grew concerned.[18] The new political calculus, which would result in a more representative government, also could lead to decreased attention to downtown development. Would support for downtown dissipate? More specifically, would public support for the Herberger Theater dissipate?

Mallery discerned a few upsides to the new political environment. Keith Turley, with the aid of the mayor's chief of staff C. A. Howlett and others, had succeeded in convincing the state legislature to pass a complicated gasoline tax bill, which resulted in a $400 million transportation block grant to the city. The funds specifically were intended for freeway construction. Turley chaired the committee that selected the location of the new Squaw Peak Parkway, which promised to make downtown more accessible to the north. These transportation developments would influence any attempts to depart radically from the downtown momentum for the theater.

Still, Mallery believed that the wisest course of action was to obtain a formal vote from the city of Phoenix on the Herberger Theater project before the next election. Ideally, he wanted a written agreement before the end of 1983. Mallery suggested to Mayor Hance and the city council that they dissolve the Central Phoenix Theater Study Committee and recognize its successor organization, the Phoenix Performing Arts Center, as the entity to complete the task of building the theater. Mallery then offered the land acquired from Monroe-Second Associates to the city expressly for the theater. As Mallery had stated in his earlier proposal to the Civic Plaza Building Corporation in 1982, this conveyance allowed the city to include the property within the existing lease to the corporation. In turn, this empowered the Civic Plaza Building Corporation to issue bonds to finance the city's 49 percent share. The theater design phase was to be under the aegis of the Phoenix Performing Arts Center board of directors, with the construction to be overseen by the city of Phoenix.

The city council quickly agreed; however, they delegated the plan's execution to Selden Kent, who served as the administrative services manager for the city of Phoenix. Kent reasoned that because the city would own the building, they should be involved in running the theater and in sharing in any surplus revenues. He conceived a structure where the city would "contract" with the Phoenix Performing Arts Center for the management of programming and operations. Kent sent Mallery a letter in October 1983 outlining his "sensible" new approach, pointing out that City Manager Marvin Andrews and others agreed with his concept.[19]

Mallery refused to go along with Selden's idea. If the city contracted with the Phoenix Performing Arts Center, it might choose not to renew the contract and, ultimately, to run the theater itself. It was crucial to keep an arms-length distance, if not an impenetrable barrier, between the city and the Phoenix Performing Arts Center. Mallery did not want to leave an opening for government bureaucrats or political meddlers to take over the theater.[20] After a few weeks of telephone calls with key board members of the Civic Plaza Building Corporation and Denny Maus, director of Phoenix Civic Plaza, Mallery met with Kent and skillfully directed the agreement back to the original concept. To solidify their discussion, Mallery personally delivered a letter to Kent on November 8, 1983, detailing their discussion, which became the key document defining the Phoenix Performing Arts Center's relationship with the city.[21] Mallery's letter stated: "In its conveyance of the Monroe property to the city of Phoenix, the board of directors of Phoenix Performing Arts Center shall reserve and *be solely responsible* for the management and operation of the completed performing arts facility, including, but not limited to, establishing the basic philosophy for its use; determining the actual use of the performing arts facility; raising the necessary administrative expenses; overseeing the programming and operational activities; supplying administrative, supervisory, and technical personnel for the activities; raising funds for such administrative expenses; and taking all the steps necessary to carry out the policies and programs necessary for the performing arts facility."

Outlining the city's role, he wrote: "As the owner of the performing arts facility, the city of Phoenix will be responsible for all building maintenance and operating expenses relating to the performing arts facility, including, but not limited to, the costs of insurance, maintenance, repairs, custodial and security services, and utilities."[22] Mallery wanted to minimize costs for the arts organizations, and with the city providing these maintenance items, it created, in effect, a permanent subsidy for the theater. Regarding the surplus revenue issue, Mallery made it clear that these monies were to remain under the control of the performing arts center board, and they were not subject to being shared with the city: "In the event Phoenix Performing Arts Center has a surplus after paying the administrative, programming, operational, and other expenses for which it is responsible, relating to the performing arts facility, such surplus shall be utilized by Phoenix Performing Arts Center for the purpose of either making additional capital improvements and renovating the performing arts facility or establishing an endowment for the benefit of the performing arts facility."[23] On November 17, 1983, Mayor Hance and the city council unanimously approved Mallery's keystone plan. Two weeks before the approval, Phoenix elected its new mayor, none other than Terry Goddard.

7

Prince of the City

Richard Mallery welcomed the election of Terry Goddard as mayor of Phoenix. Goddard had demonstrated a passion for downtown revitalization; he believed that theaters, the arts, and historic preservation were its keys. Goddard wanted Phoenix to have a new theater, and Mallery impressed him with his thoughtful, in-depth handling of the project. Mallery had commissioned the Morison study, conceived of the public–private partnership, attracted community and corporate leaders committed to the vision, and convinced the Herberger family to step forward with the galvanizing $2 million challenge grant.[1] Goddard allied with Mallery going forward with the project.

Goddard was an elected official, however, which set him apart from Mallery in fundamental ways. Goddard embraced broad citizen participation and sought public input in debating issues that shaped the city's future. He vowed to promote open government, a hallmark of his administration.[2] Mallery, in contrast, operated with singular discretion, eschewing what he perceived as unnecessary or cumbersome social and civic relationships, preferring instead to move forward with dispatch.

Open government was more than campaign rhetoric to Goddard. Soon after he entered office, he removed the prison-like security system that surrounded the offices of the mayor, the city council, and the city manager. Goddard conducted city council meetings in the evenings so that working people could attend, and he held regularly scheduled press conferences. His accessible style captivated the media, which soon dubbed him a "white knight" and the "new prince of the city."[3]

Goddard also created the Phoenix City Club, which drew its membership from every section of the city and reflected the city's political diversity. The club became a vehicle for citizen participation in developing city policy and led to the

Terry Goddard being sworn in as mayor of Phoenix by Arizona Supreme Court Chief Justice Frank Gordon Jr. Goddard's mother looks on. *Arizona Republic*, January 8, 1988. Photograph by Tom Tingle. Used with permission.

"Goals for Phoenix Forum," which placed thousands of residents and businesses in an advisory role to the mayor and the city council.[4] Goddard's populist style, an unlikely mix of Ivy League bearing and a tall, lanky Huck-Finn-type charm, resonated with the urban and suburban electorate; his reelection every two years became a foregone conclusion, until he sought the governor's seat in 1990.[5] The voting public knew Goddard as an Arizona native who had the good sense to obtain his law degree close to home, at Arizona State University in 1976.[6]

From the outset of his first term, Goddard focused on the Herberger project. In reviewing the new city council, Goddard knew that the representatives of the two downtown districts, Calvin Goode (District 7) and Mary Rose Wilcox (District 8), needed no convincing. They viewed the proposed theater as a wonderful amenity for their constituents. Goddard could depend on the support of Ed Korrick, a descendent of a Phoenix pioneer family with a tradition of supporting the arts, who represented District 6. Barry Starr, who represented District 1, also favored downtown development.[7] Thus, the overall political framework for moving forward with the theater project was in place.

The majority of the newly created Phoenix Performing Arts Center board, however, remained leery of government bureaucracy and open public forums.

They were, after all, members of the Phoenix establishment who were accustomed to operating behind closed doors and to controlling outcomes. Having witnessed too many good projects derail because of large, unwieldy groups unable to reach a consensus, they worked diligently to avoid inertia. Nowhere was this more apparent than in the method they devised to select an architect for the theater. The board members of the Phoenix Performing Arts Center decided to do it themselves.

Because Gary Herberger was an architect, he became the board's advisor on how to select an architect. Herberger had attended both Pomona College and the Massachusetts Institute of Technology, and he had been a fellow with the legendary Frank Lloyd Wright.[8] Herberger also wanted to limit bureaucratic procedures and delays that often were caused by city government. Cautious and resourceful, he sought expert guidance from Bradley Morison to learn how other cities had approached a similar situation. In late February 1984, Morison met with both Gary and his father, Bob, over lunch to talk about architect selection.

Gary strongly supported local architects, and he urged that they be given a legitimate chance to secure the contract. He believed that Phoenix possessed a strong pool of talented architects, and the idea of bringing in some big name "from outside" held no appeal for him.[9] Morison listened carefully and then spoke at length about the complexities in building a professional theater and the importance of hiring theater design experts and professionals schooled in stagecraft, lighting, acoustics, and other technical areas of expertise. Special skill sets, he argued, were needed to create a first-class theater, one that "really worked for the art of theater."[10] Morison's arguments struck a chord, and the Herbergers conceded that architects with these specific types of expertise were not practicing in Arizona.

To get around the problem, they decided to challenge local architects to organize a team of theater design experts from anywhere in the world, with the caveat that the lead architect be tied to an Arizona firm. Using a collaboration of experts had gained traction in the design field, and this concept would allow architectural firms in Arizona to be competitive with outside firms vying for the theater project. Gary Herberger developed a list of 442 Phoenix-area architectural firms, and he drafted a letter that described the collaborative team approach. His letter invited those who were interested in the theater complex to submit information about themselves and their proposed teams by May 31, 1984. Mallery reviewed the letter and assured the Herbergers and Morison that there was enough "wiggle room" if the board subsequently decided on a different methodology.[11]

A problem surfaced when Mayor Goddard learned of Gary Herberger's letter to local architects. He fired off a letter to Herberger and Mallery, protesting,

"There have been no attempts to coordinate with the city of Phoenix. Such treatment is hardly consistent with a partnership with the city."[12] Herberger referred the matter to Mallery, who arranged to meet with Goddard; Mallery asked Dino DeConcini to accompany him to the parley. Mallery and DeConcini calmed Goddard by telling him that the Herberger letter to the architectural firms was experimental. Since they were uncertain that the letter would produce anything of value, they thought it would have been premature to consult with the mayor; but they now informed Goddard that the Phoenix Performing Arts Center board had received twenty-four letters of interest from local architectural firms, and Gary Herberger, in recent days, had spelled out a viable selection process.[13] Mallery and DeConcini now sought to obtain Goddard's opinion on the matter. This assuaged the mayor.

Mallery, DeConcini, and Goddard spent a lot of time on the delicate issue of who would serve on the selection committee. Herberger's list included a city representative selected by the mayor, but Goddard wanted more. He pressed Mallery and DeConcini for the appointment of additional city representatives, and they agreed. It was not really a concession, but rather a constructive way to involve the city and one that might deepen the city's commitment. They agreed on the appointment of four city representatives: two city council members, Ed Korrick and Barry Starr; Marvin Andrews, city manager; and Richard Counts, city planning director. In addition, the group agreed to add Newton Rosenzweig, president of the Civic Plaza Building Corporation, and Denny Maus, director of Phoenix Civic Plaza. The meeting ended on a high note, as Mallery and DeConcini had engaged Goddard in designing the architect selection process.

The final selection committee grew in number and was made up of the six-member Phoenix Performing Arts Center board—Mallery, Darrow "Duke" Tully, Dino DeConcini, Keith Turley, Gary Herberger, and Hattie Babbitt—as well as Mayor Goddard's six appointees.[14] At Gary Herberger's suggestion, Gerald McSheffrey, dean of the College of Architecture at Arizona State University, became a committee member, as did Deborah Whitehurst, from the Arizona Commission on the Arts, who would represent the arts groups.[15] Morison, advisor to the board and selection committee, would act as the board's liaison between the arts groups and the chosen architectural team. Because direct involvement of arts groups in the design process was a rare occurrence in theater projects nationwide, Mallery and Herberger took special pains to include them, a mark of their enlightened leadership.[16] The result was to be a remarkably well-designed theater for the spoken word.

Meanwhile, Gary Herberger recommended hiring Morison to update the feasibility study, which was now three years old. Morison assisted the board in reviewing the twenty-four architectural firm submittals, winnowing them down to eight. These eight firms would make presentations before the selection committee in the fall of 1984, offering their design ideas for the new theater and showing examples of their previous work. After the completion of all presentations, the committee would thin the competition by one-half.[17]

Herberger grew increasingly pleased with his role on the Phoenix Performing Arts Center board. He enjoyed working with Mallery on a daily basis and found the attorney and theater proponent stimulating. The entire process reminded him of the creative synergy that filled his days when designing and building his own home. Herberger and Mallery agreed that so much was possible in Arizona. They shared common views on architecture. They believed that function—that is, how a space fits its purpose—was paramount. They also agreed that good design enhanced the functional use of space. Almost as important was the ability of architecture to create a sense of place, admittedly a more elusive concept to define, but one they described as a building "in harmony with its environment" in choice of materials and design, one that "fit Arizona," yet "pointed to a new direction" for the look and feel of downtown.[18] Herberger embraced the ensuing challenges. Furthermore, he hit upon the idea of asking students at the Arizona State University School of Architecture to add their creative energies to the mix. The Herberger family had donated to various Arizona State University schools and programs, so the dean of the School of Architecture welcomed this idea, and students began submitting their designs.[19]

Meanwhile, Keith Turley, who headed the fund-raising efforts for the theater, had begun the far more difficult task of raising $2 million to match the Herberger challenge grant. A driving force in the leadership of Phoenix, Turley was a veteran fund-raiser for civic causes, so he felt up to the task. Known and respected by the arts community, Turley served as president of Arizonans for Cultural Development, a newly formed advocacy group. The theater project benefited from Turley's visibility in the highest echelons of Phoenix's power structure and from the fact that he was greatly admired for his integrity, confidence, and unwavering commitment to the community.[20] Turley and Mallery made their first overtures to corporations, reasoning that large grants or pledges might come forth quickly. They immediately snared several firm pledges of $100,000 that were payable over three to five years. When interviewed by the *Phoenix Gazette* in late January about the theater's fund-raising efforts, Mallery replied with assurance, saying they "have been proceeding quietly and effectively" in the corporate sector.[21] Buoyed by their initial success, Turley and Mallery created the Phoenix Performing Arts Center Challenge Committee, composed of nineteen men who were mainly fellow chief executive officers and Phoenix 40 members. (See "Phoenix Performing Arts Center Challenge Committee: 1984.")

Although all committee members brought money to the table, Turley and Mallery were the largest corporate fund-raisers. Others who brought in signif-

Phoenix Performing Arts Center Challenge Committee: 1984

Edward Carson	President, First Interstate Bank
Herman Chanen	Chairman, president, and chief executive officer, Chanen Construction
Donald Cline	Arizona vice president and chief executive officer, Mountain Bell Telephone
Karl Eller	Chairman and chief executive officer, Circle K Corporation
William Franke	Chairman, president, and chief executive officer, Southwest Forest Industries
William Gresser	President, American Greyhound Racing
Leonard Huck	President and chief executive officer, Valley National Bank
Russ Lyon Jr.	Managing partner, Westcor Partners
Thomas Madden	Senior vice president, American Express
Richard Mallery	Senior partner, Snell & Wilmer
A. J. "Jack" Pfister	General manager, Salt River Project
William Schulz	Owner, WRS Investments
William Shover	Director of public affairs, Phoenix Newspapers
James Simmons	Chairman and president, United Bank of Arizona
Robert Swanson	Chairman and chief executive officer, Del Webb Corporation
John Teets	Chairman and chief executive officer, Greyhound Corporation
Donald Tostenrud	Chairman and chief executive officer, Arizona Bank
Darrow "Duke" Tully	Publisher, Phoenix Newspapers
Keith Turley	Chairman, president, and chief executive officer, Arizona Public Service

icant funds were apartment magnate William Schulz, United Bank president and board chair James Simmons, Phoenix Newspapers director of public affairs William Shover, Chanen Construction president and chief executive officer Herman Chanen, and American Greyhound Racing president William Gresser. By April 1984 they had raised $775,000 and identified another $600,000 in possible donations.[22] Still, they were shy of their $2 million goal.

On May 10, 1984, Darrow "Duke" Tully, publisher of Phoenix Newspapers, including the *Arizona Republic,* hosted a special meeting of the Phoenix Performing Arts Center board of directors.[23] Keith Turley recommended that the board invite potential donors to a luncheon, as well as those who already had made commitments, to bring new supporters into the fold. Tully and Mallery agreed to cohost a luncheon in the San Xavier Room of the Plaza Club on the top floor of the United Bank building; the date was set for June 6, 1984. Gary Herberger suggested that the Arizona State University student architectural models be presented, which were on display at Valley National Bank. The board eagerly endorsed his idea.[24]

Coincidentally, that the group had scheduled the luncheon on the day after a bond election, which would triple the space for performing arts groups in Phoenix if successful. In effect, the city asked voters to authorize the purchase of two landmark downtown theaters: Palace West, a 1929 Spanish colonial theater with 1,800 seats located at 203 West Adams Street; and Phoenix Union High School auditorium, a 1,400-seat venue at Seventh Street and Van

Palace West, a Spanish colonial theater built in 1929 and located at 203 West Adams Street, is a landmark in downtown Phoenix. Voter approval of the 1984 Proposition 15 bond election would have allowed the city to purchase and restore the theater. *Arizona Republic,* May 7, 1984. Photograph by Earl McCartney. Used with permission.

Buren built in the 1930s.[25] These bond issues reflected Mayor Goddard's initiative to use historic preservation and the arts to revitalize downtown. Goddard advocated an even grander vision for his city than simply building one new theater. He wanted a multifaceted cultural district for the performing arts.[26]

Unfortunately, both propositions became mired in controversy, despite the fact that a citizen subcommittee had recommended the purchases. Even Morison injected controversy into the debate by saying publicly that the theaters were too big for anything except symphony orchestras or opera performances.[27] Not one of the approximately thirty performing arts groups Morison had studied, many in desperate need of performing space, would be served by these theaters, he claimed. They were just too big. Phoenix architect Ted Alexander disagreed with Morison; he believed that the size issue could be resolved by renovations and that the theaters could be used for large touring groups as well. James Forsberg, director of the Downtown Phoenix Redevelopment Agency, pushed for the renovations, saying, "The city must get a cultural district under way.[28] Other cities, such as Dallas and Atlanta, know that cultural districts are critical to economic health. Phoenix cannot rest on its sunshine anymore. We will go backwards if we do."[29]

Mayor Goddard wondered if the leaders of the Phoenix Performing Arts Center feared the proposed theater renovations as a threat to their own goals. It seemed likely that they viewed these restored theaters as competition and that they could not get beyond their limited self-interest. Goddard also had to confront the long-held view by many Arizona leaders that there was not enough money in the state, or in any county, to support much more than one of anything, particularly in the arts. Such reasoning set the stage for Arizona Theatre Company, Arizona Opera, and Ballet Arizona to become statewide organizations. Although perhaps unintentional, this attitude deflected energies that otherwise might have led to the creation of professional arts organizations in cities throughout the state.[30]

Voter turnout for the bond issues was low, and they failed. Proposition 15 had called for the purchase of Palace West, but it fell victim to the opposition, which preferred to funnel money into housing or other commercial developments downtown. Proposition 8 fell into a maelstrom of controversy over charges alleging a conflict of interest involving Mallery, although not because of his role with the Phoenix Performing Arts Center. The redevelopment of the Phoenix Union High School campus, which included the historic auditorium, had the backing of the Phoenix Community Alliance, a newly formed organization of 120 business and civic leaders, with Mallery as a cofounder. Its goal was to create a dynamic, modern downtown. The alliance's plan for the twenty-seven acre site was ambitious: a city-owned cultural center, a museum, a theater, and possibly a domed stadium.[31] When word got out that Mallery and twenty-three partners from his law firm, operating as Taypolk Associates, had purchased land adjacent to Phoenix Union High School, it created the impression that the Phoenix Community Alliance project might be merely a front to benefit a few clever power brokers. In fact, the Taypolk land had been purchased to make room for the possible expansion of Snell & Wilmer offices, and negotiations had begun well before the Phoenix Community Alliance had formed or had shaped their idea of retooling Phoenix Union High School. At the time, developers were in the process of buying the Phoenix Union property, although that deal eventually fell through. Nonetheless, scorching news coverage cast a big shadow over Proposition 8, and it failed.[32]

Another conflict of interest allegation against Mallery, although baseless, had arisen a few months earlier. His mother-in-law, Forest Burgess, owned land a few blocks north of the site chosen for the new theater, which was seen by some as a conflict for Mallery, as if he had maneuvered to have the new theater near her property to increase its value. In fact, her interest in this property was common knowledge and even publicly announced in1976—well before any discussion about building a theater nearby had begun—when she donated a 100-year-old historic carriage house that was on her land to the city for placement in Heritage Square.[33]

Mallery appeared unruffled by the controversies, but the public scrutiny and criticism took its toll, especially the widespread criticism in the press. Mayor Goddard also weighed in, saying, "The Taypolk maneuver typifies the old way of doing business here."[34] Civic leadership in Phoenix had grown treacherous indeed. Despite the negative media, Mallery resolved to persevere in his role with the Herberger Theater. The fund-raising luncheon at the Plaza Club proved successful, as Mallery's fellow business leaders and friends rallied in his support, and the Phoenix Performing Arts Center Challenge Committee inched closer to their $2 million goal.

Approximately one month after the successful fund-raising luncheon, Morison began updating the three-year-old feasibility study. He developed a current list of arts groups that would use the new building, and he detailed their scheduling demands and reviewed cost estimates for construction now that the location was definite. Analysis of this data helped him determine that the Herberger theaters should be designed primarily for dramatic performances, with music, dance, and other arts receiving secondary design consideration.[35]

Next, he turned his attention to the site. Because the land was not among those considered in the original study, he had to reevaluate the location in terms of urban planning, which could influence architectural design concepts and capital costs. Was the acreage too small? Could it accommodate the required building? He remained silent until he could thoroughly think it through, but he could not help hinting about a potential bombshell in his report. Morison completed the update in two months and submitted a revised feasibility study on October 10, 1984. In an earlier letter sent on September 12, 1984, to the Phoenix Performing Arts Center board, he suggested that one of the greatest challenges facing the architectural team would be how to fit the theater within the limited one-half block site.[36] Privately, Morison already had arrived at the conclusion that the site had to be expanded, maybe even to encompass the entire block. Now he faced the dilemma of bringing the Phoenix Performing Arts Center board and the city around to his point of view without derailing the project.

8

The Architect

Cities build a theater once in a generation, if at all, and a key decision is the selection of an architect. The committee charged with this responsibility had little knowledge about how to go about it, as Hattie Babbitt saw all too well. Into this vacuum stepped Bradley Morison with his knowledge and verve.[1]

Morison impressed upon the selection committee the advantages of designing a theater that *works*, defining in detail what he meant, as he previously had for the Herbergers and for Mallery.[2] Regardless of the theater's exterior design, the interior must suit both the artists and the audience. The house needed to feel intimate, and a key element of that intimacy involved excellent acoustics for the spoken word. As for the audience, seating must be comfortable and staggered so that the most distant seat felt close to the stage and had good sight lines. Intimate seating also benefited the performers, who fed on the connective energy they sensed emanating from the other side of the footlights, a distinguishing element of live theater.

Morison tutored the committee about stage design. They learned that performers depended on a stage with large wings for their exits and entrances, as well as sufficient room for varied, and sometimes numerous, stage props. Another necessity was a crossover behind the stage to allow the performers to cross easily from one side of the stage to the other as the script indicated. Dressing rooms had to be located nearby to facilitate quick costume changes. In addition, the rehearsal hall stage must exactly mirror the dimensions of the performance theater stage.

At the technical end of design, the stagecrafters required a full-sized fly loft above the stage for a wide range of scenery changes, as well as the capability to hang a variety of lighting instruments, with a connecting master board to

Hattie Babbitt, attorney and a founding board member of the Phoenix Performing Arts Center, served on the architect selection committee for the Herberger Theater.
Arizona Republic, December 7, 2003. Photograph by Dierdre Hamill. Used with permission.

control the lighting. Additional technical design requirements included a communications system between the technical booth at the back of the theater and the stage manager in the wings, wardrobe and equipment rooms, and ample loading docks. Provisions needed to be made for a greenroom backstage, which traditionally was a place for actors to gather and bond, as well as to receive critiques from the director after a rehearsal or performance; in modern times, greenrooms often are used for small receptions with patrons and dignitaries.[3] Musical theater had its own set of demands, such as an orchestra pit to accommodate up to twenty-six musicians, storage requirements for a piano and other instruments, as well as a warm-up room for musicians. Ideally, the orchestra pit should be hydraulic, so that when musicians were not needed, the pit could be raised to stage level to form a thrust stage or it could be lowered from stage level for additional audience seating.

After all the stage and technical design needs were met, they could address the aesthetics of designing the structure to embody an intangible ambiance that creates a sense of occasion. Quoting Tyrone Guthrie, Morison noted, "It is far more difficult to create the pure magic of a great performance in a drab and dreary space than within an environment that makes your spirit take flight by its very presence."[4] Mallery concurred with Morison on the importance of superior interior design features.[5]

The selection committee soon understood why Morison's architectural team approach was the best way to bring together the expertise needed to create a first-rate theater. No single architectural firm employed all the specialists required. There were only a handful of experienced theater acousticians in the world, the majority of whom lived outside the United States. The best acoustics experts routinely traveled to wherever a theater was being constructed or renovated. To a lesser extent, the same was true in the fields of theater design and theater lighting, whose practitioners tended to operate independent of architectural firms.[6]

Bringing a team of theater design experts together was not enough, Morison counseled. Compatibility among the team members was imperative, particularly between the theater design architect and the theater consultant. "The secret," Morison said, "is to select an architectural team that includes theater design architects and theater consultants of equal talent, expertise, and imagination who can and will work together in a balanced partnership of cooperative creativity."[7] Therefore, part of the selection process was to scrutinize the dynamics and balance of power among team members.

The Phoenix Performing Arts Center board previously had winnowed the twenty-four competing architectural submittals to eight. The selection committee's task was to review each of the eight teams thoroughly and select the top four. On September 28, 1984, the selection committee viewed four team presentations. The remaining four teams repeated the process on October 3. The selection committee and the presenting teams met in the boardroom on the top floor of the Valley National Bank building. The large corner boardroom had nearly floor-to-ceiling glass windows that provided views of downtown Phoenix, such as it was in 1984. One architect asked Gary Herberger, "Which direction is downtown?" Herberger patiently pointed out the window, "Here," he said, "Right here...you are looking at it." He smiled at the look of incredulity that flashed briefly across the architect's face.[8]

Mallery was adamant that the proposed site be in full view. He wanted the selection committee members and the architects to be conscious of where the theater would be and to see the site in relationship with the surrounding buildings, such as Symphony Hall and St. Mary's Basilica.[9]

Each team paraded into the boardroom, displayed their exhibits, and presented their ideas for the new theater. The lead architect of each Phoenix-area architectural firm introduced the theater design architect, the theater consultant, the acoustician, and the lighting expert; each of these individuals then spoke about their expertise, their enthusiasm for the project, and their initial impressions about the new theater for downtown Phoenix. They showed pictures, slides, drawings, and set up three-dimensional props to enliven their performance. Creativity filled the room, dazzling the committee, which almost hated the show to end.[10]

Keith Turley chaired both meetings, but everyone knew that Mallery had the most sway; therefore, it seemed perfectly natural for the selection committee to turn to Mallery on October 11, 1984, to lead them through the assessment of each team as they worked to pare down the list. The discussion was lively and, after some time, they agreed on the top four teams. Mallery read out the names of the Phoenix-area firm heading each team: Architecture One; Robert R. Frankenberger; Howard, Needles, Tammen, and Bergendoff; and Metz Train Youngren of Arizona.

In fact, the architects who made the greatest impression on the selection committee were not from the firms that organized the teams. What drew them to Howard, Needles, Tammen, and Bergendoff, for example, was the firm's very strong partnership with both Arcop Associates of Toronto as theater design architects—particularly architect Fred Lebensold, the partner-in-charge—and George Thomas Howard Associates as theater consultants. Both firms were acknowledged leaders in their fields, and they had made powerful presentations. It helped, too, that Arcop Associates had recent experience with performance spaces, such as the award-winning National Arts Centre in Ottawa, Canada, and that the team's acoustician was the renowned Abraham Meltzer from Israel.[11]

Robert R. Frankenberger also organized an excellent team that included ELS Design Group as theater design architects, Theater Projects Consultants as theater consultants, and Chicago-based acoustician Larry Kierkegaard. This team previously had worked together for two years designing the esteemed Portland Center for the Performing Arts.[12]

Architecture One made an impact on the committee by choosing the renowned Hardy Holzman Pfeiffer Associates as theater design architects, Jules Fisher Associates as theater consultants, and Jaffe Acoustics and Paul Marantz as acoustical and lighting consultants. Hugh Hardy had established an enviable reputation for his performing arts facilities and was widely respected nationally and internationally in the cultural field.[13] Everyone agreed that the team's presentation was spectacular, almost a piece of theater in itself, although a few grumbled that it might have been a little too flashy.[14]

The most famous architect was part of the Metz Train Youngren team, with the formidable I. M. Pei and Partners as theater design architects. Although not as well known as Pei, theater consultant Robert Davis was highly regarded in the theater field as well. Pei had not attended that day, but the committee was assured that Pei, and not one of his partners, would be the architect for the theater.[15] The committee expressed a degree of skepticism, however, about Pei's direct involvement. Pei subsequently flew to Phoenix to meet privately with Mallery and Gary Herberger. This intense artist amazed Mallery and Herberger. Mallery described him as "a man who clearly lived his art."[16]

With the selection committee's work complete, Mallery and the Phoenix Performing Arts Center board now had to select one team from the pool of talent. Mallery sought the advice of Gary Herberger. Before making a final decision, the two men wanted to tour other theaters built by the theater design architects. They were particularly interested in how well the completed buildings worked for the users, what the entire building process had been like for the clients, and if the architect was able to stay within budget and complete the project on time. They decided it would be worthwhile to visit some theaters and meet with the users and clients.[17]

In a memo to the four design team finalists, Herberger asked for examples of theaters "you feel most closely relate to our program, particularly with similar seating capacities and with the primary use being dramatic arts presentations."[18] He requested that they detail "who on your team was involved; theater architects, theater consultant, the acoustician, and the theater lighting consultant" and to send information on the users and clients.

The responses revealed that three of the four teams had designed buildings in Oregon. ELS Design Group and Theater Projects Consultants, part of the Robert R. Frankenberger team, had built the Portland Center for the Performing Arts. Hardy Holzman Pfeiffer Associates, part of the Architecture One team, had built the Hult Center for the Performing Arts in Eugene. George Thomas Howard Associates, part of the Howard, Needles, Tammen, and Bergendoff team, had consulted on an amphitheater and two additional theaters for the Oregon Shakespeare Festival in Ashland. Logistically, Mallery and Herberger could complete their on-site research in one trip.

On February 22, 1985, an entourage that included Mallery and Herberger; their wives, Francie and Jeanne; and Kax Herberger, the family matriarch, arrived in Oregon. Their first stop was the Portland Center for the Performing Arts.[19] ELS Design Group completed the 2,700-seat symphony hall that had been converted from an existing movie house in September 1984. Currently under construction were two additional theaters, one with seating for 900 and the other with seating for 450.[20] Pat Harrington of the Portland Center for the Performing Arts conducted a complete tour of the building, pointing out an array of acoustical and technical solutions that might be of value to the Phoenix project. She noted subtleties of the building, such as finishes, fixtures, and colors. Before attending a Chubby Checker concert, they dined with Harrington to inquire further about the working relationship with the theater design architects and theater consultants.

The next morning they drove to Eugene, where Bob Schutz took them on an extensive tour of the Hult Center for the Performing Arts. Hardy Holzman Pfeiffer Associates had completed the center in 1982 for $25 million, including the 500-car garage. The center had two multipurpose theaters, a large 2,500-seat facility used primarily for music, and a 500-seat theater used primarily for drama. Architect Hugh Hardy designed the building with generous amounts of glass and mammoth concrete beams that eliminated the need for vertical support columns in its soaring hall because of the concrete's strength and length.

Similarities existed between the Eugene project and the proposed Phoenix project, even though Eugene's population was much smaller.[21] The Hult Center for the Performing Arts was part of a larger civic center complex that also included a new Hilton Hotel, with the performing arts center joined to the convention center by a pedestrian walkway. The new performing arts center and civic center complex played an invaluable role in reshaping the core of downtown Eugene. The world-class arts facility already had sparked civic pride after a gritty ten-year campaign to fund and to build the facility. Schutz said that the citizens now call it "a dream come true."[22] The Hult Center for the Performing Arts was named after Nils and Jewel Hult, of Eugene, for their $3 million gift to the center.[23] The group attended a concert by the Oregon Mozart Players after their tour and dinner.

The following morning, the group drove to Ashland to meet Paul Nicholson of the Oregon Shakespeare Festival. They spent several hours with Nicholson looking at the three theaters on which George Thomas Howard of the Howard, Needles, Tammen, and Bergendoff team had worked. They viewed a 1,190-seat outdoor amphitheater (Elizabethan Stage/Allen Pavilion); a 600-seat theater with a semithrust stage and soft proscenium (Angus Bowmer Theatre); and a black-box theater, a late-twentieth-century innovation consisting of a simple, unadorned space that usually has black walls and a flat floor.[24]

After lunch, the group attended a performance of *King Lear* in the Angus Bowmer Theatre. Named after the founder of the Oregon Shakespeare Festival, this playhouse left a strong imprint on them. Although the theater looked "like a World War II bunker on the outside," inside it was a magical, intimate performance space.[25] The audience felt close to the action throughout the entire play. By the time the group arrived back in Phoenix, which was close to midnight on Sunday, they had deepened their understanding of theater design and the intricate process of working with architectural teams. They also felt that, above all, they wanted to create a theater that had the magical intimacy they had experienced at the Angus Bowmer Theatre.[26]

Meanwhile, in October 1984, Morison and Peter VanDine completed the revised feasibility study. Although the main impetus for the revision was to provide updated information for the finalists, the study was an essential tool for the Phoenix Performing Arts Center board to reassess the original plan, focusing only on the new theaters, not on the other renovations Morison had recommended in his earlier study. During his research for the updated study, Morison focused on the thirty organizations most likely to use the new theaters. He narrowed that group down to twelve, which he interviewed extensively to learn how their needs had evolved since 1981. It now was clear that there was a far greater demand for the proposed two new theaters than could possibly be met.

The Arizona Theatre Company had grown substantially in the three years since the initial study, especially in the Phoenix area. The company now projected that they could fill 30 consecutive weeks in the larger theater and another 120 days, not necessarily consecutive, in the smaller theater. "It is quite apparent,"

A scene from Death of a Salesman, *performed by Arizona Theatre Company during their 1984–1985 season.*
Arizona Theatre Company Archives. Photograph by Tim Fuller. Used with permission.

Morison stated, "that Arizona Theatre Company will be the primary user of the new building. Their space and equipment needs should be the primary consideration in the design of the theater."[27] Morison stated unequivocally that the larger theater should be designed as a single-purpose drama theater.

Now, more than ever, it was obvious that the smaller second theater was imperative. It could not be delayed because of the pressing needs of the smaller arts groups. As for its design, although the smaller theater would be used extensively by drama groups, he suggested that it "should be designed with a slightly wider range of use in mind."[28] Morison noted that the best layout should be flexible, with a modified or convertible thrust stage. Eliminating an orchestra pit would simplify the design. He also noted that there no longer was a need for the smaller theater to open to outdoor terraces in order to operate as an indoor–outdoor cabaret, as suggested in the original study.

The increased needs of the arts groups led to Morison's recommendation that the theater complex also house an additional, but highly simplified, performance space, with the addition of a black-box theater. This third performance space could be provided economically by designing the rehearsal hall in such a way that it had black-box capability. In addition, he emphasized that the arts groups wanted exterior amenities, such as appealing spaces for the audience to congregate and engage with others before, during, and after performances. Another paramount concern was that the building impart a sense of occasion, which could enhance the theatrical experience. Capital costs, unfortunately, had risen by approximately 12 percent from three years earlier, to a minimum of $12 million for construction only, not including land acquisition, outdoor plazas, or landscaping. Morison's cost estimates were not detailed elaborately and were intended only to register an overall cost increase due to the passage of time.

Morison's most serious finding, however, pertained to the building site. "Even with possible variations and adjustments," he argued in his report, "it does not appear that the site can accommodate a building large enough to contain the needed spaces."[29] The one-half block of land was 41,000 square feet in total and, according to Morison and VanDine, the footprint of the theater building alone required a minimum of 45,000 square feet, although 60,000 square feet was far more realistic. These figures did not include footage for open-space ordinances, an outdoor plaza, arrival areas, or landscaping, nor did they include the very important off-street loading dock areas omitted in the original study.

Morison pointed out that the present site's orientation and proportions did not "lend themselves to the development of shared backstage and service facilities and shared front of the house facilities," an important cost-saving measure outlined in the original study.[30] Morison left it to VanDine to illuminate the site problem in greater technical detail. VanDine raised the issue of "insensitive future development of the north half of the block," which possibly could overpower and dominate the theater. He alluded to explorations that had occurred to examine several possibilities for expanding the site, suggesting expansion that would encompass the entire block. Among the advantages VanDine foresaw were that "the entire site would be developed as a theater arts complex in keeping with the spirit and feeling of the cultural and convention center."[31] He added that the extra space might also allow for the inclusion of a much needed rehearsal hall for the Phoenix Symphony in the complex. Then VanDine posed a tantalizing question, "Should the city acquire the northern half of the site?"

9

Expansion

Richard Mallery was at his best when the going got tough, and the prospect of trying to buy the entire block would thrust him into the fire. Money was the stumbling block, and he broke down the solution into two parts. Mayor Goddard and the city council needed to be persuaded into buying the additional land, which with five current owners would cost approximately $1.8 million to $2 million. He also had to approach Bob Herberger for an additional $1 million donation. As for the mayor and city council, Mallery concluded that he probably could convince them of the need to purchase the additional land if the funds came from the Civic Plaza Building Corporation. By comparison, approaching Herberger appeared to be the more formidable challenge.

Even so, there were signs that the Civic Plaza Building Corporation board might not be as malleable as they had been in the past.[1] Mallery's earlier success with obtaining support for the new theater produced imitators, as a growing number of citizens committees sought help from the board. The Phoenix Symphony vividly illustrated this phenomenon when it turned to the board the previous year to bail them out of a $650,000 shortfall to remain afloat.[2] The Civic Plaza Building Corporation board had become increasingly skeptical of such entreaties. Board president Newton Rosenzweig was particularly irked by Arizona Public Service president Mark DeMichele's impolitic comment in the media where, speaking in his role as president of the Phoenix Symphony, he commented that the contribution had been a good use of the Civic Plaza Building Corporation's "excess funds."[3,4] Rosenzweig denounced DeMichele's comments, saying, "These so called 'excess funds' are necessary to pay the interest on the bonding obligations, to acquire capital equipment, and meet operating deficits. Sound business judgment says that we should stop 'siphoning off' civic plaza funds."[5]

It was in this charged environment that Keith Turley announced at the Governor's Arts Award dinner that the Herberger challenge grant of $2 million had been matched by the private sector.[6] It was a benchmark, Mallery realized, that distinguished the theater project from other struggling groups and positioned him well with the Civic Plaza Building Corporation board. As Mallery planned his second appeal for funds from the board, he and Gary Herberger continued to evaluate the architects.

They held lengthy discussions about I. M. Pei before eliminating the team, led by Metz Train Youngren.[7] Although Pei's buildings were acclaimed for their stunning designs, Morison reported that they had received mixed reviews for their usability. Pei's buildings also were notoriously expensive, the company's fees were somewhat excessive, and Pei's firm had relatively little experience in theater design.[8]

By April 1985 Mallery and Herberger had narrowed the candidates down to two teams: Howard, Needles, Tammen, and Bergendoff and Architecture One. Although both teams were equally qualified, their differences lay largely in aesthetics. Morison weighed their differences. "Arcop [part of the Howard, Needles, Tammen, and Bergendoff team] has extensive experience in designing performing arts facilities, even more than Hardy Holzman [part of the Architecture One team]. Arcop's clients are pleased with their results and the process of working with them."[9] Then he added, "Arcop's buildings, while generally pleasing, tended more towards the conservative and traditional." The designs by Hardy Holzman Pfeiffer Associates, on the other hand, were "unusual, exciting, often startling, and sometimes controversial."[10] Their selection, however, would involve a certain amount of risk. Morison recommended Architecture One with Hardy Holzman Pfeiffer Associates, saying, "I like taking chances, gambling on the possibility of greatness."

Mallery and Herberger went back and forth between the candidates, even asking other board members for their thoughts.[11] Finally, they chose the team of Howard, Needles, Tammen, and Bergendoff, with Arcop Associates as theater design architects. The team of architects had struck a cord with them, and they appreciated that the proposed design would be in keeping with neighboring buildings. In fact, only the Howard, Needles, Tammen, and Bergendoff team had considered the surrounding architecture in their design discussion, particularly St. Mary's Basilica, an unusual example of Mission Revival architecture, with twin towers and a red-tiled roof.

With the exception of St. Mary's, critics labeled the architecture surrounding the Phoenix Civic Plaza as a type of "bland borrowing from California."[12] Even though they may have wanted to trump this stereotype, they were skittish about what likely would be a very dramatic design by Hardy Holzman Pfeiffer Associates. Instead, they favored a classic theater, such as those Mallery had enjoyed in London and New York that stressed intimacy. Furthermore, Howard, Needles, Tammen, and Bergendoff embraced a collaborative ethic, exhibiting a willingness to work with the Phoenix Performing Arts Center board and the arts groups to create the most functional and pleasing interior, with an emphasis on the needs of artists and audiences. Mallery and Herberger were confident that they had chosen the best architects.

Meanwhile, Mallery prepared for his presentation before the Civic Plaza Building Corporation board, scheduled for May 22, 1985. In the previous month, the board had been occupied with other proposals for downtown developments, as Keith Turley, speaking as president for the Phoenix Community Alliance, discussed new commercial high-rises, venues for cultural activity, and housing for all economic levels. "We want to make downtown a people-oriented place that goes twenty-four hours around the clock. We want to give Phoenix an identity that it doesn't have at present."[13]

In another development, Edward "Bud" Jacobson, a partner of Mallery's at Snell & Wilmer and chair of the mayor's ad hoc Advisory Committee on the Arts, addressed the city council on April 16, 1985, in a forum packed with arts supporters.[14] Jacobson recommended the creation of a Phoenix arts commission, a new city agency that not only would offer grants to Phoenix arts groups, but also would improve the city's appearance through a fund to commission art and sculpture as part of any new construction.[15] He spoke movingly about how "artless places melt into the faceless sprawl of anonymous development."[16] Based on previous successes in other American cities, Phoenix's "One Percent for Art" program would be funded by a mandatory developer's fee on any new city-bonded development and a voluntary fee for any private development, retroactive to 1984. The city council unanimously endorsed the plan, and the Phoenix Arts Commission was born.[17]

Despite these positive developments, Mallery suspected that the Civic Plaza Building Corporation board viewed funding increases for the theater project with skepticism. Therefore, he loaded the board's meeting docket with persuasive individuals. Gary Herberger; Mayor Goddard; Dennis Burke and Ron Engelen, both from the mayor's ad hoc Advisory Committee on Downtown; Stephen Dragos, executive director of Phoenix Community Alliance; and James Forsberg, director of Downtown Phoenix Redevelopment Agency; among others, were scheduled to address the board on the theater's behalf.[18] Mallery briefed the board on the need to expand the site.[19] He cited Morison's updated

Edward "Bud" Jacobson, a partner of Mallery's at Snell & Wilmer and chair of the mayor's ad hoc Advisory Committee on the Arts in 1985, recommended the creation of the Phoenix Arts Commission and a One Percent for Art program, saying, "artless places melt into the faceless sprawl of anonymous development."
Snell & Wilmer Archives, Phoenix, Arizona. Used with permission.

study, insisting that the current site was too confined and would require a vertical design that would not be conducive for a state-of-the-art theater. Mallery argued that they needed to acquire the entire block to create the type of theater complex that suited a city the size of Phoenix. He then introduced Gary Herberger, who described the architect selection process. Herberger noted that there was an acute demand for the new theater and that construction should commence as soon as practical.

Mallery closed with the new plan that the Phoenix Performing Arts Center board had devised to deal with the escalating cost estimates; the private sector would contribute over $6 million toward the $12 million construction budget for the theater, an increase of $1 million from earlier estimates, with $4 million in private money already raised.[20] The larger site would not only allow for a better design, but it also would provide desirable open space. He speculated that a restaurant or other retail entities, which the larger site would allow, could generate income for the arts groups. Mallery advised the board that he would ask the city of Phoenix to purchase the northern half of the block, and he was hopeful that Civic Plaza Building Corporation funds could be used to finance this expansion. Mayor Goddard strongly endorsed the larger scale project, as did Denny Maus. Mallery then polled the board members' willingness to formally endorse a resolution recommending that the city of Phoenix purchase the north lots and agree to raise the construction ceiling of the theater from $11 million to $12 million. Board president Rosenzweig, anticipating a consensus, directed the staff to include the resolution in the next board meeting.

One week later, the Civic Plaza Building Corporation board reconvened. The meeting was long and contentious. Phoenix Civic Plaza director Maus reported on the Phoenix Civic Plaza fund status; on future downtown projects, including the expansion of the Herberger Theater; on the building of a third downtown hotel; and on the refurbishing of Phoenix Union High School auditorium.[21] One option was to move the Phoenix Symphony to the Phoenix Union auditorium and to use Symphony Hall for touring Broadway shows and ballet and opera performances.[22] Maus also mentioned Palace West, which was being held in escrow for the city. This venerated, much larger structure, with upwards of 1,500 seats, posed no threat to the Herberger Theater because it was not a well-suited venue for dramatic theater.

Mallery returned to the podium to discuss the need for additional funds for the Herberger Theater land acquisition.[23] He reiterated his belief that it ultimately would be a better facility on a full block with two theaters, which would allow for greater community use and the possibility of drama and acting classrooms above the retail and restaurant areas that the expanded site would allow. The theater complex also would benefit from the overall aesthetics of more open space. Mallery emphatically stated that private sources would not finance the purchase of the northern half of the property; the land would have to be purchased by the city of Phoenix, with Civic Plaza Building Corporation funds as the most logical source.

David Bixler, a representative of the Home Builders Association of Central Arizona, turned the discussion in a different direction.[24] He asked outright that the *original* commitment of funds for the Herberger Theater be the final project funded through Civic Plaza Building Corporation, implying that their funds should not be used to purchase the northern half of the block. Instead, Bixler argued that the city council should impose a new broad-based tax from general taxpayers for future downtown projects. He ended his comments by asking the board to pass a resolution stating that Civic Plaza Building Corporation funds would not be used for any additional projects and that a target date be set to end taxation for funding the Civic Plaza Building Corporation. In other words, Bixler wanted to dissolve the Civic Plaza Building Corporation board.

In an attempt to regain control of the meeting, board president Rosenzweig called for an adjournment because of the late hour. Mallery pressed forward, however, fearing that any momentum he had gained might be lost. He deluged the board members with facts. An architect had been selected for the Herberger Theater project, his board must keep faith with Arizona Theatre Company and other arts groups who were in desperate need for a performing space, and both the mayor and Maus had endorsed the purchase of the northern half of the block with 100 percent public funding. Mallery assured the board that the Civic Plaza Building Corporation would not be held liable should the new theater incur any operating deficits. "This is a defining moment," he said, "a great opportunity to create a world-class theater that would determine the future of the performing arts in Phoenix." Finally, after further discussion and strong supporting arguments from Burr Sutter, secretary of the Civic Plaza Building Corporation, the board approved the purchase of the northern half of the block for the theater, which they referred to as the Van Buren property. The board also approved the increased construction budget of $12 million. The meeting adjourned without finishing its other business because of the late hour.[25] Thus ended one of the longest meetings on record of the Civic Plaza Building Corporation board.

The city council unanimously ratified the Civic Plaza Building Corporation resolution on July 2, 1985.[26] Mallery wasted no time in approaching Bob Herberger for an additional gift of $1million. He had asked Gary Herberger about approaching his father for additional funds, and Gary responded that he thought the timing propitious. Earlier, Mallery and Hattie Babbitt had taken Kax Herberger to lunch at the Plaza Club, and she also encouraged Mallery.[27] In early August 1985, Mallery visited Bob Herberger at his home, and he opened his remarks by pointing out how successful Herberger's first challenge grant had been in prying loose private and public money. Mallery described the architects and the trip that he, Gary, their wives, and Kax had taken to visit theaters in Oregon to learn about the essentials of theater building. He explained how and why the project was being expanded. Mallery told of the resolution of support from the Civic Plaza Building Corporation board and the mayor's support for the project. Herberger listened intently, but nothing in his demeanor indicated that he suspected Mallery had come to ask for more money.

Mallery, therefore, openly broached the subject of money. As the conversation ensued, Mallery saw that Herberger was not eager to increase his financial support. He had to come up with something compelling in order to persuade Herberger. Then, he said, "You know, Bob, people have started referring to this theater as the 'Herberger Theater.' It is a name that is catching on, even though its real name is the Phoenix Performing Arts Center. I like calling it the Herberger Theater. It sounds right; but, we are going to have two theaters now, and that presents two naming opportunities. The larger one, of course, can still be called the Herberger...as one part of the overall complex. Then, if we get a big donor for the smaller theater, it would be named after that person."[28]

Although Bob Herberger had not sought to have his name on the building, the media and the public indeed had been calling it the Herberger Theater. Herberger warmed to the idea. Mallery then named a specific figure, an additional $1 million challenge grant if the entire complex were named the Herberger Theater. He framed his argument around the nobility of the cause and its enduring impact on the performing arts in Phoenix. Persuaded by Mallery's arguments, Herberger agreed to donate another $1 million, making his total gift $3 million for the performing arts center. It was the single largest monetary gift to the arts made by any individual in the history of Arizona.

On October 15, 1985, a panoply of elected officials and supporters who had labored on the project held a press conference in the parking lot that would be transformed into the theater complex. Mallery kept a low profile, allowing others to take center stage. Mayor Goddard announced the expansion of the project to the full block, which had been endorsed by the Phoenix City Council in July. He also presented the architectural team and introduced Michael Hallmark of Howard, Needles, Tammen, and Bergendoff, who graciously took questions from the press. Keith Turley told the crowd about the new Herberger gift. He introduced Bob Herberger, who stepped forward and said, "It was obvious to us from the reaction to our first challenge that people really need and want a first-rate theater center here. Under those circumstances, we're delighted to offer a second challenge to help them get it."[29]

Margaret Hance with Bob Herberger at the October 15, 1985, press conference announcing the selection of the architectural team for the Herberger Theater project. Hance was mayor of Phoenix when Richard Mallery first proposed the project.
Herberger Theater Archives. Used with permission.

Turley used the occasion to highlight the efforts underway by the Herberger Theater board to match the new Herberger gift.[30] The match for the first Herberger challenge had been raised in a low-profile appeal to corporations. "For this next million, we hope to have a more visible campaign. We want as many people as possible to participate, because we want the people of this community to have a real sense of ownership."[31] The arts groups who would use the theater were there, too, along with Gary Gisselman, artistic director of Arizona Theatre Company. Xicanindio Artists Coalition treated the crowd to their special brand of South American jazz.[32] As the buzz and excitement of the press conference ended, Mallery surveyed the empty lot, looking across the plaza at Symphony Hall and over to the east to the twin campaniles of St. Mary's Basilica. He stood in the middle of this desolate, nondescript piece of land and savored his vision, transforming it once again in his mind's eye into what years ago only he could imagine; but other challenges were soon to emerge.

Jeanne Herberger (center) talks with Henry Sargent (right) at the October 15, 1985, press conference, while her husband Gary Herberger (left) looks on. Sargent served on the board of the Civic Plaza Building Corporation, as well as on the board of Arizona Theatre Company.
Herberger Theater Archives. Used with permission.

10

The Design

By mid-1985 Phoenix's economy began to sputter; growth slowed, unemployment rose, and inflation exceeded the national rate. Optimists considered the downturn temporary, but they underestimated the economic storms ahead. Public policy at both the federal and state levels exacerbated the problem. In June 1985 the Arizona state legislature approved a measure that allowed out-of-state banks and savings and loan institutions to acquire or merge with Arizona financial institutions. By the end of 1985, outside financial institutions had bought up three large Arizona banks. Security Pacific Bank of Los Angeles bought Arizona Bank, the third largest bank in the state; Union Bancorp of Los Angeles acquired United Bank, the state's fourth largest; and Citicorp of New York purchased Great Western Bank, Arizona's fifth largest bank. These mergers, among others, knocked political and business leaders back on their heels, and the fund-raising efforts for the Herberger Theater were hit hard as the new leadership of the merged or acquired banks had less interest in local and civic issues.

Financial deregulation was part of President Ronald Reagan's promise "to get government off the backs of Americans."[1] Its historical point of departure started in earnest on August 15, 1982, less than two years into Reagan's presidency. He invited a small gathering of supporters to witness the signing of one of his administration's major pieces of deregulation legislation, the Garn-St. Germain Act of 1982. Reagan told the audience—a mixture of savings and loan executives, public officials, and journalists—that the bill took a major step in the deregulation of American financial institutions by loosening federal regulations on savings and loans. For more than half a century, Americans had relied on savings and loans to finance their homes, but regulations dating from the Great Depression prevented these institutions from competing effectively in the financial marketplace of the 1980s. Reagan promised that the Garn-St. Germain bill would right the imbalance. As he put it in his closing remarks that day, the bill was "the most important legislation for financial institutions in fifty years."[2] He added that it meant more housing, more jobs, and growth for the economy. "All in all," he concluded, "I think we've hit the jackpot."

In effect, savings and loan associations—also called thrifts—were decidedly deregulated. Among other things, the new rules allowed them to invest in commercial and residential real estate. Over the course of the 1980s, many of these thrifts made overly risky commercial real estate loans. As the Federal Home Loan Bank Board, which regulated the thrift industry, uncovered these questionable deals in the mid-1980s, it sought to impose stricter regulations to prevent increasing instability of savings and loans. Some of this reregulation required congressional approval and new legislation. The federal government ran into problems in its attempts to fix an industry that could not control itself in the changing environment of deregulation. By the mid-1980s, it had become an industry on the edge of collapse.[3]

Adding to the upheaval, the Herberger Theater board and its cause suffered a serious blow when the publisher of the *Arizona Republic* and *Phoenix Gazette,* Darrow "Duke" Tully, one of the most powerful men in the state, was exposed as an imposter. The bizarre nature of the story attracted national attention, causing much collective embarrassment. Tully had claimed to have an impressive, heroic military record. He often bragged about his experiences as a combat pilot in Korea, where he was shot down and later awarded the Purple Heart. Tully avowed flying more than 100 missions during the Vietnam War, for which he was decorated with a host of medals, including the Distinguished Flying Cross, the Air Force Commendation medal, and the Vietnam Gallantry Cross. At social occasions and other formal events in Arizona, he often would arrive attired in a full-dress Air Force uniform, bedecked with a command pilot's insignia, and adorned with ribbons and medals.[4] The truth—Tully never had served in the military, not one day. When Maricopa County Attorney Tom Collins exposed the charade in a press conference, Tully resigned in disgrace and left town. His colleagues—including his protégé, then-Congressman John McCain—were stunned. The Herberger Theater board lost a powerful voice and ally.

Darrow "Duke" Tully in western regalia atop his horse as grand marshal of the Phoenix Rodeo. As publisher of the Arizona Republic *and the* Phoenix Gazette, *Tully was one of the most powerful men in the state, until he fell into disgrace in 1985.* *Phoenix Gazette*, March 9, 1981. Photograph by Russell Gates. Used with permission.

Despite these difficulties, Phoenix and Maricopa County continued moving forward with aplomb. Mayor Terry Goddard was able to get a transportation-financing plan off the ground that secured state funding for freeway construction in the Greater Phoenix metropolitan area and Maricopa County. Indeed, in 1985 only 13 percent of urban traffic flowed on freeways compared to 30 to 35 percent for other major metropolitan areas. Robert Robb, president of the Phoenix Chamber of Commerce, helped crystallize support with his call to raise the state sales tax by one-half cent for the next twenty years. This move yielded $1 billion for mass transit, which in Arizona parlance meant freeways. Mayor Goddard lobbied the business community, and House Majority Leader Burton Barr, a powerbroker of the first order, shepherded the plan through the legislature. The freeway plan would make downtown Phoenix more easily accessible to suburbanites and theatergoers of the future Herberger Theater.[5]

Meanwhile, Richard Mallery and Gary Herberger focused their attention on the design side of the new theater. Beginning in October 1985, they met with the architectural team every other week, a schedule that continued unabated for the next year. Bradley Morison and board member Dino DeConcini often joined them and, at Morison's insistence, arts groups attended key meetings.

Michael Hallmark of Howard, Needles, Tammen, and Bergendoff led the project in his role as project manager. A rising star in the firm, Hallmark joined the company in 1980 after graduating from the Arizona State University College of Architecture. Hallmark's counterpart at Arcop Associates was to have been theater design guru Fred Lebensold, but Lebensold unexpectedly died just as the Herberger Theater project started. Concerned about how Lebensold's death would affect the project, Morison stated, "He was the kind of person you just automatically expected would go on forever. I imagine that his passing will cause you and the board of the Herberger Theater to have some reservations about proceeding with the Howard, Needles, Tammen, and Bergendoff/Arcop Associates architectural team, and I think it is probably well to at least review your choice in that light."[6] Fortunately, Lebensold's studio was strong and notable for its enviable group of expert theater design architects. Art Nichol and Brian Hall assumed Lebensold's role. Nichol had worked closely with Lebensold as a partner for several decades, although his understated manner was a contrast to Lebensold's more dramatic style, which had captivated clients. Nichol's design for Tampa Bay's $45 million three-theater complex was nearing completion to local acclaim, but Mallery and Herberger still felt a bit ambivalent about the changed situation, since Lebensold's creative energy had much to do with the hiring of Arcop Associates in the first place. Mallery and Herberger invited Nichol and Hall to Phoenix to meet with the Herberger Theater board to discuss the change and its possible implications. Nichol and Hall demonstrated an equal intelligence and vigor, assuaging all lingering doubts about their architectural leadership and abilities; the board voted to move forward with the two.[7]

On a backstage tour of Arizona Theatre Company's Tucson facility, artistic director Gary Gisselman (right) discusses the new Herberger Theater Center with theater design architect Brian Hall of Arcop Associates (left) and theater design consultant George Thomas Howard (center).
Herberger Theater Archives. Photograph by Steven Trubitt. Used with permission.

Work on designing the building began in earnest, moving through three distinct phases that were hashed out in the offices of Howard, Needles, Tammen, and Bergendoff on East Camelback Road and Twenty-second Street. In the first phase, designated "the program," the exact requirements for the theater complex were set out. During the second phase, the schematic design, the vision came alive in drawings and models. The third phase was a complex dance of refinements and changes that finalized the plans. Mallery and Herberger demanded that no changes be made after finalizing the third phase. At that point, changes would be too costly, and extra expenses had to be avoided.

To ensure that the arts organizations had a say in the design process, Morison arranged for them to meet with the architects before any meetings were held with the Herberger Theater board.[8] The arts groups exhibited their expertise in countless ways, helping with both the back-of-house and front-of-house design. Their contributions made the difference between creating a first-class, workable theater rather than one that was a source of unending irritation.[9] The denouement was exemplary. The theater design architects designed the main stage with a forty-six-by-twenty-six-foot proscenium opening, with a fly loft above of sixty-six feet. The moveable orchestra pit could be raised to create a thrust stage or lowered to allow for additional seating in the house. State-of-the-art theatrical lighting and sound equipment augmented videotaping and closed-circuit television capability. Throughout the design meetings and the inevitable permutations and modifications, Mallery remained focused, saying, "We want to put the money inside the theaters, to make them magical performing spaces. We want the acoustics to be perfect, so you can hear a pin drop on the stage. And we want the seating designed so that the audience is close to the stage, so they can be swept up in the drama occurring onstage."[10]

Audience comfort was a top priority. To accommodate wide seats with ample legroom, Arcop Associates designed all seats in the main theater to be twenty-two inches wide, not the standard seventeen to nineteen inches. They arranged more than one-half of the seating on the main floor, with a balcony of eight

Robert Jensen (center, standing), architect and principal-in-charge for Howard, Needles, Tammen, and Bergendoff, points out the site of the new Herberger Theater Center to artistic directors (from left) Kenneth Daugherty of Black Theatre Troupe and David Saar of Childsplay. At right is Michael Hallmark, project manager for Howard, Needles, Tammen, and Bergendoff.
Herberger Theater Archives. Photograph by Hal Martin Fogel. Used with permission.

rows wrapping toward the stage, plus boxes along each side. The 801-seat theater also needed a feeling of intimacy. Arcop Associates rose to the occasion by designing the main theater, now called Center Stage, with a maximum viewing distance of no more than sixty-six feet, a point of pride when the design was made public. If you were sitting in the last row of the balcony in Center Stage theater, for example, you would be closer to the action than if you were sitting in the thirteenth row of nearby Symphony Hall.

Mallery held strong opinions about the exterior design. He told the architects that he had long admired the architecture at Stanford University, where he had attended law school.[11] Mallery telephoned the president of Stanford, and he asked him to have the university archivists cull the collection for photographs of all the buildings and their environs. He received over 300 photographs, showed them to the architects, and said, "I want to keep it simple for you. I want this theater to look like Stanford. I don't want anything else. This is the look of the Southwest. It is beautiful—and it is inexpensive—just stucco and glass."[12]

Not surprisingly, the architects endeavored to please their client. As the exterior design took shape, they described the architectural language in a memorandum to the Herberger Theater board as that of a "Mediterranean vernacular, appropriate to the climate and character of the Southwest."[13] To be compatible with its next-door neighbor, St. Mary's Basilica, the roof must be red tile, which would also harmonize with the Mercado shopping area being planned a few blocks to the east.[14]

Much talk centered on how to relate the theater building to the raised plaza in front of Symphony Hall, which was eight feet above the sidewalks. From the street, patrons climbed ten steps to reach the huge plaza that fronted Symphony Hall. In contrast, the new theater would not have an extensive plaza, nor would it be raised above street level. The architects wanted the theater to feel as intimate on the outside as it would on the inside, as well as to create an inviting place for public life.[15] Even at street level, the new building needed to complement its neighbor across the street, Symphony Hall. The best way to do so, the architects suggested, was to place the main entrance to Center Stage on an axis aligned with Symphony Hall. The smaller theater could then parallel Center Stage, allowing both theaters to share a large lobby, which would also encourage the two audiences to intermingle. As the lobby plan developed, Herberger suggested a two-story rotunda, with arcades on the second level, skylights, and outside balconies where possible to take full advantage of Phoenix's salubrious climate. Later, Herberger and Mallery reworked the grand staircase that rose to the second level of the rotunda to make an even more elegant statement.[16]

Practicality influenced many aspects of the design. The smaller second theater, for example, could be sealed off so that air-conditioning and security were unnecessary when the theater was not in use. The interior design for the smaller theater, now called Stage West, caused months of discussion and heated disagreement. These issues never were fully resolved.[17] The architects designed Stage West as a changeable theater space, which everyone wanted. It could be configured with traditional seating; as an arena in-the-round theater; or as a cabaret, with theater seats removed for tables and chairs to be placed in the audience seating area. The entire floor would be built in panels, with individual lifts for raised seating or a myriad of other configurations. Disagreement centered on the shape of the audience chamber, with the two tiered balconies designed as a gallery that wrapped around the side of the house, each with one row of seats on the side and two rows in the back. Morison and other individuals argued that the sight lines would be unacceptable from the balconies, especially the flanking seats. In the arena arrangement, moreover, the audience would have to look down on the action occurring on stage, disrupting their sight lines. The architects' answer to these concerns was simply to not use balcony seating when the theater was configured in the round. Morison found their response unacceptable. He knew the arts groups wanted as much seating as possible to generate income, and only the most highly trained actors could project their voices as far as the balconies. Morison declared that this type of design would discourage groups from using the arena option. It negated the flexibility of the space, and if the design curtailed the flexibility, then the design was faulty.

Mallery and DeConcini requested the mock-ups for each seat's sight lines in Stage West. Dissatisfied, they further questioned the layout. To settle the issue, Herberger, accompanied by Arcop Associates' Brian Hall, traveled to Canada to see firsthand the small theater at the Calgary Centre for the Performing Arts, which had a similar gallery design. Morison's assistant, Julie Dalgleish, went on a similar scouting mission to see the small theater at the Tampa Performing Arts Center. In the end, the architects made some minor changes; but the essential design remained unchanged.[18]

The architects voiced serious concerns about the $12 million construction budget. In a letter dated October 8, 1985, Hallmark warned Mallery and Gary Herberger that the "entire design team is most concerned about the budget for the project, which we feel is quite low for all the accommodations needed."[19] At his urging, the Herberger Theater board engaged a cost consultant before they went ahead, although Mallery stood firm about the $12 million construction budget ceiling. Nevertheless, on November 8, 1985, Arcop Associates submitted a preliminary plan for the building, with a total cost of $18.92 million. It was not an extravagant design, but it was finely wrought and similar in quality to the Tampa Performing Arts Center. They also submitted a $12 million option, which they dubbed "a barely operable facility."[20] To arrive at the reduced option, the architects had set aside twenty-three features, some of which could be added later when more money became available. Seeking compromise, Herberger quickly figured that reinstating five of the features would bring the construction total to $13.82 million, which he rounded to $14 million. That figure, although still too high, seemed more palatable than the nearly $19 million budget submitted. The upshot of all the haggling was that $14 million became the benchmark figure for what would be needed for a usable theater. Mallery, however, was deeply concerned because he understood how important it was for the project to remain within the approved $12 million construction budget. He knew that there was only the slimmest chance that the Civic Plaza Building Corporation board would support a larger budget.

There was no way around it. Mallery and his board would need to tap private sources for substantially more money. Mallery and Herberger brainstormed; perhaps some of the building materials or labor costs might be donated or, if not, perhaps given at cost from the contractor.[21] They explored all types of further cuts. One feature—designing the large rehearsal room so that it could be turned into a space for black-box performances of new or experimental works—failed to make the program because of these cost-cutting measures. Other outlays entered into the mix, too. The land around the theater, everything beyond five feet of the building line, would require landscaping. Mallery suggested that the city of Phoenix assume this responsibility. Even so, cost estimates continued to rise at an unacceptable rate.[22] As they escalated, Arcop Associates jettisoned some innovations, such as the additional buildings on the east side of the property that were to be used as office space for arts organizations, as well as restaurant and retail space to generate income for the performing arts groups. These buildings had been designed to create a festive environment that would attract people to the area, but all of this had to be postponed until there was a more favorable economic environment for fund-raising.

Meanwhile, Morison started the ball rolling on a nationwide search for a theater manager. The consummate manager would oversee the construction of the theater complex and, once it was up and running, would schedule the use of the two theaters, as well as develop special events and bring in shows from the likes of New York or Los Angeles. The primary responsibility of a theater manager, however, was to work with each ensemble in technical stagecraft and marketing. In short, the Herberger Theater board wanted an "imaginative and resourceful promoter, as well as an experienced arts-facility administrator."[23]

Morison surmised that the ideal candidate would not be actively in the job market, but would already be employed with a theater.[24] He enlisted his colleague, Joseph Zeigler, who was based in New York, to aid him in the search. They scrutinized sixty candidates, narrowed the field to six, and put forward the names and résumés to the Herberger Theater board. By mid-February 1986, four candidates stood out, and the board invited each candidate to Phoenix for an interview. On May 20, 1986, the Herberger Theater board announced that Gary Moore, from Bartlesville, Oklahoma, would serve as executive director of the two-theater complex and as secretary of the Herberger Theater board. In a press release, Mallery said of Moore's appointment, "We are delighted to find someone who has a strong background in facilities management as well as theater. He not only has a formal education in drama, but also has worked in

A scene from Glengarry Glen Ross, *performed by Arizona Theatre Company during their 1986–1987 season.*
Arizona Theatre Company Archives. Photograph by Tim Fuller. Used with permission.

the theater as an actor, director, designer, and administrator. Since the new facility is designed primarily for theater and its flagship tenant will be the Arizona Theatre Company, Gary's unique experience will contribute greatly to the successful creation of this performing arts center."[25]

Indeed, Moore's résumé was impressive.[26] He currently was serving as the managing director of the Bartlesville Community Center in Oklahoma, a Frank Lloyd Wright-inspired building developed with major funding from Phillips Petroleum. Even though Bartlesville had a population of only 35,000 residents, the community center offered extensive programs in the arts. Moore had overseen the last nine months of construction. The Bartlesville Community Center had an 1,800-seat auditorium, a studio theater, exhibit gallery, and convention spaces. It had been established with a public–private partnership between Phillips Petroleum and private donors, as well as with a one-cent increase in the city's sales tax.[27] In 1975 Moore had supervised the design and construction of the Cultural Activities Center in Temple, Texas, a performing and visual arts center. His background was all theater. He had worked both onstage and behind the stage as an actor, a director, and an administrative director of the Dallas Theater Center. Moore also knew his way around marketing and audience development. As one of the top professional arts managers in Oklahoma, and widely admired, he had received a Governor's Arts Award. Furthermore, Morison knew Moore. They previously had served on an advisory panel for the Mid-American Arts Alliance, a regional arts agency serving the Midwest. Moore assumed his new position in Phoenix on September 1, 1986.

Morison also had been busy setting other initiatives in motion. He urged the board to draft a mission statement and operating plan before Moore's arrival. Morison suggested that the board consider adding new members and form a national artistic advisory council or an international advisory board. He prodded the Phoenicians to see themselves and their new theater complex as the creative energy that would spur Arizona's cultural evolution.[28]

Without question, the mid-1980s were a turning point in the cultural history of the desert metropolis. A Chicago consulting firm, Fantus Consulting, released a report that explained Phoenix's continued low rating in national quality-of-life surveys. The city's population growth had outstripped its arts scene and its facilities. "One of Phoenix's problems," said Fantus Consulting vice president Philip Phillips, "is it isn't a big corporate headquarters town. So the people who give money to these facilities are not heavily represented."[29] Morison countered the dispiriting message, "There is a new awareness of what it means to be a city here....This place, over the next five to ten years, may be ready to take on a new cultural character."[30] In some respects, Phoenix reminded Morison of his home base of Minneapolis–St. Paul as it was fifteen years ago. "The Twin Cities formed a pretty pedestrian community after World War II....It really wasn't aware of its possibilities," he said.[31] Then, in the 1950s and 1960s, there were what Morison called stirrings, as a new generation assumed leadership of the community. Since that time, the region had blossomed artistically, and Morison cited the Guthrie Theater, built in 1963; the development of a prestigious contemporary art museum, the Walker Arts Center; the St. Paul Chamber Orchestra, the Minnesota Composers Forum, the Children's Theater Company, along with several smaller theater companies. "The leadership transition from one generation to another doesn't have a parallel in Phoenix," Morison surmised, "but the sense of cultural awakening does."[32] Another veteran Phoenix arts booster, Edward "Bud" Jacobson, echoed Morison's sentiments, and he likened the nascent cultural landscape in Phoenix to pots in various soup kitchens, saying, "What you have now are people in kitchens all over the arts world chopping up carrots and potatoes. If they all come to a boil, we will have a very different valley."[33] The Herberger Theater Center, Jacobson suggested, could serve as the main ingredient in the collective stirring of the pot in a culturally maturing Phoenix.

11

Tucson's Temple of Music and Art

As Phoenix forged ahead with downtown revitalization and cultural development, its smaller and arguably more culturally mature counterpart, Tucson, took similar steps; however, Tucson's first cultural champions in this case came not from established civic or corporate arenas, but from a small group of artists.[1] Rather than start with a new building like its rival, Old Pueblo citizens focused their energies on an historic building already in their midst, the Temple of Music and Art at 330 South Scott Avenue near Armory Park. This half-century-old Spanish Colonial Revival cultural center surfaced among supporters as an ideal home for Arizona Theatre Company.[2]

Since 1972 the theater company had performed at the Leo Rich Theater in the Tucson Convention Center, a step-up from their previous home in the old Santa Rita Hotel building. Although not unworkable, it certainly was not perfect. Its wide, oversized stage and seating area must have been designed by "a committee of politicians" and not by anyone who knew anything about producing plays and performances.[3] Then things changed. An editorial in the alternative *Tucson Weekly,* published on November 21, 1984, turned the community's attention to the revered, but deteriorating and underutilized Temple of Music and Art. A campaign led by a young group of artists to restore the fabled temple gained traction, and supporters cried out, "[The Temple of Music and Art] is, without a doubt, one of the finest facilities of its kind west of the Mississippi...it is essential that action be taken to stop the desecration of this building."[4] A campaign was waged and, in the end, Arizona Theatre Company found a new home.

A plan put forward by a group of Colorado investors who had owned the Temple of Music and Art since 1982 called for its partial demise in the interest of securing tax credits for the restoration and adaptive reuse of historical structures.[5] The owners hoped to take out 6,000 square feet in the back of the building—part of the stage and stage house—and convert it into a five-story

Tucson's Temple of Music and Art, an elegant building with a spacious courtyard, graceful arches, and tiled roof, was the cultural focus of Tucson in the late 1920s and for decades thereafter. The historic building looks almost the same today as it did when it opened in 1927. The city dedicated the performance facility as the permanent home of Arizona Theatre Company in Tucson in 1988.
Arizona Historical Society, Tucson (photo BN201924). Used with permission.

office tower.[6] The second-floor greenroom and dressing rooms would be turned into a law library for attorneys who would lease offices in this radical conversion. Citizens of Tucson objected. The entire battle was nothing less than a metaphor for Tucson's twentieth-century cultural growth and development.

In 1907 when the Old Pueblo's population numbered scarcely 10,000 souls, Madeline Heineman (who had come to Tucson in 1897 and would later become known as Madeline Dreyfus Heineman Berger) sought to edify a raw frontier environment by encouraging high-level performing arts that brought prestige and nobility to the desert Southwest. She invited a group of musically astute friends to her home on Paseo Redondo to start the Saturday Morning Musical Club. These women were not rank amateurs. In order to join, one had to play from memory a Beethoven sonata, a Bach suite, and a modern composition. The club first met as a study group, but as their musical interests grew, the women wanted to branch out and to bring top professional artists to perform in Tucson. Their ambitions, however, required an auditorium much larger than anything available. Thus, the construction of a building—where the women could perform, teach, and bring peerless artists to Tucson—became the club's raison d'être.[7]

They incorporated as a nonprofit corporation and set about fund-raising. In 1923 a wealthy East Coast philanthropist, Alexander Berger, donated $100,000 because his daughter, Mrs. William Jennings Bryan, was an active member of the club, and she coaxed him into talking with Heineman.[8] There was a touch of romance involved in Berger's donation, as Madeline Heineman soon married Alexander's brother, Henry. Besides playing a role in his brother's courtship, Alexander's generosity served as a memorial to his wife.[9] The other Tucson landmark that he funded, the fountain in front of the University of Arizona's Old Main, served as a memorial for University of Arizona students who had died in World War I.[10] Cost overruns for the theater ran to $195,000. Local banks were of no help, so Berger arranged for a mortgage with the Juilliard Foundation, the first time that organization had loaned money to any arts group in the American West.[11]

On Tuesday, November 30, 1926, Italian coloratura soprano, Madame Amelita Galli-Curci, who at the time was one of the highest paid opera stars in the world and recently had appeared with Enrico Caruso in Buenos Aires, turned the first spade full of earth for the new building in front of 1,000 Tucsonans.[12] The cornerstone bearing the names of the various Saturday Morning Musical Club officials was laid, and less than one year later—on October 21, 1927—the dedication ceremony took place. The mossy green colored program featured a drawing of the new theater surrounded by willowy green Muses; Alexander Berger's portrait was on the cover. Former University of Arizona President Rufus von Kleinschmid (1914–1921), who had championed the cause during his years in Tucson and who at the time was serving as president of the University of California (1921–1947), returned to the Old Pueblo to address the large crowd.[13] That evening, Heineman spoke with grace and enthusiasm: "We are offering you this Temple, with its spirit of music, to be yours for all time; to enjoy, to care for, and cause to grow. Let its harmony spread from the few who are here to the many who are not here. Tonight it is young; into your kind hands and big heart we place it. Look then into the future and make it the Mecca of Art."[14]

World-renowned Italian coloratura soprano Madame Amelita Galli-Curci turned the first spade full of earth for the ground-breaking of the Temple of Music and Art in Tucson in 1926. To her left is Madeline Heineman, founder of the Saturday Morning Musical Club, who was responsible for the creation of the Temple of Music and Art. Arizona Historical Society, Tucson (photo 101662). Used with permission.

The elegant building, with its spacious courtyard, graceful arches, and tiled roof, recalled the Pasadena Playhouse after which it had been patterned. Designed by the youthful architect Arthur Hawes of Los Angeles, the Spanish Colonial Revival style theater was the cultural focus of Tucson in the late 1920s and for decades thereafter.[15] The grand opening concert featured twenty-seven-year-old Jascha Heifetz, who played to a full house. The 25,000 square foot performing arts center featured a 947-seat theater with perfect acoustics. On the second floor were dressing rooms, scene shops, a smaller recital hall used for lessons and auditions, and an art gallery, where portraits hung on cream-colored walls.

Despite its auspicious beginnings, the Temple of Music and Art was always in debt, even though every season saw international artists grace its stage, including two more appearances by Heifetz in 1936 and 1942. During the middle decades of the twentieth century, the Temple of Music and Art hosted the virtuosos Ernestine Schumann-Heink, Geraldine Farrar, Arthur Rubinstein, Efrem Zimbalist, John Philip Sousa, Ignace Paderewski, Ruth St. Denis, Ted Shawn, Sergei Rachmaninoff, and Martha Graham. The Tucson Fine Arts Association and the Tucson Boys' Choir both got their starts at the Temple of Music and Art. Despite financial losses and unrelenting struggle, the Saturday Morning Musical Club operated the theater until 1963, when the members sold it. Indeed, the Temple of Music and Art's financial history was one of on-again, off-again, but just not quite making it.[16]

In 1963 a private for-profit company headed by Ernest Hoffman purchased the building and renamed it the Tucson Music Center. Hoffman struggled for nine years before he sold the property to Frances and Salvador Galvan who operated it as the Cine Azteca, a Spanish-language movie theater. In 1976 William Nichols and Roger Gentry bought the building and returned it to its original name and purpose. It also received historical status in the National Register of Historic Places. Then, after a brief ownership by Steve and Marcia Hutchinson, Restoration Associates partnered with the Denver, Colorado, company in 1982.[17] The Colorado investors had the resources to fix the Temple of Music and Art's aging infrastructure and to restore the original courtyard's fountain. They also hired James Woodward, a Phoenix-based specialist in historic architecture, to shear off 6,000 square feet in the back of the building and rebuild it into an office tower.

At first, the Armory Park Advisory Board, the local neighborhood agency that had to approve the plan, supported the Colorado group because at least they were attempting to do "something rather than nothing" with the deteriorating building.[18] The city granted a demolition permit, and the investors hired a crew to take out the back end of the theater. Then, the *Tucson Weekly* ran its November 21, 1984, "Save the Temple" editorial. Subsequently, the public debate honed in on the inappropriateness of the plan. The building, after all, was an historic theater, not an office building. Demolition must be stopped.[19]

It was the efforts of one young man, a University of Arizona graduate named John Hudak, who garnered the attention of the *Tucson Weekly* editors. Hudak had joined with local artists to form the Tucson Artists Coalition in 1984.[20] The coalition's goal was to install artists in studios and galleries in downtown Tucson by purchasing a building and converting it to that end. They had raised a mix of private money and grant funds to secure a piece of downtown for artists.[21] The Tucson Artists Coalition decided to fight to save the Temple of Music and Arts. On December 11, 1984, at a crowded meeting of the Tucson City Council, the Tucson Artists Coalition offered their small cache of money to stave off demolition if the city would back them. By the end of the night, the city council had agreed to enter into negotiations with the Colorado investors. They made an offer of $6,500 to delay demolition for thirty days so that the city could study the possibility of buying the building. The investors countered that $6,500 was not enough money; they wanted $25,000.[22] By then, a grassroots movement was afoot, fueled by Robert Cauthorne's extensive coverage in the *Arizona Daily Star,* Judy Carlock's coverage in the *Tucson Citizen,* and Howard Allen's coverage in the *Tucson Weekly.* "We saw that other communities had revitalized their downtown by using art, and we thought maybe it could happen here," Hudak commented.[23] The Tucson Artists Coalition envisioned an Arts District, with a number of facilities—and as anchor—the Temple of Music and Art. Early in 1985, the Tucson City Council approved the plan, and the coalition moved forward to save the Temple of Music and Art, but now with the city's leadership behind them.

On December 14, 1985, a meter reader for Southwest Gas noticed that a meter on one side of the Temple of Music and Art had been bypassed with a plastic hose. Looking closer, he found another meter rigged the same way. City building inspectors were called in; that afternoon, at 1:45 P.M., the city condemned the Temple of Music and Art for a host of building, fire, and safety violations. It was shut down immediately.[24] Two months later, the city filed formal condemnation proceedings.[25]

The city council seized the opportunity; on June 16, 1986, it voted to make the Temple of Music and Art a public facility and the new home of Arizona Theatre Company.[26] The city put $2.6 million into the renovation, using part of the money raised from the sale and leaseback of the Tucson Community Center. The city council also approved an Arts District allocation of $5.6 million and hired Arthur D. Little of Boston, a management-consulting group, to conduct a "Tucson Downtown Arts and Cultural Venue Study."[27] The new Arts

District would get underway with the restoration of the Temple of Music and Art. It marked a major victory for proponents of historic preservation and cultural investment.

James Woodward, the architect who originally had collaborated with the Colorado investors, oversaw the installation of black wrought iron fixtures; refitted seats; and electrical, heating, and plumbing fixtures at the Temple of Music and Art. State-of-the-art sound and lighting systems and a modern rigging system also were part of the reconfiguration. Arizona Theatre Company received the status of sole operator of the city-owned building. The main theater had 623 seats, approximately 300 fewer than the original, making for an intimate theater environment. It was named for Alice Holsclaw, wife of Arizona state senator Douglas Holsclaw, who gave a substantial gift for the remodeling.[28] The rededication of the Temple of Music and Art occurred amidst great fanfare on November 21, 1988.

As Tucson was finding inspiration from its cultural history to fashion a modern theater for the performing arts, as well as a permanent home for Arizona Theatre Company, Phoenix was completing its design for the Herberger Theater Center with Gary Moore engaged as its executive director. David Hawkanson, managing director of Arizona Theatre Company, seemed to be on the cusp of having two new theaters for his company, the Herberger Theater in Phoenix and the Temple of Music and Art in Tucson. Before either theater was completed, however, artistic director Mark Lamos, at Hartford Stage Company, lured Hawkanson away from Arizona in 1985 to join him as managing director. Eventually, the two men received a Tony Award for Outstanding Achievement in Regional Theater.[29] As his career took off elsewhere, Hawkanson remained in touch with his colleagues in Arizona, visiting whenever he could and sometimes offering consulting advice to his former employer.[30] In fact, Hawkanson was in Tucson on October 5, 1990, for Arizona Theatre Company's first public performance in their new Tucson home at the Temple of Music and Art. The company performed *Amadeus* for this august occasion to kick off a weeklong celebration of daytime and evening events at the newly restored theater. John Hudak, among others, was honored on opening night, receiving a broken brick with the inscription, "A piece of the Temple for having helped save it."[31]

Madeline Heineman, who had come to Tucson in 1897, sought to edify a raw frontier environment by encouraging high-level performing arts that brought prestige and nobility to the desert Southwest. Arizona Historical Society, Tucson (photo 59213). Used with permission.

A large portrait of a contented Madeline Heineman Berger, dressed in a peach-colored, sequin-trimmed dress, had been found in the condemned Temple of Music and Art. After a loving restoration, the portrait prominently graced the lobby of the theater.[32]

From its illustrious beginnings in the 1920s as the hub of Tucson's cultural life, to its miscast years as a movie theater, the Temple of Music and Art breathed grace, elegance, and style into the lives of Tucsonans. The city-owned Temple of Music and Art would be managed solely by Arizona Theatre Company, a telling departure from the arrangement being hashed over in Phoenix for the Herberger Theater. The coupling of Arizona's only regional theater with one of Tucson's most elegant buildings led to a mutually beneficial marriage and a marvelous place to create and to see theater.

12

The Groundbreaking

By the fall of 1986, the architects had completed the design of the Herberger Theater, and its board of directors released the architectural model of the new complex for public viewing. Its red-tiled roof, set off by cream-colored stucco walls, complemented nearby St. Mary's Basilica. Large windows, a huge skylight, and balconies graced the two-story octagonal main entrance rotunda. A bank of glass doors flowed to one side, with a colonnade outside the doors that led to the second theater, Stage West. Numerous ramadas and overhangs added shade, while two large six-story towers—one behind the rotunda and one to its side—housed the fly lofts above the stages.[1] Unlike any other downtown building, it fit pleasingly into its existing environment and had a definite southwestern feel. As Gary Moore, executive director of the Herberger Theater told reporters, "It's going to be a damn good building!"[2]

Meanwhile, Mallery kept his attention on the construction budget. By 1986 it became clear that although construction might stay in the vicinity of $12 million, other outlays—architectural fees, engineering fees, construction management fees, and land costs—were likely to bring the total costs closer to $17 million. There was no way to reduce the figure. Richard Mallery had to reappear before the Civic Plaza Building Corporation board and the city council for approval of the increased budget. Together with Denny Maus, Mallery recalculated the numbers and presented the revised budget at the October 15, 1986, board of directors meeting of the Civic Plaza Building Corporation. At the same time, he unveiled the spectacular model for the new theater, a maneuver designed to assuage any doubts among the supportive, but skeptical board members. Mallery then introduced the new executive director of the theater, Gary Moore. After Moore's remarks, Maus explained the reasons for the increase from $15 million to $17 million. The increase in the building's size to accommodate two theaters, a construction price increase from the 1984 updated study estimates, landscaping, and other items combined to push up the cost estimates.

Architect's model of the Herberger Theater complex, including additional low-rise buildings (on the right) that were intended to provide office space for arts organizations, classrooms, restaurants, and other retail space to generate income. These buildings were designed to create a festive environment to attract people to the theater, but their construction was postponed until a more favorable economic environment would allow additional funds to be raised. Herberger Theater Archives. Used with permission.

Kevin Keogh, finance director for the city of Phoenix, then presented a funding mechanism through the Civic Plaza Building Corporation's bond program that would cover the increase. He noted that by taking the $1.8 million cost for the northern half of the block out of the equation, the city retained its 49 percent share, with the remaining 51 percent share provided by private sources. After much discussion and questioning, the Civic Plaza Building Corporation board approved the increase.[3]

Everyone involved in the Herberger Theater project looked forward to the groundbreaking ceremony scheduled for March 1987, but the complexity of the project required that it be delayed. Then, a fire at the mechanical engineer's office destroyed the plumbing and electrical plans.[4] Despite these setbacks, excitement grew as the media alerted the public to the onset of a new cultural era in Phoenix. Even *New Times,* the alternative weekly, ran a huge spread that featured large photographs of the architectural model.[5] Theater aficionados dreamed that Phoenix would join Chicago, Minneapolis, and maybe even New York City in the world of great theater towns. The opening of the Guthrie Theater in Minneapolis had added luster and definition to that great urban area. Phoenicians prepared themselves to leave behind a theater scene of tiny companies struggling "to stay alive as they performed in converted churches and spaces behind supermarkets; where up until a few years ago national touring companies feared to venture for lack of potential audiences; where some local troupes are forced to make do with high school auditoriums."[6] The reporter asked Moore how as many as twenty arts groups could use the stages at the Herberger Theater; he replied that although it was an "unusual concept without precedent" in the theater world, it seemed appropriate for Phoenix.[7]

Still, Mallery had to focus on fiscal discipline. Mallery had the never-ending challenge of raising enough private-sector funds so that construction could begin and the 300 pages of flat architectural drawings could be transformed into three-dimensional spaces. His board and Turley's challenge committee had raised $5 million through the Herberger challenge grants and pledges, but most of the more than $2.5 million cash received thus far had gone to pay for land, architects, and other fees, plus salaries and operating cost. Mallery now estimated that they would need an additional $6.25 million from the private sector because all construction funds had to be in hand before the city of Phoenix would give the project the green light. In a remarkably short time, Mallery convinced a consortium of banks to front the money, with a portion of the land as collateral. Valley National Bank, MeraBank, and First Interstate Bank loaned $1 million each; Western Savings and Loan, Arizona Bank, and United Bank loaned $750,000 each; and Citibank of Arizona and Chase Bank of Arizona loaned $500,000 each. These funds allowed the Herberger Theater board to maintain a line of credit for the full amount, which would be repaid as the board received pledges. Valley National Bank agreed to act as agent for the line of credit.[8]

This new infusion of capital arrived just as the design process and the cost estimates made the inevitability of yet another increase clear. On April 22, 1987, Mallery and Maus again approached the Civic Plaza Building Corporation board for an additional $1 million increase to $18.06 million.[9] Although incremental increases in budgets were not unusual for projects of this scale and scope, Mallery had not relished another appeal before the Civic Plaza Building Corporation board. Yet, his fervor was contagious. "This is not an ordinary building," he began, standing before the now familiar faces, "it is like building a giant Swiss watch."[10]

Mallery assured the board that all nonessentials, such as the ornamental ceiling, had been excised and that they would be added back only if additional private-sector funds became available. Increased architectural fees because of the complexity of the design, coupled with the city's requirement for a construction manager to oversee progress on a daily basis, were the key elements that triggered the latest budget adjustment.[11] The Herberger Theater board also added a contingency budget.

Mallery then submitted the Herberger Theater board's plan for financing their share of the costs. He told the Civic Plaza Building Corporation board that he had obtained a $6.25 million letter of credit from a consortium of Arizona banks. The banks accepted the remaining pledges and a portion of the land as collateral, in accordance with banking regulations. Because the city must own the building free and clear of any liens, the theater and the foundation upon which it rested could not be used as collateral for the construction-financing loan; therefore, Mallery had devised a plan that only could be hatched by an agile mind. His plan realigned the land ownership. The city would own the land directly under the theater (42,235 square feet) and the Herberger Theater would own the perimeter land (42,656 square feet) on an interim basis during the construction phase. The bank lien would be on the perimeter land until the Herberger Theater board paid off the line of credit, at which time full title would be turned over to the city.

Mallery assured the Civic Plaza Building Corporation board that the lien would still allow for a public right-of-way to the theater during the time the land remained under ownership of the Herberger Theater. The banks had wanted a comfort letter from the city of Phoenix indicating the city's possible interest in purchasing the perimeter land if the Herberger Theater defaulted on the loan. Mallery noted that this letter did not commit the city to the purchase. Finally, two independent cost analysis prepared by experts at HuntCor and Chartwell validated the current construction estimates of $12.6 million as accurate and likely to hold. Although the Civic Plaza Building Corporation board grilled Mallery on every detail, they still voted to approve the budget increase to $18.06 million.[12] The city council subsequently ratified the budget increase on May 5, 1987.

On the previous day, May 4, 1987, the project went out to bid, with a deadline of June 18, 1987. Moore began planning the groundbreaking ceremony for early July. Unfortunately, the lowest construction bid came in approximately $1 million over the estimates. When Mallery brought the news to the Civic Plaza Building Corporation board meeting on July 9, 1987, he had to explain the inaccuracy of the two independent cost analysis conducted in April.[13] It turned out that the analyses were based on only 78 percent of the completed drawings because the other 22 percent of the drawings had been lost in a fire at the mechanical engineer's office. Instead of a projected $12,600,000 for construction, the lowest bid was for $13,557,559, issued by the Nielsen Construction Company. Westbrook Construction Company came in at $13,600,000, while Sundt Construction Company was the high bidder at $14,360,000.[14] At last, after much bureaucratic wrangling, Nielsen Construction Company secured the contract.

The Civic Plaza Building Corporation board, after responding to repeated requests to amend budgets, had to ponder once again the notion of higher costs; they questioned if the contingency budget of $400,000 was enough to cover surprises if something unforeseen happened during construction.[15] Mallery pointed out that the Nielsen Construction Company would be bonded on a fixed contract and that change orders would be minimal, if any. He personally had made a careful study of the plans and specifications, which had gone through five addenda to clarify construction. Although there was no guarantee that the costs would remain fixed, Mallery would do everything humanly possible to keep time and cost overruns from happening. The Civic Plaza Building Corporation board voted its approval for the increase, with the total theater project now projected to be $19.06 million.[16] This was the last Civic Plaza Building Corporation board meeting for Newton Rosenzweig, whose term of office was over, but he left the boardroom feeling immense satisfaction for the part he had played in helping to make the Herberger Theater a reality.

A crowd gathers in the parking lot on Monroe Street for the groundbreaking ceremony for the Herberger Theater. *Phoenix Gazette*, July 23, 1987. Photograph by Russell Gates. Used with permission.

The groundbreaking ceremony for the Herberger Theater finally took place at 8:30 A.M. on July 23, 1987, at the height of Phoenix's legendary summer heat. The heat did not matter, for everyone's spirits remained high. The 300 attendees grasped their fan-shaped programs and listened with rapt attention as Mallery opened the event, saying, "This early morning celebration symbolizes the beginning of a new dawn in Arizona for the performing arts."[17] He proceeded to introduce Phoenix City Council members, city staff, Civic Plaza Building Corporation board members, and Denny Maus. Mallery also introduced representatives from Arizona Theatre Company, Ballet Arizona, and the Xicanindio Artists Coalition who had played their music while the audience gathered. Michael Hallmark from Howard, Needles, Tammen, and Bergendoff and Howard McCrady, the vice chairman of Valley National Bank who had recently joined the Herberger Theater board, received recognition and applause. Mallery also singled out Keith Turley for his work in matching the first Herberger grant and called him the "most effective doer in

At the groundbreaking ceremony for the Herberger Theater, seated left to right, are Mayor Terry Goddard, Keith Turley, Kax Herberger, and Bob Herberger. *Phoenix Gazette*, July 23, 1987. Photograph by Russell Gates. Used with permission.

Bob Herberger, holding a shovel, and Mayor Terry Goddard, holding a jackhammer, as they prepare for the ground-breaking for the Herberger Theater. Next to Goddard are Richard Mallery, Kax Herberger, and Keith Turley, with Howard McCrady (standing in rear).
Herberger Theater Archives. Used with permission.

this community."[18] Turley, Bob Herberger, and Mayor Terry Goddard gave brief statements, and then the climatic moment occurred. Bob and Kax Herberger and Mayor Goddard stepped forward to break the ground. Actually, Goddard wielded a jackhammer to symbolically dent the asphalt and the crowd applauded wildly. At that moment, the bells of St. Mary's Basilica rang out, an unplanned coincidence that added magic to the occasion. Mayor Goddard presented a commemorative gold shovel to Bob Herberger, which he kept in a corner of his office for the rest of his life.[19]

A decision was made to delay the start of construction until after September 14, 1987, when Pope John Paul II visited Phoenix and drew over 500,000 people to the Phoenix Civic Plaza area. Nielsen Construction Company then received the go ahead, and the heavy equipment moved in to clear the land. Completion estimates ranged from 18 months to 24 months, and the theater staff optimistically targeted an opening date for the spring of 1989. With the Herberger Theater project a reality, other developments in downtown Phoenix fell into place.

The much talked about Superblock project of offices and retail centers, diagonally across from the back of the Herberger Theater, was about to begin. The city and the Phoenix Community Alliance's efforts to convince the Rouse Corporation to develop the project finally had borne fruit. Once the Herberger Theater project was definite, Rouse Corporation agreed to develop the Superblock. "It was a key piece showing that Phoenix was committed to downtown," said Mayor Goddard.[20] "Of course, it wasn't the whole story, but it helped Rouse to feel they were connected to the coming attraction."[21] The Superblock was instantly hailed as the next jewel of downtown redevelopment. Arizona Public Service, the state's largest private utility, signed on to become the first major tenant, taking up one entire office building.[22] Later renamed the Arizona Center, the Rouse Corporation expected to break ground on the Superblock complex just after the groundbreaking ceremony for the Herberger Theater. The Superblock complex would take up six full blocks.[23] A few blocks southeast of the proposed Arizona Center was the site of the soon to be Mercado, a mixed-use shopping complex with a Mexican theme, being developed by Chicanos por la Causa and the Symington Company. Nearby, the mayor's office planned to build a new heritage and science park. The Phoenix Art Museum, one mile north of these developments, also was expanding. Finally, there was a proposal for a new multipurpose stadium downtown, and developers were swarming to build it. It appeared that Phoenix had unleashed a dazzling array of urban economic energy, and the city stood on the precipice of transformation.

Heavy equipment operator Robert Bowles, of Crown Construction, loads dirt from the excavation at the site of the future Herberger Theater. The twin towers of St. Mary's Basilica peek through the background. *Arizona Republic*, September 26, 1987. Photograph by Sean Brady. Used with permission.

Beneath the surface, however, serious problems persisted. The Phoenix Economic Growth Corporation had commissioned a report from Fantus Consulting that concluded that Phoenix lacked the industrial base necessary for long-term job needs and urged the city to improve areas vital to attracting new industry, specifically transportation, environment, and cultural amenities.[24] Much to the consternation of the area's conservative

The land is being cleared to make way for the future Herberger Theater. St. Mary's Basilica is on the left, with the roofline of the Phoenix Civic Plaza convention center in the background. *Phoenix Gazette*, September 25, 1987. Photograph by Rick Giase. Used with permission.

voters, Fantus Consulting also suggested enacting an economic development tax to fund efforts to bring in new businesses.[25] Although there had been a surge in recently announced downtown projects, a construction industry slowdown had begun by the end of 1986. The bedrock of Phoenix's growth, commercial and new home construction, showed palpable signs of weakness. The unemployment rate jumped sharply as well, another indication that the Valley's image of prosperity might be illusory.

Nationally, the savings and loan industry was starting to show serious signs of trouble. Empire Savings of Texas failed in 1984, and Ohio had to declare a bank holiday in March of 1985 to stave off the failure of Home State Savings Bank of Cincinnati. Savings and loan association failures in Maryland followed two months later. Arizona's problems were yet to surface, but when they did in 1989, they led to an economic meltdown that indelibly changed the political, economic, and power structure of not only Phoenix, but of the entire state. The meltdown affected every sector of the economy, including the Herberger Theater project. In the afterglow of the Herberger Theater's groundbreaking in July 1987, no one could foresee the trials that lay ahead. The focus was to continue raising money and to start planning the gala opening.

Nevertheless, warning signs persisted. In addition to the gathering clouds of recession, the citizens of Arizona elected Republican maverick and ultraconservative Evan Mecham as governor of Arizona in a shocking outcome to a three-way gubernatorial race in November 1986. Although he remained in office for only fifteen stormy months, from January 1987 until April 1988, he became one of the most controversial and divisive figures in Arizona political history. Mecham faced an attempted recall, a successful impeachment that removed him from office in 1988, and finally a criminal trial in 1988. In many ways, public attention turned to the Mecham political sideshow while Arizona's economy drifted off course.[26]

In this dynamic, but changing, economic and political climate, the Herberger Theater board had raised $5 million in cash and pledges. They had spent over 50 percent of that amount to acquire the southern half of the block and to pay architect fees and other expenses. Based on the new budget of $19.06 million, the Herberger Theater board's share was $8.80 million. Subtracting the $5 million already raised, that left an additional $3.80 million to be raised from the private sector.[27] At this point in 1987, Mark DeMichele took over as fund-raising committee chair of the Herberger Theater board, replacing the stalwart Keith Turley, whom he also previously succeeded as president of Arizona Public Service. DeMichele already had established himself as an arts leader, having helped Tony Snow, chair of the Phoenix Symphony, stave off an economic crisis at the Phoenix Symphony in 1984. He also had played a key role in fund-raising efforts for the Arizona Opera and Ballet Arizona. DeMichele's passion for the arts extended back to his early childhood in an Italian immigrant family in Syracuse, New York. His father inculcated in him a love and respect for his Italian heritage by exposing young Mark to opera and teaching him about the contributions of the great artists of the Renaissance, including Michelangelo and Leonardo Da Vinci. "I would have much preferred to be out playing baseball," he remembered, "but this is the long-lasting legacy in my life."[28] He also was fortunate that the arts were an integral part of his education in Syracuse; his appreciation for the arts stayed with him throughout his life. DeMichele had dabbled in the arts, trying out acting in high school and college, and even considering a career in radio and television; however, he ended up in marketing and public relations, first in New York with Mohawk Power and then in Arizona when Turley hired him to come to Arizona Public Service in 1978.

DeMichele attempted a renewed grassroots fund-raising campaign for the Herberger Theater. Launched earlier in the spring of 1986 to match the additional $1 million Herberger donation, the effort faltered. With the arrival of Gary Moore, and then the massive undertaking to design the theaters themselves, little time or energy was left for anyone to rev up the campaign, although Moore did raise small amounts whenever and wherever possible. Moore formed a group of volunteers, called the Associates, to help with fund-raising and audience development. One of their first projects was to work with the Valley Innkeepers Association for a fall 1987 wine auction to benefit the Herberger Theater. Their efforts netted over $10,000.

As building costs escalated, Moore voiced the need to launch a major campaign to DeMichele and the Herberger Theater board in May 1987. They decided to aim the fund-raising campaign primarily at individuals and small businesses because the majority of the major corporations in town already had pledged substantial funds. With urging from Gary Herberger, Moore also sought to establish an endowment that would subsidize rents for arts groups and provide operating funds for the Herberger Theater.

DeMichele agreed to chair the campaign. To make the appeals more attractive, the board would let contributors designate their money toward parts of the building, which would then bear a plaque inscribed with the donor's name. For major donors, entire sections of the building were earmarked for donations; for example, the rotunda, a rehearsal hall, the greenroom, and even dressing rooms could be inscribed with the name of a theater patron. If all the items on the list found a donor, it would total $3 million, which was very close to their overall goal. To interest small contributors, they organized a seat sale. If they could sell every seat in both theaters, they would accrue another $1.3 million. Although it was unlikely that every seat would be sold, the board found the potential energizing. One of the first takers was a group called the Society for Marketing

The foundation for the new theater is dug, and construction begins on the complex maze of technical areas below the stage and lobby. Herberger Theater Archives. Used with permission.

Professional Services. Jeffery Feeney, vice president of the engineering firm of Read Jones Christoffersen and president of the Society for Marketing Professional Services said, "Since we make our living in the design–build industry off of what grows and develops in the town, we felt there are things that need to be put back into this community."[29] At a luncheon on November 19, 1987, the group presented Mallery, Herberger, and Moore with a check for $3,750; the seat sale got off to an optimistic start.[30] DeMichele's efforts to make the campaign more visible were helped when Erma Bombeck agreed to be honorary chair. The board formally announced the seat sale in September 1988. They held a party in the Valley National Bank conference suites on the thirty-sixth floor to kickoff the seat sale, with the model of the theater as the centerpiece and a spectacular view of the ongoing construction below. Erma Bombeck attended the party and said excitedly, "The theater's coming to town!"

13

Stabilization and Meltdown

In 1987 Myra Millinger, another individual who shared a passion for the arts, brought a new mechanism to advance the arts in Phoenix. Millinger was associate director for the arts at the Flinn Foundation, the state's largest grant-making organization. She had been with the Flinn Foundation for four years and devoted considerable time convincing the National Arts Stabilization Fund to make Arizona a funding recipient. The prestigious Flinn Foundation served as the local administrator of the program. The fragile base of financial support within the state for major arts organizations required a constant struggle for survival dollars. Millinger worried that this hand-to-mouth existence had a deleterious effect on creativity. Established to counter these dangers, the National Arts Stabilization Fund had achieved a notable record of success with arts organizations throughout the country.

The Ford, Mellon, and Rockefeller foundations created the New York-based National Arts Stabilization Fund to strengthen the financial and managerial skills of major performing arts and visual arts organizations.[1] Millinger, who had come to Arizona from the Ford Foundation, not only knew Marcia Thompson, the president of the National Arts Stabilization Fund, but she also had a strong understanding of the program's stabilization concept. If the arts were to flourish in Arizona, Millinger speculated, they would need a huge influx of capital, and the most likely source for this capital was the National Arts Stabilization Fund. She also had an interest in the financial acumen that arts organizations would develop by participating in the rigorous program. Millinger convinced the National Arts Stabilization Fund to conduct a financial analysis of Arizona's principal arts organizations as a prelude to qualification. The National Arts Stabilization Fund accepted Arizona into the program in 1988, the first time an entire state was chosen for arts stabilization funding. The Flinn Foundation committed $1.5 million to the stabilization effort, more than doubling its previous financial commitment to the arts.

The fund's stabilization mechanics were intricate and sophisticated, and they took more than ten years to implement. The National Arts Stabilization Fund required arts organizations to develop sound managerial and financial practices. The fund advanced two types of so-called balance sheet strategy support over a multiyear period in a disciplined process that would enable the arts organizations to achieve a series of financial goals. Arts organizations were required to adopt financial practices that shored up their balance sheets, looking beyond yearly operating expenses. This approach initially confounded the Arizona organizations. Receiving new funding from the National Arts Stabilization Fund; however, made the efforts required very worthwhile. An arts organization first had to clear all accumulated debts. The fund offered a powerful incentive. If an organization could raise 50 percent of the sum in which their liabilities exceeded their assets within a one-year period, the fund would liquidate the organizations remaining debts. The organization could then begin anew with a clean financial slate.

The National Arts Stabilization Fund would then provide the arts organization with a restricted working capital reserve equal to 25 percent of their operating budget. This capital reserve positioned the organization to act as their own banker, enabling them to lend themselves money to cover their shortfalls within each fiscal year. (Arts groups, and particularly performing arts groups, often have huge swings in cash flow needs.) The organization had to repay all loans from the capital reserve fund, with all reserve funds in hand at the close of each year. If successful, the organization could then keep the 25 percent to reuse as a capital reserve, or they could put aside a portion of the capital reserve toward the establishment of a permanent working endowment. The fund would continue to give 25 percent of the operating budget for five years, as long as the monies donated were replenished by the end of each fiscal year. Each organization received the National Arts Stabilization Fund's rigorous technical assistance in strategic planning, board development, fund-raising, and marketing and management strategies.

The National Arts Stabilization Fund committed $1.5 million to the Arizona stabilization effort, and the Flinn Foundation matched the amount. The newly established Arizona Arts Stabilization Committee needed to raise another $1.5 million; by 1986 the committee had raised 85 percent of that amount. Howard McCrady, vice chairman of Valley National Bank, and also deeply involved in the Herberger Theater project, agreed to become the first committee chair.[2] Others taking leadership roles in the Arizona Arts Stabilization Committee included arts patron and Snell & Wilmer attorney Edward "Bud" Jacobson, Arizona Bankers Association president D. Gordon Murphy, philanthropist and arts supporter Mary Dell Pritzlaff, and Tucson arts patrons Helen Schaefer and Tina Lyons. The program ultimately delivered an additional $4.5 million for the arts in Arizona. This money made long-term fiscal stability of the participating arts organizations possible.[3]

Nine of the most highly prized Arizona arts organizations were invited to participate in the National Arts Stabilization Fund's program: Arizona Opera, Arizona Theatre Company, Ballet Arizona, the Heard Museum, the Museum of Northern Arizona, the Phoenix Art Museum, the Phoenix Symphony, the Tucson Museum of Art, and the Tucson Symphony. The museums were the first to jump on board in January 1989. Performing arts groups joined the National Arts Stabilization Fund's program over the next five years. Arizona Theatre Company, for example, began the program in October 1993; by June 1997 the company had received $817,168 through the fund. Never had so much money been raised for the arts in Arizona. Although the funds were doled out gradually, they changed Arizona arts significantly. By the end of the 1990s, the nine arts organizations had improved their current liquidity by $2.4 million, they had increased their working capital reserves by $2 million, they had enhanced their endowments by $9 million, and they had augmented their earned income by 65 percent. In recognition of her vision and leadership, Millinger received the Governor's Arts Award in 1995.[4]

Ironically, while the arts organizations in Arizona were balancing their budgets, building working capital, and tossing around words such as working capital reserve and current liquidity, the savings and loan industry was starting to fall apart by ignoring these very same principles. Unquestionably, the savings and loan debacle of the 1980s was more complex. This national financial crisis had evolved over the decade, leading to the biggest banking failure in U.S. history up to that time. In Arizona, it was the biggest financial failure in the state's history.[5]

Savings and loans associations, also called thrifts, had been in trouble for some time after the Reagan administration passed the Garn-St. Germain Act of 1982. This legislative act gave thrifts a green light to venture into new areas, such as commercial real estate, high-yield junk bonds, and other risky assets. This giant step toward financial deregulation, which gave thrifts powers equal to banks, was made even more attractive because it increased the thrifts insured deposits from $40,000 to $100,000 and added forbearance, a looser accounting standard that made a thrift's net worth appear greater than it actually was. In effect, it made insolvent thrifts look sound.[6] The Garn-St. Germain Act also allowed one individual to own a thrift instead of the previously required 400 stockholders. In the final coup de grâce of errors, the Federal Home Loan Bank Board severely reduced their regulatory staff because of budgetary stringency and political pressure for smaller government, leaving the regulatory agency understaffed, underpaid, and out of its depth in overseeing a vastly changing and booming industry.[7] Operating in the go-go climate of the 1980s, in an unfamiliar commercial-lending world, and spurred on by the high ceiling for insured deposits, it took little time for many of the high-risk loans to sour. Many thrifts collapsed. By the end of September 1986, Texas led the way in failures with Empire Savings and at least sixty-five other insolvent thrifts; California counted thirty, and Illinois was not far behind.[8]

President Ronald Reagan and his administration, hoping to stem the tide, allowed banks and other corporations to buy ailing thrifts rather than have the government take them over or bail them out, even as he signed a $10.8 billion bailout bill into law.[9] This bill had the chilling effect of attracting a new breed of owner who saw the thrifts as a cash cow ready to be milked.[10] By the summer of 1987, the crisis became national in scope. To make matters worse, on October 19, 1987, the stock market crashed; by the closing bell on Black Monday, the market had fallen 508 points—losing nearly 25 percent of its value—an even bigger fall than the infamous Black Friday crash of 1929. It appeared that the nation might be facing another Great Depression.[11]

In Arizona, the savings and loan meltdown was gradual, but it "indelibly changed the political, economic, and power structure of metropolitan Phoenix and Arizona."[12] The effect on the fund-raising efforts of the Herberger Theater board and its committees was profound. Although Arizona had a smaller number of thrifts, in the end, it became the poster child for the entire problem in the charismatic, risk-taking, and lavish-living Charles Keating Jr. He had come to Arizona in 1978 as board chair of the American Continental Corporation; by 1982 he was the leading homebuilder in the state. American Continental Corporation soon became the sixth largest employer in Arizona, and Keating poured nearly $1 billion into Arizona real estate, where he built shopping centers, housing subdivisions, hotels, and other real estate enterprises.[13]

Keating may well have been the largest single source of capital in the state after his 1984 purchase of a California thrift, Lincoln Savings and Loan. With an unregulated thrift in his hands, Keating gained almost total freedom to act and to issue billions in junk bonds far in excess of the net value of his companies and investments. By April 1987 Lincoln Savings and Loan was a ticking time bomb, as its complicated and excessive money machinations drew regulators' attention. Meanwhile, the egomaniacal Keating built his testament to himself, the lavish Phoenician Hotel in Phoenix, where over $300 million vanished into 600 rooms. The hotel opened on October 1, 1988, to much local fanfare, but the federal government subsequently seized it on November 16, 1989.[14] Unfortunately, the American Continental Corporation, the Phoenician, and other Keating enterprises had pledged substantial contributions to the Herberger Theater.

Seven months earlier, on April 13, 1989, the American Continental Corporation declared itself in Chapter 11, taking eleven of Lincoln Savings and Loan's subsidiaries into its legal tent. The following day, federal authorities seized Lincoln Savings and Loan and found it to be at least $1 billion short of funds. By September 1989, racketeering and other charges were brought against Keating and several officials in his companies for the largest bank fraud in U.S. history. Keating and his officers were charged with bleeding over $1 billion of federally insured deposits out of Lincoln Savings and Loan through various stratagems. According to Michael Manning, a federal investigator at the time, Keating was the only individual he had come up against who had mastered every known form of bank fraud.[15]

Keating was not the only Arizona-based thrift operator who played fast and loose with weakened rules and regulations. A few miles from Keating's office on Camelback Road was Western Savings and Loan, a local thrift that had been under the management of the same Mormon family for generations. With the availability of "hot money from brokered accounts," Western Savings and Loan transformed from a conservative family firm into a player, with loans to Mesa developer Conley Wolfswinkel totaling close to $100 million. Western Savings and Loan loaned another $200 million to a Tucson operator for a Colorado land deal and also built a new $32 million headquarters. Then it went under.[16]

In the end, all eight of Arizona's savings and loans collapsed, including the largest, MeraBank, along with Western Savings and Loan, Southwest Savings, and Pima Savings, all of which were once household names in the state, plus a handful of banks. This left Arizona's real estate economy, previously the foundation on which the state's financial strength and growth stood, "dead on the desert floor."[17] Along with the real estate bust went appraisers, mortgage loan companies, title companies, contractors, architects, and assorted others. Downtown redevelopment stalled for a decade. Innocent investors, many of them elderly, lost their life savings.

The savings and loan meltdown washed out a generation of Old Guard businessmen and community leaders, such as Gary Driggs of Western Savings and Loan; Pinnacle West Capital Corporation board chair Keith Turley; Gene Rice, then head of MeraBank; and former Governor Fife Symington, a real estate developer whose downtown Mercado project became an enormous economic and political albatross. It brought diversified owners of utility companies, Arizona Public Service and Tucson Electric Power, to the brink of bankruptcy. The desperate situation also triggered financial giants Bank of America and Wells Fargo to hasten into the Valley and replace homegrown institutions like MeraBank and Western Savings and Loan.

President George H. W. Bush, who succeeded Reagan in 1989, could no longer tamp down the unmitigated financial disaster. He saw to the passage in August 1989 of federal legislation called the Financial Institutions Reform, Recovery, and Enforcement Act, which was a taxpayer-financed bailout measure that also created a new government agency called the Resolution Trust Corporation to liquidate insolvent institutions. Over 50 percent of U.S. savings and loan associations had failed.[18]

By 1990 the Resolution Trust Corporation swept into Phoenix and the city became an occupied territory. Over 300 government agents descended on the Valley to clean up the wreckage. Their job was to take over the thrifts, clean them up, and package their holdings for sale, often at huge discounts. In all, the Resolution Trust Corporation seized more than 3,000 properties in Arizona, which were worth an estimated $10 billion to $15 billion. The properties, on average, were sold for 40 cents on the dollar, further deflating the Valley's real estate market and prolonging its recovery.[19] Nationally, over 1,000 thrifts failed in "the largest and costliest venture in public misfeasance and larceny of all time."[20]

While the introduction of the National Arts Stabilization Fund into the Arizona arts community generated long-term hope, the Herberger Theater effort would be dealt a serious setback because of the savings and loan meltdown. The seriousness of their situation would not become apparent until the new building was complete and the opening curtain had been raised. Then, the theater's board and staff would have to search their souls and their shattered financial goals for elusive answers.

14

The Opening

In the late fall of 1988, after eight years of fiscal struggle, political mobilization, and community recruitment, steel and cinder block began to rise at Monroe and Second Streets. The strange configuration of the two, six-story fly towers, which overlooked an unusual, but graceful octagonal structure that would become the lobby pavilion, suggested something innovative was afoot. First-time observers commonly asked, "What's going on here?"

Excitement gripped the arts community as construction began. The media reported on the day-to-day developments, with long feature stories, photos, and quotes from Herberger Theater insiders. Each morning Richard Mallery stopped at the construction site, checked on the progress, and met with key Kitchell CEM construction management employees. He then headed to his Snell & Wilmer law office, where his window looked down upon the construction site, which allowed Mallery to keep a close eye on the goings on. Gary Moore often took Bob and Kax Herberger on VIP tours as the work on the theater continued in earnest.[1]

The construction of the Herberger Theater fly loft for Center Stage begins.
Arizona Republic, March 19, 1988. Photograph by Dave Nelson. Used with permission.

A few blocks away, between Fifth and Seventh Streets, the Mercado was under construction, with a scheduled opening at approximately the same time as the Herberger Theater. Behind the theater, the new Superblock was underway, with Rouse Corporation as the developer. Rouse Corporation's Arizona Center, the new skyscraper home for Arizona Public Service, anchored the six city blocks. The corporation also planned an additional elegant skyscraper that would house the law offices of

(Left) *The Center Stage fly loft takes shape in May 1988, rising six stories over stage level to house stage machinery.*
Herberger Theater Archives. Used with permission.

(Right) *A construction worker stands on the highest steel beam of the Herberger Theater building. He is directing a string of beams being lowered into place by a crane.*
Arizona Republic, July 2, 1988. Photograph by Suzanne Starr. Used with permission.

Snell & Wilmer and overlook a stylish swath of restaurants, shops, and a lushly planted, shaded park. In the midst of all these transformations, Phoenix voters approved Proposition 5 on April 5, 1988. This bond election provided funds for the restoration of the historic Palace West, for doubling the size of the Phoenix Art Museum, and for other cultural projects. The restoration would return Palace West to the grandeur it once knew when it had opened in 1929 as the Orpheum Theater, the most luxurious movie house west of the Mississippi.[2] This venerable old building had been added to the National Register of Historic Places in 1985. The restored Orpheum Theater would complement Symphony Hall and the Herberger Theater, as well as bring into being the beginnings of a theater district where none had existed before, thereby achieving a goal that Mayor Goddard had worked toward from the time he first took office. The bond election also approved the building of a new science museum, now called the Arizona Science Center; a history museum, now called the Phoenix Museum of History; as well as a Solar Oasis on the plaza in front of Symphony Hall, which would transform the plaza into two acres

An aerial view of the Herberger Theater construction site in December 1988.
Herberger Theater Archives. Kitchell CEM photograph by Marianne Boich. Used with permission.

Construction of the Herberger Theater Steele Pavilion main lobby shown framed by scaffolding.
Phoenix Gazette, March 10, 1989. Photograph by Randy Reid. Used with permission.

of dense, cool greenery.[3] In addition, it funded a new central library, named the Burton Barr Central Library in 1994 after the longtime Arizona house majority leader. Downtown Phoenix was undergoing a physical and cultural rebirth, and the Herberger Theater was at the heart of it all.

The national magazine *Horizon: A Magazine for the Arts,* attracted by the frenetic pace of downtown development, featured a major story on the genesis of the new Herberger Theater. Mallery summed up the eight-year process by saying, "In Phoenix, we have been free to study, design, build, and then operate a performing arts facility, synthesizing the best ideas from all over America and Europe, and at the same time, learning from the mistakes of others. We are trying to achieve artistic excellence, economic soundness, and financial efficiency. Though our facilities have been designed specifically for the needs of our community, our methods are applicable to any city."[4]

In the meantime, Gary Moore had hired staff. He lured Leon Scioscia from Arena Stage in Washington, D.C., to become the theater's general manager. Moore also hired a technical director, Harold "Chip" Ulrich, with whom he had worked in Oklahoma; as well as an administrator, Cecilia Pinkston, another Oklahoma associate. The Herberger Theater board of directors had

Gary Moore, executive director of the Herberger Theater (seated), and Leon Scioscia, general manager of the theater, with the model of the Herberger Theater Center in their offices in the basement of Valley National Bank.
Arizona Republic, September 10, 1988. Photograph by Sean Brady. Used with permission.

expanded to twenty-three members, adding corporate and civic leaders to their roster. The new board members included Donald Bliss of Mountain Bell, Norman Buchan, Gary Driggs of Western Savings and Loan, Robert Duckworth of First Interstate Bank of Arizona, G. Robert "Bull" Burham, Stevie Eller, John Graham of Sunbelt, William Gresser of American Greyhound Racing, William Hogan of *Arizona Republic*, Robert Mathews of Arizona Bank, A. J. "Jack" Pfister of Salt River Project, Gene Rice of MeraBank, James Simmons of United Bank, Richard Snell of Ramada Inns Incorporated, and John Teets of Greyhound Corporation. It was not coincidental that the Herberger Theater board resembled the leadership of the Phoenix 40.

Moore and his newly assembled staff planned a season of performances unlike any Phoenix had ever seen.[5] They put together an elaborate series of events for the anticipated opening in mid-April 1989, which would continue through June 1989, featuring primarily Arizona performing groups. In fact, Moore booked performances through September 1990, claiming, "There will never be a time when something is not happening at the Herberger."[6]

The premiere resident company, Arizona Theatre Company, could at long last count on using Center Stage as its Phoenix home. Moore invited Actors Theatre of Phoenix to be the resident company of the smaller Stage West, where they would perform mostly contemporary fare.[7] As part of the opening calendar of events, Moore invited both companies to perform their final shows of the 1988–1989 season in the new Herberger Theaters.

Moore also spent time developing relationships with dance companies he intended to book into the Herberger Theater. He courted Ballet Arizona, a company raised from the ashes of three previous attempts to establish a viable ballet presence in the Valley; the dance company was established through a merger that combined Ballet West Arizona, the Arizona Dance Theatre, and the Phoenix Ballet into Ballet Arizona in 1986. Although Ballet Arizona performed their large ballet pieces in a big concert hall similar to Symphony Hall, the company still saw the benefits of performing their smaller ballet pieces at the new Herberger Theater. Moore also met choreographer Frances Smith Cohen at a dinner and encouraged her to assemble a new modern dance company. Cohen followed through with Moore's suggestion; the new dance company became the Center Dance Ensemble and a resident company of the Herberger

Theater Center.[8] Previously, Cohen had put together the University of Arizona's dance department between 1971 and 1978; before that, she had showcased her Tucson-based company, Kadimah Dancers, throughout Arizona in 1955. Moore then encouraged Ann Ludwig, a professor of dance at Arizona State University, and her company, A Ludwig Dance Theatre, to join the roster of resident dance groups.[9]

The opening ceremonies, scheduled from April 14 through April 16, 1989, were packed with special preview evenings for major contributors, volunteers, public officials, and educators. The contributors would be treated to a concert version of Verdi's opera, *Giovanna D'Arco (Joan of Arc),* directed by the general director of the Arizona Opera, Glynn Ross.[10] The performance would feature prominent soloists and a full chorus and orchestra. The Arizona Community Foundation and the ARCO Foundation would pay for the opening performance, which would be followed by a champagne reception in the theater foyer. During the day, visitors would enjoy an open house at the theater and guided tours.

One week later, between April 20 and April 23, 1989, the first public performances would grace Center Stage. The internationally acclaimed Phoenix Boys Choir, under the direction of Dr. Harvey Smith, would feature the western U.S. premieres of three works by American composers.[11] The composers included Milton Babbitt, the highly celebrated twentieth-century composer and professor at Princeton University; Daniel Pinkham, chair of the Department of Early Music at the New England Conservatory of Music; and Ned Rorem, Pulitzer prize-winning opera and symphony composer.

In addition to serving as a showcase for Arizona arts organizations, Moore and his staff viewed the state-of-the-art theater as a potential Broadway-type house, hosting dramas or small touring musicals. They were excited to launch the national tour of Stephen Pouliot's *Grandma Moses: An American Primitive,* starring Emmy- and Oscar-winning actress Cloris Leachman in the title role. This premiere would mark the first theatrical performance on Center Stage, and the audience would be the first to bask in the acoustics of a theater designed especially for the spoken word.[12]

Over the next two months, the Herberger Theater staff scheduled numerous and diverse performances. At the same time that Center Stage was to be in full swing, Childsplay was to open the smaller Stage West theater with a production of *The Miracle Worker.* Shortly thereafter, Ballet Arizona would open on Center Stage with a performance of new choreography by artistic director Jean-Paul Comelin. The newly choreographed performance within the intimate setting of Center Stage would draw the audiences' attention to the subtle dance movements and gestures that might be lost in a larger theater like Symphony

Hall. During the performance of the new ballet, the orchestra pit also would be used for the first time.

In mid-May, Actors Theatre of Phoenix would debut on Stage West in a production of *And They Dance Real Slow in Jackson* by Jim Leonard, playwright-in-residence at Arizona State University. Saving the best for next to last, Arizona Theatre Company would claim Center Stage as their new home with a production of Lee Blessing's Tony-nominated drama, *A Walk in the Woods.* After Arizona Theatre Company's production closed, Center Stage would feature the world premiere of *Cowgirls,* a musical based on the lives of Arizona ranch women, with original music by Dolan Ellis, a Phoenix singer and composer who was Arizona's Official State Balladeer.[13]

As the performing arts community reveled in the promise of the new Herberger Theater, fund-raising foundered. When asked to explain the situation to a reporter from *Phoenix Magazine,* Moore equivocated, saying that once the first Herberger family challenge had been met "we were…[absorbed] in the process of designing the building and we weren't sure what the final costs might be; we decided to hold off and not do another fund drive to match the last million [the second Herberger family challenge] until we were sure of the total costs."[14] The Herberger Theater board and its finance committee still had to raise at least $4 million, $1 million to match the second Herberger gift, plus a minimum of an additional $3 million, a figure fated to escalate even further. Mark DeMichele, who had taken over as fund-raising committee chair of the Herberger Theater board in 1987, needed to get the ball rolling. He explained publicly, "The corporate drive is by no means complete. The first $2 million raised represented the involvement of only about fifty-five companies in the Valley. So there are many other firms that had not participated. And we intend to approach them as part of the first prong of this campaign."[15] In fact, DeMichele had been slow out of the gate, and perhaps he voiced his secret hope when he told *Phoenix Magazine,* "Now that the theater itself is taking shape right down there on the street, I'm hoping there will be a significant outpouring of support."[16]

On March 11, 1989, the Herberger Theater board members walked through the new building, now so close to completion. They then gathered in the Kitchell CEM construction trailer to hear an ominous report from Richard Mallery. He had been notified that the contractor expected a forty-five-day to sixty-day delay in the completion of the building beyond the scheduled April 14, 1989, opening because of an earlier three-month delay in the delivery of structural beams. Although the Nielsen Construction Company had been able to make up one month of that delay, it now was clear that they could not make up the

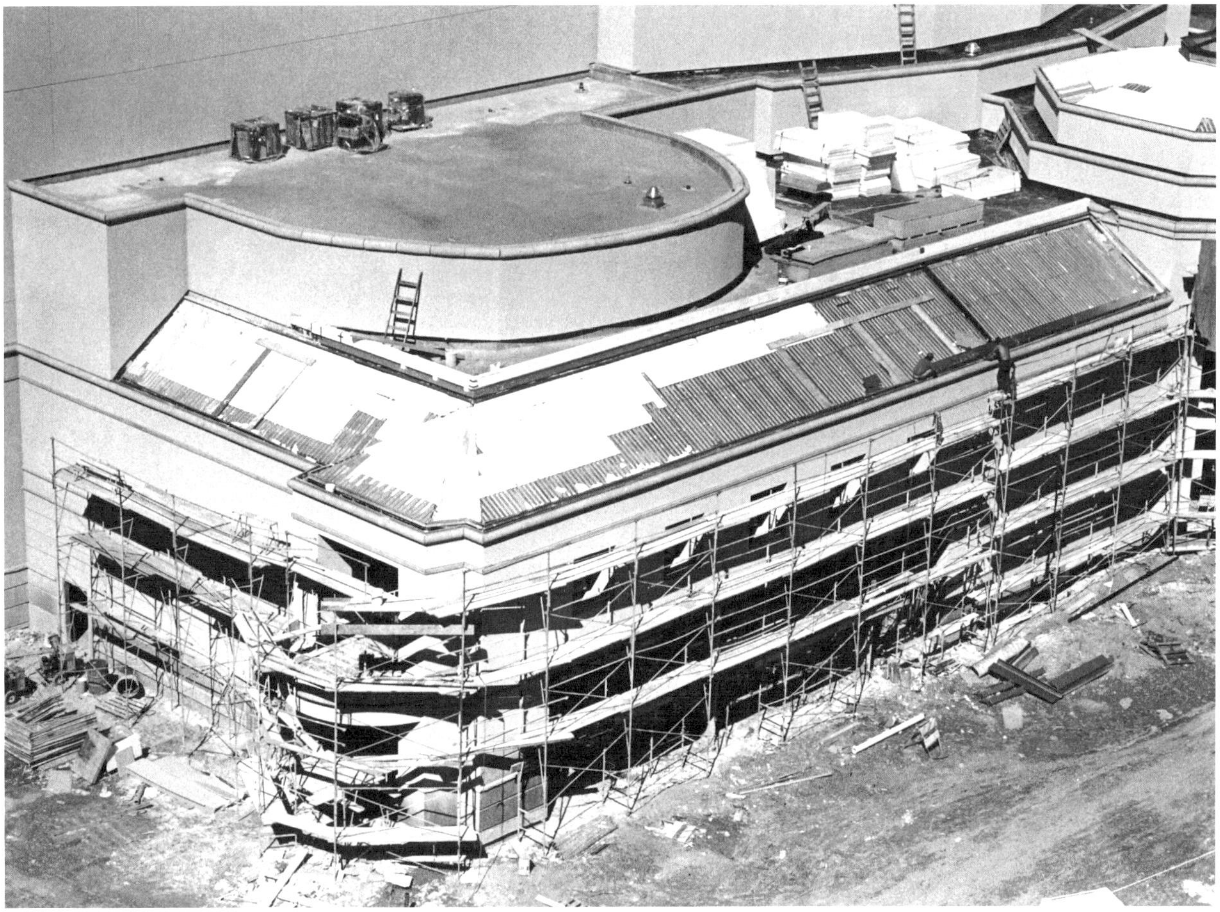

The Herberger Theater Center in April 1989 as construction comes closer to completion. The photograph was taken from the Hyatt Regency. *Arizona Republic*, April 4, 1989. Photograph by Peter Schwepker. Used with permission.

other two months, especially contending with the overall complexity of the theater itself. The Herberger Theater board grappled with the problems now before them, particularly how to rearrange all the elaborate performances Moore had scheduled.

The delay was disheartening, but they had no choice except to plunge ahead. The board members also learned that Gary Moore was in the hospital recovering from back surgery, although he did continue to work from his bed. Moore rallied the troops in true show business style, saying, "The show is going to go on, somewhere."[17] First and foremost, they needed to accommodate the two-week run of Cloris Leachman in *Grandma Moses: An American Primitive*. The staff eventually found a stage at Saguaro High School in Scottsdale, a far cry from the much-anticipated Herberger Theater, but at least some type of viable substitute. American Express donated funds to cover the extra expenses of moving the show, and the Herberger family feted Cloris Leachman in their home and at several public events. Several other performing arts groups moved

Mike Samaniego of Canyon Plastering applies adhesive to the entry area of the new Herberger Theater.
Arizona Republic, April 4, 1989. Photograph by Peter Schwepker. Used with permission.

Working on a control panel for Stage West of the new Herberger Theater is Larry Budd, an installer for Sound and Intercom Systems of Phoenix. The foreground shows cable for a fly baton.
Arizona Republic, April 4, 1989. Photograph by Peter Schwepker. Used with permission.

to the new Paul V. Galvin Playhouse at Arizona State University in Tempe; this well-equipped 500-seat house had opened on April 1, 1989, yet it still had an open summer calendar. The Center Dance Ensemble made their debut that June at the Mesa Amphitheatre and then moved to the Paul V. Galvin Playhouse. Some events were put off until the fall.

The Herberger Theater Center finally opened on July 19, 1989, with *Party of One*, an offbeat musical coproduced by Musical Theater of Arizona and the Herberger Theater. Imported from San Francisco, Musical Theater of Arizona had been operating in Phoenix for five years under artistic director Ron Newcomer.[18] Although the production of *Party of One* was not an adequate substitute for the previously planned gala opening, the press still took notice. Linda Trezza, in her *Arizona Republic* review, commented:

"Candidly speaking, it isn't the kind of grand-scale production one would expect to mark the inception of a major new theater....Despite an occasional camera flash and drinks served in elegant stemware, you might not have suspected that was the 'historic event' that Gary Moore referred to it in his remarks before the performance."[19] But audiences loved the theater, and they loved the show so much that *Party of One* had an extended run through August 27, 1989. The show clearly was a success. The gala opening events now were planned for the fall, rather than at the opening production of *Party of One*, because Phoenix is a searing urban nightmare in July, which discouraged the trappings of a grand opening. The delayed grand opening events did not dampen hopes that the Herberger Theater would stimulate Phoenix artists and performing arts organizations to excel. "This brings us into the twenty-first century," noted Erma Bombeck.[20] "We should have a working theater here where people can try out things and be daring and take chances." Mayor Goddard added, "I think symbolically, it's very important, because it makes a commitment to quality theater that has never been made in this state."

Kax and Bob Herberger attended the first Friday night performance of *Party of One*. They arrived early and received a special tour from Mayor Terry Goddard and Richard Mallery. "It's a very moving experience," said Kax.[21] The pair sat in seats close to the front because Bob Herberger's eyesight was failing. "Time goes by so fast and Bob's eyesight is almost totally gone," she candidly revealed in an interview, "and it just kind of broke my heart to think

The new theater is ready! A view of the entrance to the Steele Pavilion.
Arizona Republic, August 19, 1989. Photograph by David McIntyre. Used with permission.

Bob Herberger (left) is given his first tour of the completed theater complex that bears his name by attorney and civic leader Richard Mallery.
Arizona Republic, July 21, 1989. Photograph by Barrett Stinson. Used with permission.

that he wouldn't be able to see a performance in the theater."[22] She also expressed misgivings about the delayed opening, "Late April would have been such a divine, ideal time for the opening of the theater." Bob consoled her: "Well, we'll have what we call in retailing a soft opening. We do that with department stores...and a month later, you give them a full treatment. It doesn't concern me very much because I think a lot of people expect delays on construction."[23]

Finishing touches on the Herberger Theater continued, with the completion of Stage West the following month. The theater opened on August 11, 1989, with a production of *Geech...The Moosical,* with lyrics written by Jerry Bittle, based on his cartoon strip, and the musical score written by Angelo Badalamenti. The

Theatre League of Phoenix and Kansas City, Missouri, premiered this new musical production at the Herberger Theater after a preview run in Kansas City. Theater patrons and performers praised the small Stage West theater for seeming vast and intimate at the same time.

Patrons head to the Herberger Theater for one of the opening performances.
Arizona Republic, September 9, 1989. Photograph by John Blackmer. Used with permission.

The gala opening festivities for the Herberger Theater Center ran from October 6 through October 9, 1989, with performances of a musical tribute titled *The Great Women of Broadway*, starring Nancy Dussault and Karen Morrow. The opening events included a black-tie, invitation-only affair to thank the financial supporters of the Herberger Theater. They enjoyed a champagne reception before the performance and a desert buffet after the final curtain. Volunteers and public officials were honored the following evening. For the last performance, held on October 9, 1989, the audience was made up of educators. They were invited in the hope of generating not only a personal interest in the Herberger Theater, but also in generating an interest for the all-important school matinees to come. AT&T funded the entire weekend of gala opening events.[24] Gary Moore embraced the spirit of Sir Laurence Olivier at the opening, commenting, "He [Sir Laurence] saw the potential of artists and tried to provide a place that would nurture and help them do their best work."[25] The Herberger Theater intended to follow Olivier's lead and do the same.

Guests celebrate the opening of the Herberger Theater in the lobby of the Steele Pavilion.
Arizona Republic, September 9, 1989. Photograph by Stephen Mounteer. Used with permission.

Resident companies of the Herberger Theater were listed as Arizona Theatre Company, Ballet Arizona, Actors Theatre of Phoenix, Childsplay, the Center Dance Ensemble, and A Ludwig Dance Theatre. Affiliated organizations were the newly formed Arizona Jewish Theatre Company, whose original home was Scottsdale's Stagebrush Theatre; the Aurora Mime Theater; the Black Theatre Troupe; the Desert Dance Theatre; Teatro del Valle, the Theatre League; and the Musical Theater of

Executive director Gary Moore sits in one of the plush seats of the Herberger Theater's Center Stage. The farthest main floor seat is only sixty-six feet from the proscenium.
Arizona Republic, July 19, 1989. Photograph by Gary Ulik. Used with permission.

Arizona. In describing how so many organizations could call this new theater home, Moore said: "It is a fairly unique operation in this country. The individual companies could not afford to build this magnificent facility, but collectively, it creates a place where talented people can work together backstage. The dancers may have the rehearsal hall from 9 A.M. to 2 P.M. and then a theater company will move in. They comingle and watch each other's work. Also, both stages are used year round rather than sitting empty between productions."[26] There was a new spirit of cooperation between all the arts groups, and according to Moore, "This is what we hoped would happen....We are all in this together and if one succeeds, we all succeed."

The Herberger Theater Center, downtown Phoenix's new theatrical jewel, distinguished itself in its initial year, winning unanimous praise for aesthetic and technical excellence.
Arizona Republic, May 6, 1990. Photograph by John Samora. Used with permission.

"Phoenix was elevated to theater heaven," according to Michael Burkett of the *Arizona Republic*, in a special publication on the Herberger Theater.[27] With two beautiful and intimate state-of-the-art theaters built especially for the spoken word, and with just as much attention lovingly paid to audience comfort as to the technical prowess of its staging devices, it was truly a place to make art, as well as to share that art with the people of Phoenix. The general manager of the Herberger Theater, Leon Scioscia, spoke for many who had been involved from the beginning when he said, "The architects' model doesn't give you the sense of what it's actually like to look up through the pavilion's skylight and see the stars."[28] As for his particular role with the theater, he said, "It adds something to a life, to be in on the ground floor of a project that evolves into a structure that will outlive all of us and be around for generations."

The lobby of the Herberger Theater for the premiere performance by Arizona Theatre Company.
Arizona Republic, May 6, 1990. Photograph by John Samora. Used with permission.

A scene from Quilters, *Arizona Theatre Company's first performance in the Herberger Theater in the fall of 1989.*
Arizona Theatre Company Archives. Photograph by Tim Fuller. Used with permission.

In November and December of 1989, the spotlight illuminated Arizona Theatre Company when they performed for the first time on Center Stage. They chose *Quilters,* by Barbara Damashek and Molly Newman, a play about the joys and struggles of America's pioneers. It was Arizona Theatre Company's most requested play since they had first performed it six years earlier. This was, in fact, a season of firsts for Arizona Theatre Company, as they had just moved into their new home in Tucson at the restored Temple of Music and Art. Now they performed in two glorious theaters in the two most populous cities in the state. These advances transformed the company, as well as professional theater in Arizona.

For Richard Mallery, the completion of the Herberger Theater Center was the culmination of nearly a decade of work, which was exhilarating at times, but also taxing, as he doggedly overcame obstacle upon obstacle. It is safe to say that no one else experienced his particular level of satisfaction and triumph.

15

The Work Out

One month before the Herberger Theater opening, the Federal Home Loan Bank Board stunned Pinnacle West Capital Corporation with a $180 million capital call at its MeraBank subsidiary, Arizona's largest savings and loan institution. The capital call on June 24, 1989, was made under terms of a keep-well agreement that Pinnacle West Capital Corporation had signed when it purchased MeraBank in 1986. This agreement held the firm responsible for maintaining the thrift's net worth. Pinnacle West Capital Corporation board chair Keith Turley took decisive action to dispose of the troubled savings and loan before it pulled the entire corporation down.[1]

The corporation formed two committees to explore ways to sever the thrift and to negotiate some type of settlement with federal regulators. To further distance the corporation from MeraBank, Pinnacle West Capital Corporation pulled four of its interlocking directors off the savings and loan board and replaced them with individuals who had no affiliation with the parent corporation. According to a spokesperson, Pinnacle West Capital Corporation did this so that "the best interests of each company can be served without conflict."[2] The Wall Street firm Salomon Brothers began working on a restructuring plan for Pinnacle West Capital Corporation.

Federal regulators seized Western Savings and Loan on June 14, 1989, even as its new chair, Robert Stallings stated that he believed "consolidation was still viable."[3] Stallings had planned to combine a number of troubled Arizona savings and loan associations—Western, Sun State, Security, and Universal—into one institution. This did not happen. Federal regulators placed Western Savings and Loan into receivership, a move that wiped out the value of the institution's stock, as well as about $115 million in subordinated debt.[4] Regulators then seized Sun State Savings and Loan, followed by Security Savings and Loan and Universal Savings and Loan.[5] Each of these thrifts wound up in receivership, as did the rest of Arizona's thrifts, along with a handful of banks. Arizona's banks were also in deep trouble, with portfolios now encumbered with nonperforming loans. Valley National Bank added $181 million to its loan loss reserve on June 22, 1989, and for the second quarter in a row reported a loss in share value. There were rumors of pending write-downs at Valley National Bank, but the $181 million sum shocked the Arizona business community, especially the new chair-elect of the bank, Richard Lehman. "Things deteriorated in the last three weeks," according to United Bank president and board chair James Simmons.[6] "The heart of the problem is property appraisals. They are coming in 50 percent below what they were at the first of the year." The declining values prompted many borrowers to walk away from developments and raw land holdings. There was concern about further deterioration in the Arizona real estate market, and all the negative publicity added to the gloomy scenario.

Although still aglow from the opening of their beautiful new theaters, the Herberger Theater board was not immune to the financial havoc in their midst. They also were in trouble. Fund-raising efforts virtually had ground to a halt. Richard Mallery knew he had to act to reinvigorate the board of directors to meet the challenge. He also considered stepping aside as board president if the right person could be found to assume the position. Mallery had devoted sizable sums of his time since 1980 to the mission of seeing a new theater in downtown Phoenix come to fruition, and he must have been exhausted, understandably so. He decided to bring Pamela Grant, president and chief executive officer of Goldwater's department stores, into the foreground to head up the fund-raising campaign to erase the building and operating debt, which now stood at over $6 million, while he stepped into the background.[7]

Grant introduced Jack Marks to the Herberger Theater board at its January 24, 1990, meeting. Marks had spent years at Arizona State University directing their $100 million capital campaign. Everyone hoped that these two newcomers to the cause could help avert a crisis. Grant and Marks's methods, however, initially digressed little from past practices; they tried to pump new life into the seat-underwriting campaign, and they worked hard on acquiring major gifts. Even so, Grant's energy and commitment provided a ray of hope that held the board together during its toughest times to come.[8]

Besides the frightening economy, Grant faced another difficulty. Banks traditionally had been the source of major gifts to nonprofits in Arizona, but that was before most of them had been bought out by major national banks that had little knowledge of, or history with, the local community. In the Herberger

Theater's case, it was the banks themselves that had to be paid; therefore, they could hardly be a source of new contributions.

By the end of March 1990, David Sprenthall, an attorney at Snell & Wilmer who had offered the board his services pro bono to help refinance the debt balance, reported that negotiations were continuing, but nothing had been settled.[9] The banks wanted the city of Phoenix to guarantee the interest on the loan, and the city signaled that it had little interest in assuming that obligation. Grant lamented that even though the theater had $1.2 million in outstanding pledges, it was not clear if all, or any of the pledges, would be paid because of the deteriorating economic situation in the state. Forging ahead, she noted that Steven Kolesar had joined the effort to invigorate the seat-underwriting campaign.[10]

The situation worsened in May 1990 when the Herberger Theater could not pay its quarterly interest payment to the banks that had been due at the end of March. Not only that, but $100,000 was needed by June 30 to cover current operating expenses.[11] At the May 30, 1990, meeting of the Herberger Theater board, Sprenthall conveyed that negotiations with the banks were at an impasse because the banks still were trying to persuade the city to take responsibility for some of the debt.[12] Grant pointed out that the current negotiations for restructuring the outstanding loan had paralyzed corporate and individual gifts. She had learned that no one would give to the Herberger Theater until the board resolved the debt restructuring matter. The board meeting closed with the election of Mark DeMichele as president and Grant as vice president.

As fund-raising committee chair, DeMichele realized that trouble loomed for the Herberger Theater. He also knew how difficult it was to raise money in Phoenix, even in the best of times; 1990 was plainly the worst of times. He accepted the presidency anyway, for personal and noble reasons: "The primary reason was that the theater was so important to the arts, in my view, that I hated to see it get tarnished; and for a while it was tarnished because the rumor mill in the community was that it was going to go into bankruptcy. I didn't want to see that happen; and then secondly," De Michele continued, "my predecessor in this company [Arizona Public Service] was Keith Turley, who was one of the visionaries [of the Herberger Theater]. He was the guy responsible for raising the money. He had enough troubles as it was with all the things that happened with Pinnacle West and MeraBank. I just didn't want to see the Herberger added to it, so the combination of the two things was important to me to see it through and get it done."[13]

Negotiations with the banks continued throughout the remainder of the year. Representatives from the city attended the meetings, including Ray Bladine, deputy city manager, and Kevin Keogh, finance director for the city. Denny Maus, who had been promoted to director of community and economic development for the city of Phoenix, also attended. In his new role, Maus no longer was responsible for the Phoenix Civic Plaza or the Herberger Theater; however, he felt a commitment to the project. Maus wanted to help it through this difficult time.

At times, the bank meetings grew heated. Except for Valley National Bank, every one of Arizona's banks had changed hands and was now owned by out-of-state financial institutions with no deep connections to Phoenix. "They had no involvement with the theater, its conceptualization, or its meaning in the community," said DeMichele, who led most of the conferences, with Mallery steadfastly by his side.[14] "These were very, very contentious meetings. We were dealing with the work-out people, people who work out bad loans." As anyone who has ever faced them knows, the really tough guys in banking are the ones known as the work-out guys. That made the discussions quite different than if DeMichele had been dealing with colleagues whom he had served with on other committees and boards.[15]

The first item the work-out guys seized upon was the comfort letter from the city that Mallery had prepared for the banks when they first made the loan to the Herberger Theater. The banks sought to use this comfort letter to force the city to pay the default money, or at least to pay the outstanding interest; however, Mallery had crafted the letter in such a way that, legally, the city could not be forced to come up with any additional money.[16] Once the bankers consulted their attorneys, they were furious. At one point, the work-out guys threatened to sue Valley National Bank because it had acted as agent for the line of credit. Of course, they also threatened to sue the Herberger Theater board and the board's directors personally. There were other threats, such as seizing the land around the Herberger Theater, which had not yet been given to the city, and installing a chain-link fence to cut-off all access to the theaters, despite the likely public relations disaster such an unnecessary stunt would cause the banks. The bankers' heavy-handed approach displeased DeMichele, who found the atmosphere poisonous. He knew the banking community well; although DeMichele intended for the Herberger Theater to pay off the loan over time, he also understood that the loan for the Herberger Theater had already been written off by the banks.

As it turned out, the most egregious bank was one based in New York City that conducted a good deal of business with Arizona Public Service and its parent company, Pinnacle West Capital Corporation. DeMichele discretely contacted the bank's headquarters "in an effort to use whatever influence we as a major customer of the bank could exercise to get them to tone down the negotiations and work toward a solution." In this instance, going over the heads of the negotiators worked.[17]

On September 24, 1990, Maus presented a comprehensive report to the Herberger Theater board on the bank negotiations.[18] He told the board members that the banks wanted \$2.3 million from the city. The city, on the other hand, was exploring the idea of placing a large sum of money into a trust fund, from which they would give \$1 million to banks and the remaining amount could be used to help subsidize the operations of the Herberger Theater. Although the city was willing to help the theater, it had its own financial stresses; for example, the restoration of the Orpheum Theater and the construction of the new history museum had been delayed because of the city's reduced income projections. Peter Hill, vice president of special credit administration at Valley National Bank, said that the banks were willing to give the Herberger Theater five years to pay off the loan if the board paid \$1 million now. Perhaps the banks had noted that the board recently had received a \$1 million grant from the Horace C. Steele Foundation, earmarked for the marble tile to be laid in the lobby pavilion.[19] Maus proposed that the Horace C. Steele Foundation money be invested instead and that the interest earned be used for an operating subsidy. He further advised that \$20,000 a month from fund-raising proceeds should be kept in-house for operating expenses.

DeMichele clarified the current offer from the banks. The banks would put a \$2.3 million lien on the parcel of land surrounding the theater, which had secured the original line of credit to the Herberger Theater board. The city would pay this amount to the banks, thereby purchasing the land. The banks then would forgive approximately \$2 million of the debt if the board raised \$1 million by end of 1990. The board would have to promise to raise the balance of the principal by 1991 and all outstanding interest by 1992. In effect, the board would be obligated to raise \$2.2 million by end of 1991, even though Grant only had projected a goal of \$1.3 million. The board rightfully worried about their ability to raise such large sums in the existing economic environment. Grant especially had concerns about raising the first \$1 million, which would need to be raised in a matter of months. The board asked DeMichele to negotiate better terms. He responded that he would try, but he made it clear that if the deal dissolved completely, the Herberger Theater might be turned over to the city of Phoenix. While the board operated in crisis mode, Gary Moore had cut his staff by 40 percent and eliminated the entire marketing and public relations staff. As the months progressed, Moore even loaned the theater money out of his own pocket to meet payroll, as did several members of the board of directors.[20]

The final outcome of the loan negotiations with the banks resulted in a more realistic modification of the previous offer. DeMichele had bargained successfully for better terms, conditioned upon city council approval. The Phoenix City Council, under the new mayor who had succeeded Terry Goddard, Mayor

Paul Johnson, adopted the compromise plan.[21] Stakeholders considered the settlement a good solution to an impossible situation, where all parties shouldered some of the burden. Grant and Moore emphasized the theater's successes at the city council meeting, before Grant described how careful negotiations with the city, the Herberger Theater, and the banks were able to avoid a loan default. The city approved an expenditure of $2.3 million from Civic Plaza Building Corporation bonds for the acquisition of the parcel of land surrounding the theater, and the banks forgave $1.7 million of the theater's loan. These two compromises reduced the loan from the banking consortium by $4 million. The banks also agreed to freeze the interest until 1992, and they capped the interest at $194,000. The Herberger Theater board promised to have signed pledges for the remaining amount of $2.8 million by the end of 1993.

Five years later, after Grant had become president of the Herberger Theater board, the banks forgave even more of the loan through negotiations that were spearheaded by DeMichele, even though he no longer served on the board of directors. Altogether, the banks forgave $4 million of the loan, which in effect made the banks the theater's biggest donors, followed by the city of Phoenix. Although some bank executives grumbled, upon reflection, their investment in a major performing arts facility for the largest city in the state demonstrated a certain type of cultural and economic leadership. As one community leader stated, "We could never have convinced them to give donations in that amount, so this was an indirect way of receiving the kind of support that maybe they should have been giving all along."

As for the arts, the Herberger Theater accomplished what Mallery had envisioned in 1980. The Phoenix arts scene was awake and audiences were growing. Arizona Theatre Company saw its single-ticket sales increase by 164 percent in Phoenix. "I've been saying for years that the Herberger will do this for us and it did," said Gary Gisselman, Arizona Theatre Company's artistic director.[22] "In fact, it has been even better than we expected." Every arts organization that used the theater was full of praise for what a magnificent and workable place it was. As the Herberger Theater fulfilled its mission for the arts in Arizona, it added luster to downtown Phoenix and became the real jewel in the center of the city.

16

A Sense of Place

The plaza in front of the Herberger Theater experienced a beautiful transformation when the John Henry Waddell sculptures, a series of twelve figures called *Dance,* were moved from their perch in front of Symphony Hall, directly across the street, to the grounds of the Herberger Theater complex under the watchful eye of Waddell. Walter Bimson and Lewis Ruskin had commissioned the sculptures for the Phoenix Civic Plaza as a gift to the citizens of Phoenix in the early 1970s. They subsequently were placed in front of Symphony Hall on the south end of the plaza. The two men's generosity is commemorated on a small plaque in the courtyard of the theater. Placing these life-sized sculptures at ground level, rather than on the elevated, protected platforms at Phoenix Civic Plaza was risky, but it was worthwhile because the sculptures now provided visitors with an intimate, tactile experience of the bronzed dancing figures. Harry Wood, chair of Arizona State College's art department, had persuaded Waddell to leave his home in Illinois in 1957 to teach art education.[1] Bimson and Ruskin, as well as Bob and Kax Herberger, became his patrons, which led Waddell to adopt Arizona as his home. He is considered one of Arizona's greatest sculptors.[2]

The 1980s were a pivotal time in Phoenix's history, as well as in the city's cultural life. During the decade, the city council evolved from at-large representation to district representation and open government, which provided more than one way for citizens to become involved in shaping the city's future. The 1980s witnessed the first real steps taken to improve transportation, which eventually gave rise to a freeway system connecting its far-flung suburban communities. Moreover, the 1980s also witnessed the first serious efforts to transform downtown Phoenix, via enterprises like the Arizona Center, the Mercado, and the Herberger Theater.[3] Shortly after their completion, a downtown sports arena, a science center, and a history museum rose from the urban landscape. Then, at the end of the decade, the boom went bust. Phoenix lost its savings and loans,

The exterior of the Herberger Theater after the installation of the John Henry Waddell sculptures, Dance. *The twelve figures were originally placed in front of Symphony Hall, on Phoenix Civic Plaza, but were later moved to the Herberger Theater to make room for the expanded Phoenix Convention Center. Waddell supervised their move and placement in front of the theater. The sculptures are greatly admired in their new home.*
Herberger Theater Archives. Photograph by Bob Rink. Used with permission.

and out-of-state financial institutions purchased all but one of its commercial banks, Valley National Bank.[4]

Culturally, the 1980s saw unprecedented growth, evidenced by the legislature's increased annual appropriations to the state arts commission, although Arizona continued to lag behind most states in public funding for the arts. The governor's office and the state arts commission created the Governor's Arts Awards; even today, these prestigious awards remain the most coveted among the city's artists

The beautiful interior of Center Stage, the main theater of the Herberger Theater Center.
Herberger Theater Archives. Photograph by Robert Reck. Used with permission.

and patrons. Arizona benefited from the creation of the first statewide arts advocacy organization, Arizonans for Cultural Development. The city of Phoenix followed suit, creating the Phoenix Arts Commission and launching a public art program. The Herberger Theater, the most conspicuous symbol of the city's cultural maturation, opened in the late 1980s, giving a permanent home to Arizona Theatre Company and a state-of-the-art facility to other performing groups. Steps were taken to save the Orpheum Theater, with the groundwork laid for its restoration. Historic preservation became a meaningful part of Phoenix's lexicon. Finally, the National Arts Stabilization Fund helped major arts organizations in the state become fiscally stable.

By the end of 1989, Arizona Theatre Company had two new stages on which to perform, the new Center Stage at the Herberger Theater in Phoenix and the restored Temple of Music and Art in Tucson. These different environments changed the nature of Arizona Theatre Company's productions and their relationships with their respective communities. In Phoenix, although the company found the Herberger Theater to be a superb facility in every way, they had precious little latitude in the use of Center Stage. It was theirs only at prescribed times.[5] In addition, they were required to pay rent for each usage.[6] In Tucson, Arizona Theatre Company was master of its fate. The Temple of Music and Art was theirs alone to conjure the art of theater; it was where the company was able to boost its artistry.[7] Phoenix audiences benefited from this boost, as all the company's productions made their way to the Herberger Theater; some productions even opened there first. The Herberger Theater was a place to *show* staged productions; however, it was not a place *to give birth* to them.

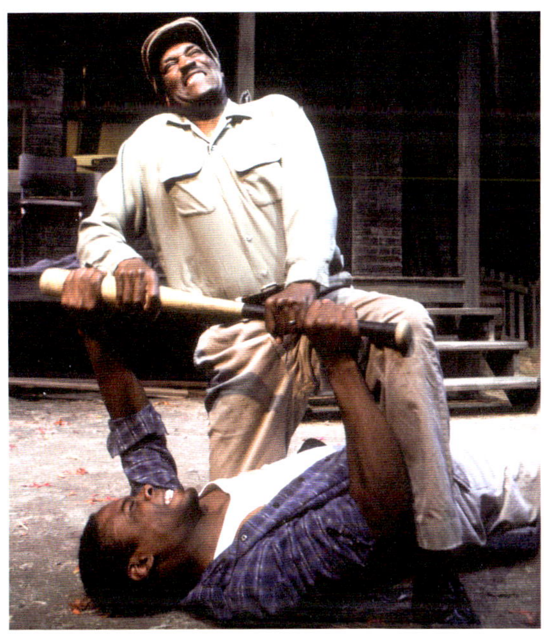

A scene from Fences, *performed by Arizona Theatre Company during their 1989–1990 season.*
Arizona Theatre Company Archives. Photograph by Tim Fuller. Used with permission.

To put the situation in context, most regional theaters in the United States have a home of their own, almost exclusively. Arena Stage in Washington, D.C.; the Alley Theatre in Houston, Texas; and the Guthrie Theater in Minneapolis, Minnesota, belong to each theater company, even if the

A scene from Cat on a Hot Tin Roof, *performed by Arizona Theatre Company during their 1988–1989 season.*
Arizona Theatre Company Archives. Photograph by Tim Fuller. Used with permission.

buildings are legally owned by their respective cities. In fact, a banner that exclaimed, "Not a Hotel for Theatre, but a Home" best illustrated the regional theater movement, which began in earnest in the early 1960s.[8] It was at Tucson's Temple of Music and Art that Arizona Theatre Company went about the complicated and intangible activity of creating art. Perhaps the lack of close identity with one theater company added to the steep challenges the Herberger Theater board faced in raising money. People do not donate to a building as much as they donate to what happens inside and to the organizations that create what happens inside. Pamela Grant, although deeply committed to the value of the Herberger Theater, recalled years later, "To many in the community, the Herberger did not have a heart...the Herberger was nothing but a building with a name. It meant nothing, in that sense."[9] Put another way, Grant lamented the fact that since the Herberger Theater was a place for many arts groups, it was not possible to establish a meaningful identity of its own.[10]

To be sure, the Herberger Theater founders had nothing but the best intentions when they broadened their focus from a one-company facility to a multicompany facility. The Herberger Theater's founding leaders had come to that decision after seeking counsel and studying what little the city had to offer its performing arts groups. As Gary Moore summed up at the opening, "We're not ready for a Guthrie or an Alley or an Arena Stage, where you have the following and support to run a building year-round. The only way it could function is on a cooperative basis. The more I've come to know Phoenix, the more I've come to believe that this is the most appropriate vehicle to serve the needs of the moment."[11] In retrospect, there was no way Arizona Theatre Company could have taken on the complex management or the enormous debt that beleaguered the Herberger Theater in its early years.[12]

Today, twenty years later, the situation is dramatically different. The Herberger Theater's debt is paid; Arizona Theatre Company gained valuable experience successfully managing a theater building in Tucson. As the Herberger Theater celebrates its twentieth anniversary, it is time to revisit its genesis. As Everett King, actor turned businessman, community leader, and Arizona Theatre Company board member recalled, "Nobody had the idea in their head to build a theater downtown until the company making art came and said, 'We need a place to play.' That's how it happened. Buildings do not create art. Art creates the building."[13] This remains pivotal, because presenting organizations like the Herberger Theater, whose main function is to rent their facility and not create the art that is shown there are, by definition, one step removed from the art itself; they also may be less geared toward creating an atmosphere that is conducive to art making and to artists.

Even so, despite myriad challenges—artistic, fiscal, and practical—Arizona Theatre Company happily resides at the Herberger Theater. In 2010 they are one of three resident companies, sharing space with Actors Theatre of Phoenix and the Center Dance Ensemble.[14] It might appear that the Herberger Theater scaled back since it opened in 1989 with six resident companies and seven affiliate arts organizations, but that would not be true. The Herberger Theater still manages to host nearly 700 performances annually, which was its goal from the outset. Each year the arts organizations performing at the Herberger Theater attract more than 200,000 patrons and 30,000 school children to their live performances. With the conversion of the rehearsal hall into a performance space in 2006, called the Performance Outreach Theater, lunchtime performances by various small theater groups occur almost weekly and have become quite popular.[15] To the surprise of some, three shows playing at the same time, using the two stages at the Herberger Theater and the rehearsal hall, works very well.[16]

The president of the Herberger Theater Center, Richard Bowers, took vital action to protect the theater and its environment in 2003 when the city moved to triple the size of the Phoenix Convention Center, formerly the Phoenix Civic Plaza. The $600 million project called for some inelegant structures to be built directly in front of the theater, namely a massive concrete wall and a loading dock for the convention center.[17] Bowers, who had spent twenty-three years as Scottsdale's city manager, knew his way around city politics. He persuaded Phoenix administrators to relocate the loading dock and to redesign the concrete wall's exterior to be more compatible with the theater. Although Bowers fell short in securing an open corridor between the Herberger Theater and Symphony Hall, which would have allowed the eye to move gracefully back and forth between both entrances, he did manage to convince Phoenix administrators to reduce the height of the new building from 190 feet to 170 feet.[18] Nevertheless, the domineering, imposing convention center directly across from the Herberger Theater's Steele Pavilion looms above the entire theater complex, the equivalent of seventeen stories.[19] The Phoenix Symphony, unfortunately, did not fare as well in their negotiations. No matter how much the city put into renovating the interior of Symphony Hall to compensate, it did not make up for the fact that music patrons must now squeeze into the concert hall by a side entrance because the new convention center building actually blocks the front entrance to Symphony Hall entirely.[20]

Bowers and his staff have undertaken a $16.6 million renovation of the Herberger Theater, made possible as part of a 2006 city bond election. Some of the money is being spent on infrastructure, such as new heating and air-conditioning systems, seats, and carpets, as well as providing up-to-date access for disabled patrons. More noticeable changes will occur by the fall 2010. An enlarged outdoor patio connecting the lobbies of both theaters, where drinks can be served, will be added, as well as an upstairs Donors' Lounge and a more attractive entrance for the Performance Outreach Theater on Van Buren Street. At some near future date, Bowers also intends to develop the one-half acre eastern side of the property, which he noted as "one of the few pieces of undeveloped property downtown," to create an income revenue stream, one of the original ideas of the Herberger Theater's board of directors.[21] The revenue from retail development on the site will help to offset the rents for nonprofit users, as well as to set up a long-desired endowment for the theater. Bowers, whose background is in urban planning and design, calculated that when the new Sheraton Hotel, on Van Buren Street directly behind the theater, is occupied at 70 percent capacity, it will produce approximately 2.1 million visitor foot trips across the theater's property by people on their way to and from the convention center. That amount of daily traffic, coupled with the right type of retail, could mean sizable profits for the Herberger Theater. Bowers would like to see the entire block surrounding the Herberger Theater become the "go to piazza" of downtown, where there is always something taking place.[22] Finally, he would like to build on-site offices for all the resident companies. "The benefits of that would be just huge," said Bowers.[23]

Economically, the Herberger Theater was a catalyst to the development of an arts-and-entertainment hub in downtown Phoenix and, by extension, to the region. The monthly First Friday art tours bring thousands of people each month to the growing number of galleries and studio spaces along Roosevelt Street and Grand Avenues and add a sense of place and teaming activity to downtown Phoenix. Arts, culture, and entertainment growth in many American cities in the past two decades outstripped other sectors of the economy. In recent years, these trends merged into what one study called the "experience economy."[24] In fact, Harvard University economist Edward Glaeser argued pointedly that if cities and downtowns were to succeed, one of their jobs must be to please the type of consumer looking for experiences rather than things to buy.[25] Increasingly, these experiences are creative in nature. There has been increased recognition that arts and culture are key components of the urban fabric. They make it possible for a city to attract and keep highly talented professionals, scientists, and entrepreneurs in high-growth sectors. Arts and culture have assumed their rightful place in the minds of urban planners, not as just a nice amenity, but as a true necessity.

Myra Millinger, formerly with the Flinn Foundation, understood that a vibrant, creative community was a critical partner in the economic growth of Phoenix when she accepted the position of president and chief executive officer of the newly formed Metro Phoenix Partnership for Arts and Culture in 2004.[26] This new organization conducted several key studies about this very issue to see how Phoenix stacked up. One study compared Phoenix, now the fifth largest city in the United States, with nine new growth cities that compete with Phoenix for bioscience, biotechnology, and other new growth industries, cities such as Denver, San Diego, and Austin.[27] Once again, Phoenix does not fare well. Except for urban design and architecture, per capita rankings placed Phoenix last in both for-profit and nonprofit arts and cultural organizations. A second study clarified the reason; by every standard that contributions are measured—individual, corporate, private foundations, and public money—Phoenix lagged far behind all nine new growth cities.[28] Despite its cultural achievements in the 1980s and beyond, Phoenix could not compare with these benchmark cities. This should alarm civic leaders. Clearly, much remains to be done to move Phoenix out of last position in arts and cultural organizations and in arts contributions.

A 2004 Battelle Memorial Institute and Morrison Institute for Public Policy study warned, "Unless more priority and focus are given to arts and culture...the full potential for the Valley's economic future will not be realized."[29] These experts, armed with impressive data, were explicit about the importance of the arts to Phoenix's economic growth. The report added, "A robust arts and culture sector will transform the region, making it a highly desirable place to live and visit. The gap between what we are currently investing in arts and culture and what we would need to invest to catch up to our competition appears unbridgeable unless drastic changes are made in the region's approach to and support of arts and culture."[30] Thus, Millinger and her board of directors developed a bold plan to ensure a dedicated and enduring funding source to invigorate arts and culture in the entire state. They had hoped to place a ballot initiative before voters to earmark one-tenth of 1 percent from Arizona's sales tax toward funding for the arts for a minimum of twenty years, a move that could yield over $50 million per year for the arts in Phoenix alone and approximately $100 million per year statewide. The state and its citizens would finally fund its creative communities in a way that would make a difference for the arts and for the economy of the state. Unfortunately, these plans began to change in 2009 as a severe economic recession swept the country, in part due to the nationwide failure of risky securitized mortgages that threatened the entire banking system. Eerily similar to the savings and loan crises in 1989, Arizona's real estate market collapsed and the state's budget hemorrhaged red ink. As the situation worsened, support for an arts ballot initiative waned and it was postponed, although its resurrection for the 2012 elections remains a possibility. In a sign of the seriousness of the situation, the Metro Phoenix Partnership for Arts and Culture, which in its brief life had forged new ground in upping the ante for the arts in Phoenix, ceased operation on March 31, 2010. It retained its legal incorporation in anticipation of a better economy in Arizona.

On a brighter note, the Battelle Memorial Institute had developed a detailed road map for creating a bioscience sector in Arizona a few years earlier, before its work on the creative sector. The extraordinary multibillion-dollar bioscience effort began in 2004. Once again, Richard Mallery was the driving force behind the launch of the International Genomics Consortium and the Translational Genomics Research Institute in Phoenix, placing Arizona at the international forefront of a medical revolution, not to mention the boost they gave to Arizona's economy.[31] Like the Herberger Theater project, Mallery became involved because of a family connection, his wife Francie's brave, but ultimately losing battle against a rare and aggressive form of cancer. He had learned much from the Herberger project, and he used a similar strategy for the bioscience effort. Mallery created public- and private-sector partnerships, although on a scale that dwarfed the Herberger Theater effort.[32] This time there was no lack of sponsorship by a number of major new foundations in Arizona, such as the Virginia G. Piper Charitable Trust, the Nina Mason Pulliam Charitable Trust, and the Stardust Foundation, all of which contributed millions to the bioscience effort.[33] Mallery oversaw the construction of the new, more than $100 million biomedical campus in downtown Phoenix that sits on part of the former Phoenix Union High School campus and is anchored by the offices of the International Genomics Consortium and the Translational Genomics Research Institute.

The lessons we can learn from Mallery and his fellow Herberger Theater founders is that a city's history and cultural life are inextricably bound together. What civic and political leaders do, or do not do, has a profound effect on whether a city's arts thrive. In the same vein, what the arts do, or do not do, has an effect on the type of city it becomes and the type of citizens it attracts and keeps. Conceived as a pivotal piece in the revitalization of downtown Phoenix in the early 1980s, the Herberger Theater, in spite of its fitful opening, is a beacon for the future. Many veterans of the Herberger Theater crusade have moved on or passed away, but their contributions to the larger cause of cultural development in an urban and regional context stand as testaments to their commitment and civic stewardship. Although Bob Herberger died at the family home in Paradise Valley after a brief illness on February 25, 1999, and Kax died from a stroke on April 19, 2003, the surviving members of the Herberger family—particularly Gary, Jeanne, and Judd—who embraced the cause from the outset, continue to serve as benefactors and leaders in the broader community.[34] Their generosity of spirit continues to inspire others. The memory of Bob and Kax Herberger, who experienced the opening of their namesake theater in 1989, will forever be tied to the theater as a symbol of cultural advancement, a cause to which they had a deep commitment. Elected officials, bankers, corporations, board members, and countless others who donated their time, money, and effort all deserve credit for playing their respective roles in what was a community-wide effort that helped create an identity and a sense of place for the performing arts in downtown Phoenix. Without Richard Mallery's vision, Herculean dedication, and inestimable skill in overcoming every obstacle that came his way, the civic drama might never have seen its final act completed. The Herberger Theater will remain a tribute to a generation of twentieth-century visionaries whose actions shaped the cultural, educational, and economic lives of those living in the twenty-first century.

Notes

Prologue

[1]Gertrude Stein was referring to Oakland, California, where she had spent her childhood. Gertrude Stein, *Everybody's Autobiography* (New York: Random House, 1937), chap. 4.

[2]Bradford Luckingham, *Phoenix: The History of a Southwestern Metropolis* (Tucson: University of Arizona Press, 1989), 110.

[3]Russell Pulliam, *Publisher Gene Pulliam: Last of the Newspaper Titans* (Ottawa, Ill.: Jameson Books, 1984), 129.

[4]Luckingham, *Phoenix: The History of a Southwestern Metropolis,* 106–107.

[5]"With the largest land mass of all U.S. cities, the Valley spreads over 9,200 square miles, an area larger than the state of Massachusetts." Edward Booth-Clibborn, *Phoenix: Twenty-First Century City* (United Kingdom: Booth-Clibborn Editions, 2006), 23.

[6]Arizona was the last of the forty-eight contiguous states to be admitted to the union. Howard R. Lamar, *The Far Southwest, 1846–1912: A Territorial History* (New Haven: Yale University Press, 1963), 345–347.

[7]Luckingham, *Phoenix: The History of a Southwestern Metropolis,* 51–53.

[8]*Saturday Evening Post,* June 24, 1960, 234.

[9]Luckingham, *Phoenix: The History of a Southwestern Metropolis,* 91.

[10]Frank Lloyd Wright first came to Arizona in 1927 to work on a desert resort in Chandler, but the project became a victim of the depression. He returned ten years later to what he called "the nation's Gold Spot," and bought several hundred acres of raw desert at a time when Scottsdale had only 100 residents. Taliesin West became the Valley's first National Historic Landmark. *Phoenix Magazine,* January 1987.

[11]*Phoenix Magazine,* January 1985.

Chapter One: The Leader

[1]Richard Mallery has generated significant and varied interest from journalists because of his public stewardship in Arizona's economic, cultural, political, and social spheres. Over the past thirty years, his highly successful law practice at Snell & Wilmer, coupled with his seemingly effortless access to power, has evinced both admiration and envy. See, for example, *Arizona Republic,* June 18, 1984; *Arizona Republic,* December 7, 2007. Also see *New Times* (Phoenix), June 6, 2002; "Ground Broken!" *Herberger Theater Center: A Project of Phoenix Performing Arts, Incorporated,* 1, no. 1 (fall 1987), Herberger Theater Center Collection, Herberger Family Papers, file 1, Scottsdale, Ariz.

[2]Minutes, Board of Directors Meeting, July 29, 1982, Phoenix Performing Arts Center, Arizona. Herberger Theater Center Collection, Herberger Family Papers, file 1, Scottsdale, Ariz.

[3]Kathleen Mallery, interview by author, Phoenix, Ariz., September 14, 1996; Kathleen Mallery, "In the Arena" (Authors' files, n.d., photocopy).

[4]Snell & Wilmer was founded in 1938. See Jack L. August Jr., *Dividing Western Waters: Mark Wilmer and Arizona v California* (Fort Worth: Texas Christian University Press, 2007), chap. 2, 3.

[5]Frank Snell and Walter Bimson led a group of investors who bought a controlling interest in Central Arizona Light and Power Company in 1945. The company merged with Arizona Power Company; based in Prescott, the power company served Flagstaff and the northern part of the state. In 1952 Central Arizona Light and Power Company merged with Arizona Edison, a large Phoenix-based power company that served the southern part of the state. From these mergers, Arizona Public Service was born. See Bradford Luckingham, *Phoenix: The History of a Southwestern Metropolis* (Tucson: University of Arizona Press, 1989), 166. Also, Henry Sargent, interview by author, New York, August 29, 2009.

[6]In October 1946 the self-made newspaper publisher Eugene Pulliam bought the *Arizona Republic,* the *Phoenix Gazette,* and the *Arizona Weekly Gazette,* which were organized under Phoenix Newspapers, Incorporated. The *Phoenix Gazette* ceased production in 1997, and

with the *Arizona Republic* sold to Gannett Company in 2000, more than fifty years of Pulliam family ownership ended. See "History of the *Arizona Republic*," http://www.azcentral.com/help/articles/about2.html.

[7]Born April 25, 1892, Walter Bimson entered the University of Colorado at nineteen years of age, where he initially studied journalism before changing his major to architecture. He developed an interest in banking while working as a janitor in a bank and, in 1920, Harris Trust in Chicago hired Bimson. In the early 1930s, Bimson and his brother Carl founded Valley Bank and Trust in Arizona, later called Valley National Bank. Bimson ran the bank until he retired in 1970. See http://azgenweb.org/maricopa/biosb.html.

[8]See Thomas Sheridan, *Arizona: A History* (Tucson: University of Arizona Press, 1995), 263, 274; Luckingham, *Phoenix: The History of a Southwestern Metropolis*, 136–176.

[9]William Shover, interview by author, Phoenix, Ariz., March 19, 1996; William Shover, "No Good Deed Shall Go Unpunished: The Story of Greater Phoenix Metropolitan Goals to Phoenix 40 to Greater Phoenix Leadership, 1974–1993" (Author's files, n.d., photocopy.)

[10]John Wesley, the celebrated preacher, is largely credited with founding the Methodist movement with his brother Charles. Methodists quickly became leaders in many social justice issues of the day. For the best recent account of John Wesley, see Kenneth J. Collins, *The Theology of John Wesley: Holy Love and the Shape of Grace* (Nashville, Tenn.; Abingdon Press, 2007).

[11]Richard Mallery, interview by author, Phoenix, Ariz., January 2, 2008.

[12]Eugene Pulliam, letter to Richard Mallery, January 20, 1975, Richard Mallery Papers, Snell & Wilmer, Phoenix, Ariz.

[13]Critics often derided Phoenix 40 as elitist; supporters, however, praised it for embracing the enlightened philosophy that businessmen must not only be concerned with economics, but also with ethics and a responsibility to their communities' needs. By 1993 Phoenix 40 expanded its mission and changed its name to Greater Phoenix Leadership.

[14]Richard Mallery, interview by author, Phoenix, Ariz., March 18, 1996.

[15]Dino DeConcini was born in Tucson, Arizona, to a prominent family involved in law, business, and politics. The eldest son of Ora Webster DeConcini and Evo Anton DeConcini, Dino graduated from Georgetown University School of Foreign Service and the University of Arizona College of Law. The elder DeConcini had served as attorney general of Arizona in 1948 and as a judge on the Arizona Supreme Court from 1949 to 1952. Dino had served as Tucson city attorney from 1968 to 1969 and as chief of staff for Governor Raul Castro from 1975 through 1977; it was during this period that he became friends with Richard Mallery. He subsequently pursued a diverse career in law, politics, real estate development, international business, and government service. President William Clinton appointed Dino as executive director of the Savings Bonds Marketing Office, U.S. Department of Treasury in 1995. Dino's brother, Dennis DeConcini, was the senator from Arizona from 1977 to 1995. See Dennis DeConcini and Jack L. August, *Senator Dennis DeConcini: From the Center of the Aisle* (Tucson: University of Arizona Press, 2006).

[16]President Richard Nixon appointed Nancy Hanks as chair of the National Endowment for the Arts on October 6, 1969. She served two terms, ending her role as chair on October 2, 1977. See "The National Endowment for the Arts 1969–2000: A Brief Chronology of Federal Support for the Arts" (Washington, D.C.: National Endowment for the Arts, 2000), 18, 28. For three solid works on Hanks and her administration, see Livingston L. Biddle, *Our Government and the Arts: A Perspective from the Inside* (Lancaster, Penn.: Reed Books, 1988); Jane Alexander, *Command Performance: Actress in the Theater of Politics* (New York: Perseus Books, 2000); and Donna M. Binkiewicz, *Federalizing the Muse: United States Arts Policy and the National Endowment for the Arts, 1965–1980* (Chapel Hill: University of North Carolina Press, 2004).

[17]Jack Golodner, president of the Department for Professional Employees, AFL-CIO, interview by author, Washington, D.C., December 14, 1999.

[18]Adrienne Hirsch, interview by author, Chicago, Ill., March 25, 2009. By executive order, Governor Samuel Goddard established the new state council, Arizona Commission on the Arts and the Humanities, and appointed Lewis Ruskin as the first chair on January 14, 1966. The legislature made it a permanent state agency on March 13, 1967, signed into law by Governor Jack Williams.

[19]Arizona Commission on the Arts. *Report to the Governor, Fiscal Year 2000.* (Phoenix, 2000), 36.

[20]Sam Kathryn Campana was executive director of Arizonans for Cultural Development from 1983 to 1996. She built the organization into an effective force in state arts advocacy and was named chair emeritus in 1996. The organization changed its name to Arizona Citizens/Action for

the Arts in 2005. Elected mayor of Scottsdale in 1996, Campana subsequently became vice president of the National Audubon Society and founding executive director of Audubon Arizona.

[21]"We had never had such important arts leaders come to Arizona before. Jeanne Herberger was responsible for convincing Ken Dayton, a major corporate arts supporter, to come; and I was able to convince Biddle," said DeConcini. Dino DeConcini, interview by author, Washington, D.C., April 14, 2009.

[22]Dino DeConcini, interviews by author, Washington, D.C., December 18, 2007; April 14, 2009.

[23]Dino DeConcini, interviews.

[24]Begun in the 1960s, the Combined Metropolitan Phoenix Arts and Sciences (known as COMPAS) raised money for the Phoenix Art Museum, Desert Botanical Garden, Phoenix Symphony, Phoenix Zoo, and Heard Museum until 2001. Their fund-raising activities were discontinued because these organizations had become effective fundraisers on their own. The Combined Metropolitan Phoenix Arts and Sciences had raised an estimated $10 million over the years for the five recipient organizations. See Nancy Welch, *Perfect Pitch: Considerations for a Dedicated Funding Source for Arts and Culture* (Tempe, Ariz.: Morrison Institute, 2005), 48.

[25]Dino DeConcini, interview by author, Washington, D.C., August 15, 1997.

[26]Richard Mallery, interview by author, Phoenix, Ariz., February 20, 1999. Forest Appleby Burgess, a Phoenix philanthropist and playwright, was a "major force in Arizona theater." She was an original supporter of the Arizona Repertory Theater and a cofounder of the Southwest Ensemble Theater. Burgess also was instrumental in bringing the Arizona Theatre Company to Phoenix, and she served on the company's board of directors for twelve years. When she died in 1996, she directed all contributions to the Arizona Theatre Company. *Arizona Republic*, May 5, 1998.

Chapter Two: The Patron

[1]Shortly after their marriage, Conrad Herberger found work as a horseshoer with the Burbank Stage Company on the stage route from St. Cloud to Georgetown. The family then moved to Pomme de Terre, Minnesota, where Conrad worked as a horseshoer and Catherine boarded the stage crews, jobs that paid $200 annually. In 1862 the Sioux uprising caused the family to return to the comparatively safer community of St. Cloud, where Conrad continued his blacksmithing business and, reflecting his ingenuity and ambition, started the Herberger Brewing Company with this brother Fred. See Jim Smith, *The Bob Herberger Story* (Phoenix: Jim Smith, 1990), 13.

[2]Osakis is approximately sixty miles north of St. Cloud, Minnesota.

[3]Smith, *The Bob Herberger Story*, 14. George prospered at the Osakis store, dealing in dry goods, livestock, and land. Over his career, he bought and sold stores in Alexandria, Sauk Center, Wadena, Park Hill, and Nelson, Minnesota; and in Ripon, Wisconsin.

[4]G. Robert Herberger, interview by author, Scottsdale, Ariz., December 15, 1995.

[5]Smith, *The Bob Herberger Story*, 22. Also, G. Robert Herberger, interview.

[6]G. Robert Herberger, interview.

[7]G. Robert Herberger, interview.

[8]Richard Mallery, interview by author, Phoenix, Ariz., March 18, 1996.

[9]Richard Mallery, interview.

[10]Smith, *The Bob Herberger Story*, 45, 53. Herberger's land purchases also benefited from an assured water supply when Arizona won the *Arizona v California* Supreme Court case in 1963 and the subsequent passage of the Colorado River Basin Project Act in 1968, which brought with it the construction of the Central Arizona Project and Arizona's hard-won share of mainstream Colorado River water. The value of Herberger's desert land increased exponentially. See, for example, Jack L. August Jr., *Vision in the Desert: Carl Hayden and Hydropolitics in the American Southwest* (Fort Worth: Texas Christian University Press, 1999); Jack L. August Jr., *Dividing Western Waters: Mark Wilmer and Arizona v California* (Fort Worth: Texas Christian University Press, 2007).

[11]G. Robert Herberger, interview.

[12]Richard Mallery, interview; G. Robert Herberger, interview.

[13]G. Robert Herberger, interview.

[14]G. Robert Herberger, interview.

[15]Herberger also gave cash gifts of $1,000 to 100 former and long-time present employees in 1982. He firmly believed that "any organization that disregards the feelings of its employees deserves to fail." He also stated, "What good is money if you don't spread it around and give it to people who have done something good for you?" See Smith, *The Bob Herberger Story*, 90–91.

[16]Smith, *The Bob Herberger Story,* 107.
[17]Richard Mallery, interview by author, Phoenix, Ariz., December 30, 2002.

Chapter Three: The City

[1]C. A. Howlett, interview by author, Tempe, Ariz., February 13, 1996. "One of the greatest events that anybody could hope to attend here was a political event where Margaret was mistress of ceremony and maybe Mo Udall was on with her. She was a stand-up comedian. We had to turn down many requests for her to speak, she was so much in demand," Howlett recalled.

[2]See Rosalie Crowe and Diane Tod, *Arizona Women's Hall of Fame* (Phoenix: Arizona Historical Society, 1990), 6–7. The youngest of three children, Hance was born on July 2, 1923, in Spirit Lake, Iowa. The family resettled in Phoenix, where Hance's father became senior vice president of Valley National Bank. Besides a long history of volunteerism before her period in electoral politics, Hance produced documentaries on public affairs for KINK television. During her years on the city council, from 1971 to 1975, she produced the nationally syndicated radio program, "Holiday World Travel."

[3]C. A. Howlett, interview.

[4]C. A. Howlett, interview. Howlett served under Mayor Timothy Barrow from 1974 until 1976.

[5]C. A. Howlett, interview.

[6]C. A. Howlett, interview. Mayor Milton Graham (1964–1970) led the initiative to get the first phase of Phoenix Civic Plaza built, but little happened under the subsequent two mayors. Some people have attributed this inertia to the fact that Phoenix, unlike many other cities, had a well-developed branch banking system, which gave the banks less incentive, as well as less interest, in preserving and expanding downtown.

[7]C. A. Howlett, interview.

[8]C. A. Howlett, interview.

[9]C. A. Howlett, interview. From 1887 to 1948, Phoenix had a thriving trolley line, but this form of public transit ultimately gave way to the private automobile. After a catastrophic fire, the trolley line passed into history on February 17, 1948. At its height, the line boasted, "It comes every ten minutes and goes everywhere worth going." General Moses Hazeltine Sherman, who was the territory's first superintendent of public instruction in 1880, founded the original trolley line. "The city of Phoenix bought the trolley system in 1927 and, with a voter approved $750,000 bond, completely rebuilt the rails and bought new trolleys." The city made money on the operation of the trolley. See *Phoenix Magazine,* May 2008.

[10]C. A. Howlett, interview.

[11]Richard Mallery, interview by author, Phoenix, Ariz., March 18, 1996.

[12]Critics of the growing city of Phoenix in the 1980s posited, "behind the demographic and economic growth in the area, Phoenix had to realize it goofed...in its tremendous drive to make a metropolis it left the arts out. Now it has to play catch up." See Bradford Luckingham, *Phoenix: The History of a Southwestern Metropolis* (Tucson: University of Arizona Press, 1989), 251.

[13]Richard Mallery, interview.

[14]Richard Mallery, interview.

[15]Richard Mallery, interview.

[16]Richard Mallery, interview.

[17]Richard Mallery, interview.

[18]C. A. Howlett, interview.

[19]C. A. Howlett, interview.

[20]Howlett left Arizona for Washington, D.C., in 1985 to serve as special assistant to President Ronald Reagan for intergovernmental affairs.

Chapter Four: The Arts

[1]Barbara Levy, interview by author, Tucson, Ariz., April 22, 2009.

[2]Arizona Theatre Company, like many nonprofit theater companies, had a two-pronged leadership structure. Although the responsibilities sometimes overlapped, Gary Gisselman, the artistic director starting in 1980, was directly responsible for the artistic work of the company. As managing director, Hawkanson raised the money, directed the marketing campaigns, and managed all other business aspects of running the theater.

[3]Everett King, interview by author, Phoenix, Ariz., February 13, 1996. Also see *Phoenix Magazine,* August 1980.

[4]Hawkanson knew Mark Lamos from his Guthrie Theater days in Minneapolis, and he was

able to attract him to Arizona as the artistic director for Arizona Theatre Company for one year, from 1978 to 1979, while Gary Gisselman was on sabbatical. Lamos later became a nationally recognized, award-winning theater director and producer.

[5]Scottsdale and Phoenix are geographically contiguous, and the cities are easily interchanged in discussions about either city.

[6]Deborah Whitehurst, interview by author, Phoenix, Ariz., March 24, 1996.

[7]Deborah Whitehurst, interview.

[8]Richard Mallery, interview by author, Phoenix, Ariz., March 23, 1996.

[9]Deborah Whitehurst, interview.

[10]For the seminal work on regional theater, see Joseph Wesley Zeigler, *Regional Theater: The Revolutionary Stage* (Minneapolis: University of Minnesota Press, 1973). Other books of note include Tyrone Guthrie, *A New Theatre* (Minneapolis: University of Minnesota Press, 1964; expanded edition, 2008); Peg Guilfoyle, *The Guthrie Theater: Images, History, and Inside Stories* (Minneapolis: Nodin Press, 2006); Howard Taubman, *The Making of the American Theatre* (New York: Coward-McCann, 1965); Margo Jones, *Theatre-in-the-Round* (New York: McGraw-Hill, 1965); William Beeson, ed., *Thresholds: The Story of Nina Vance's Alley Theatre* (Houston: Alley Theatre, 1968); Herbert Blau, *The Impossible Theater: A Manifesto* (New York: Collier, 1965); Stuart Vaughan, *A Possible Theatre* (New York: McGraw-Hill, 1969): Jules Irving, *Beyond Broadway: The Quest for Permanent Theatres* (New York: Hill and Wang, 1968); and Zelda Fichandler, Peter Zeisler, and Arvin Brown, *TCG Oral History Project: Voices of the American Theater*, Preserving the Legacy series, vol. 1, *Zelda Fichandler, Peter Zeisler, Arvin Brown* (New York: Theater Communication Group Oral History Project, 2003), digital video disc; and Weldon B. Durham, *American Theatre Companies: 1931–1986* (Westport, Conn.: Greenwood Press, 1989).

[11]At this time, Cohen and DeConcini were arriving at similar conclusions. Cohen had encouraged Arizona Theatre Company to expand into Phoenix, and he understood the need for a permanent facility. As president of Arizona Theatre Company's board in 1977, he arranged numerous meetings between Hawkanson and prominent arts patrons in Phoenix. Cohen and Hawkanson secured behind-the-scenes support from Forest Burgess, who was not only Mallery's mother-in-law, but also an accomplished playwright. Hawkanson and Burgess developed a close relationship.

[12]Marvin Cohen, interviews by author, Phoenix, Ariz., March 29, 1996; March 10, 2008. An article that appeared in the *New York Times* on May 26, 2008 noted, "In 1963, for example, the Tyrone Guthrie Theater in Minneapolis opened with great fanfare as one of America's great regional theaters. Since then, the regional theater movement has flourished. Almost every major community and many minor ones have at least one resident company. Through a process of decentralization, the movement has altered the face of the American stage. Especially after 1970, New York was no longer the only theater center."

[13]Bradley G. Morison and Kay Fliehr, *In Search of an Audience: How an Audience Was Found for the Tyrone Guthrie Theater* (New York: Pitman Publishing, 1968).

[14]*Arizona Republic*, March 4, 1981. Also see *Arizona Republic*, March 22, 24, 1981; *Arizona Republic*, April 2, 6, 1981; *Phoenix Gazette*, March 22, 1981; and *Phoenix Gazette*, April 2, 1981.

[15]Bradley G. Morison, William B. Fleissig, William R. Morrish, and Peter VanDine, "The Performing Arts in the Valley," chap. 5 in *The Central Phoenix Theater Study Project* (Phoenix: Arts Development Associates/CityWest, 1981).

[16]Morison et al., *The Central Phoenix Theater Study Project*, chap. 5.

[17]On this point Morison was prophetic. David Saar, artistic director of Childsplay, created the nonprofit touring group, comprised of professional adult actors, in 1977. Less than ten years later, Childsplay became nationally recognized as one of the finest theaters for children in the country. Childsplay's mission was to create "theater so strikingly original in form, content, or both, that it instills in young people an enduring awe, love, and respect for the medium, thus preserving imagination and wonder, those hallmarks of childhood that are the keys to the future." *Arizona Insight*, December 2007. Saar was the recipient of the Governor's Arts Award in 1989 for his contributions to the arts in Arizona.

[18]Morison et al., "Downtown Phoenix as Marketplace for the Performing Arts," chap. 7 in *The Central Phoenix Theater Study Project*.

[19]Richard Mallery, interview by author, Phoenix, Ariz., February 20, 1999.

[20]Everett King, interview. Although Phoenix Little Theatre tried to adjust its schedule to accommodate Arizona Theatre Company, it was increasingly difficult; in addition, Phoenix Little Theatre did not have enough fly space for Arizona Theatre Company's sets.

[21]Morison et al., "Facilities Development Plan," chap. 6 in *The Central Phoenix Theater Study Project*.

[22]Morison et al., "Three Prime Possibilities: Advantages, Disadvantages, and Costs," chap. 8

in *The Central Phoenix Theater Study Project.*

[23]Morison et al., "Facilities Development Plan," chap. 6 in *The Central Phoenix Theater Study Project.* Morison was speaking of the First Southern Baptist Church, the home of the first Baptist denomination in Arizona, constructed in 1931. Purchased by the Arizona Department of Transportation in 1972, the Phoenix Parks and Recreation Department leased the building. Morison found it to be a "strong and sturdy shell, which could be quickly and economically converted into an attractive…medium-sized theater."

[24]Morison et al., "Facilities Development Plan," chap. 6 in *The Central Phoenix Theater Study Project.* Also see *Arizona Republic,* November 18, 1981; *Phoenix Gazette,* November 18, 1981.

[25]*Phoenix Gazette,* November 14, 1981.

[26]*Arizona Republic,* November 17, 1981.

Chapter Five: Ninety Days

[1]Richard Mallery, interview by author, Phoenix, Ariz., March 23, 1996.

[2]Headquartered in Columbia, Maryland, and founded in 1939, Rouse Corporation was known as a premier real estate development company. Its portfolio of world-class retail centers included Water Tower Place in Chicago, Faneuil Hall Marketplace in Boston, Fashion Show Mall in Las Vegas, and master-planned communities in Maryland, Nevada, and Texas.

[3]C. A. Howlett, interview by author, Tempe, Ariz., February 13, 1996. Several other people close to the Rouse Corporation Superblock negotiations, for what would become the Arizona Center, clearly saw the importance of the Herberger Theater project in convincing Rouse to invest in Phoenix. Jack Tevlin, interview by author, Phoenix, Ariz., March 28, 1996; Gary Herberger, interview by author, Scottsdale, Ariz., February 15, 1996. However, according to Mark DeMichele, the key factors were the tax incentives offered by the city and the fact that Arizona Public Service agreed to be the anchor tenant. Mark DeMichele, interview by author, Phoenix, Ariz., March 27, 1996.

[4]Richard Mallery, interview.

[5]Governor Janet Napolitano renamed Squaw Peak Parkway the Piestewa Freeway in 2003 in honor of Army Spc. Lori Ann Piestewa, the first Native American woman to die in combat in the U.S. military and the first military servicewoman to be killed in action in 2003 at the start of the Iraq conflict. A Hopi, born in Tuba City, Arizona, she died in a convoy ambush on March 23, 2003; the U.S. Board on Geographic Names officially approved the name change in 2008.

[6]C. A. Howlett, interview.

[7]*Phoenix Magazine,* August 1981.

[8]The price for the Monroe-Second Associates property ultimately would be $1,115,000, with terms calling for $699,000 in cash and the remaining amount through a promissory note.

[9]C. A. Howlett, interview; Richard Mallery, interview.

[10]For most of the twentieth century, the Rosenzweig name was associated with the jewelry business in Arizona. Newton Rosenzweig's civic engagement included helping found the Phoenix Symphony and championing urban political reform. In the late 1940s, he was a cofounder of the Charter Government Committee that launched the political career of Barry Goldwater. Newton Rosenzweig died on February 5, 2002, at the age of ninety-six. See Newton Rosenzweig Collection, Arizona Historical Foundation, Hayden Library, Arizona State University, Tempe, Ariz., especially box 2, folders 1–6.

[11]For the best account of Harry Rosenzweig's relationship with Goldwater, see Robert Alan Goldberg, *Barry Goldwater* (New Haven: Yale University Press, 1995). Harry, his brother Newton, and his sister Anna grew up with the Goldwater children, including the future senator Barry, as well as his siblings Robert and Carolyn. Those close ties remained throughout their lives.

[12]*Phoenix Magazine,* October 1982.

[13]See Thomas Sheridan, *Arizona: A History* (Tucson: University of Arizona Press, 1995), 167–169.

[14]Henry Sargent, interview by author, Phoenix, Ariz., July 24, 2002.

[15]Maus so enjoyed his work with Phoenix Civic Plaza that he used the same motif from the buildings on his wedding rings. Deborah Whitehurst, interview by author, Phoenix, Ariz., April 23, 2003.

[16]Richard Mallery, interview.

[17]As Bimson had once observed, "Civilization is moved forward by restless people, not by those who are satisfied with things as they are." *Phoenix Magazine,* August 1980. Also see www.modernphoenix.net for a brief overview of Bimson and Valley National Bank. In addition,

see Thomas Sheridan, *Arizona: A History,* 165–166, which provides an accurate assessment and interpretation of Bimson's role in shaping modern Arizona's economic climate.

[18]*Phoenix Magazine,* August 1980.

[19]Richard Mallery, interview by author, Phoenix, Ariz., December 30, 2002.

[20]Richard Mallery, interview by author, Phoenix, Ariz., March 23, 1996.

[21]Jim Smith, *The Bob Herberger Story.* (Phoenix: Jim Smith, 1990), 90–93.

[22]Harriet Babbitt, interview by author, Washington, D.C., January 13, 2003.

[23]Richard Mallery, interview by author, Phoenix, Ariz., March 23, 1996; Harriet Babbitt, interview.

Chapter Six: A New Entity

[1]Margaret Hance, press release, May 12, 1983, Margaret Taylor Hance Papers, 1971–1990, Department of Archives and Special Collections, Arizona State University, box 4, file 4, Tempe, Ariz.

[2]*Arizona Republic,* May 12, 1983. Also, Richard Mallery, letter to Gary Herberger, May 1, 1983, Herberger Theater Center Collection, Herberger Family Papers, file 2, Scottsdale, Ariz.

[3]Margaret Hance, press release. Also, Richard Mallery, letter to G. Robert Herberger, March 8, 1983, Herberger Theater Center Collection, Herberger Family Papers, file 2, Scottsdale, Ariz.

[4]*Arizona Republic,* March 11, 1983.

[5]Linda Whitney's husband, Richard, was a founding member of the Arizona Commission on the Arts and served as its chair after Dino DeConcini.

[6]The citation came through the President's Committee on the Arts and Humanities. President Ronald Reagan praised Arizona Theatre Company as a national model for the way in which it built audience support and fiscal stability in both communities.

[7]*Phoenix Magazine,* January 1983.

[8]For the best and most thorough work on territorial Arizona and the Southwest, see Howard R. Lamar, *The Far Southwest, 1846–1912: A Territorial History* (New Haven: Yale University Press, 1963). Also see Gerald Nash, *The American West in the Twentieth Century: A Short History of an Urban Oasis* (Albuquerque: University of New Mexico Press, 1973); Bradford Luckingham, *The Urban Southwest: A Profile History of Albuquerque, El Paso, Phoenix, and Tucson* (El Paso: Texas Western Press, 1982); Thomas Sheridan, *Arizona: A History* (Tucson: University of Arizona Press, 1995); and Thomas Edwin Farish, *Arizona History* (Phoenix: Phoenix Manufacturing Company, 1920).

[9]Tucson was part of the Mexican Republic from 1821 to 1848, when the community became part of the United States with the Treaty of Guadalupe Hidalgo in February 1848. The literature on the Spanish borderlands frontier is rich and considerable, but the two best book treatments on this period, in what is now Arizona, are David J. Weber, *The Spanish Frontier in North America* (New Haven: Yale University Press, 1994) and David J. Weber, *The Mexican Frontier, 1821–1846: The American Southwest Under Mexico* (Albuquerque: University of New Mexico Press, 1982).

[10]*Phoenix Magazine,* September 1985.

[11]For the role of the Udall and DeConcini families in Tucson, see Donald W. Carson and James W. Johnson, *Mo: The Life and Times of Morris K. Udall* (Tucson: University of Arizona Press, 2004) and Dennis DeConcini and Jack L. August Jr., *Senator Dennis DeConcini: From the Center of the Aisle* (Tucson: University of Arizona Press, 2006). Founded by Tucson Presbyterian minister John Fife in the 1980s, the Sanctuary Movement provided safe haven for immigrants escaping from war-torn El Salvador and Guatemala. The movement eventually expanded to over 500 churches and synagogues nationwide and assisted thousands of Central American immigrants. John Fife, interview by Amy Goodman, *Democracy Now! The War and Peace Report,* National Public Radio, April 23, 2007.

[12]*Phoenix Gazette,* January 25, 1984.

[13]Bradley G. Morison, William B. Fleissig, William R. Morrish, and Peter VanDine, "Management, Operation, Budgets, and Impact," chap. 9 in *The Central Phoenix Theater Study Project* (Phoenix: Arts Development Associates/CityWest, 1981).

[14]*Arizona Republic,* May 21, 1983. Also, Richard Mallery, letters to Gary Herberger, April 4, 1983 and May 23, 1983, Herberger Theater Center Collection, Herberger Family Papers, file 4, Scottsdale, Ariz.

[15]Minutes, Board of Directors Meeting, June 5, 1983, Phoenix Performing Arts Center, Arizona. Herberger Theater Center Collection, Herberger Family Papers, file 5, Scottsdale, Ariz. Also, Richard Mallery, letter to Mayor Margaret Hance and members of the Phoenix City Council, November 17, 1983, Herberger Theater Center Collection, Herberger Family Papers, file 9, Scottsdale, Ariz.

[16]Terry Goddard was the son of former Arizona Governor Samuel Goddard Jr., who served as the state's twelfth governor from 1965 to 1967.

[17]See *Arizona Republic,* November 3, 8, 15, 22, 25, 27, 1982; *Arizona Republic,* December 3, 5, 8, 15, 16, 17, 1982; and *Phoenix Magazine*, May 1983. Also see Bradford Luckingham, *Phoenix: The History of a Southwestern Metropolis* (Tucson: University of Arizona Press, 1989), 223.

[18]Margaret Hance went on to become the national cochair of President Ronald Reagan's 1984 reelection campaign. Reagan subsequently appointed her to the Advisory Commission on Intergovernmental Relations and the Presidential Federalism Advisory Committee. In 1988 she directed George H. W. Bush's presidential campaign in Arizona. Margaret Hance died on April 29, 1990.

[19]Selden Kent, letter to Richard Mallery, October 7, 1983, Richard Mallery Papers, Snell & Wilmer, Phoenix, Ariz.

[20]Richard Mallery, interview by author, Phoenix, Ariz., March 23, 1996.

[21]Richard Mallery, letter to Selden Kent, November 8, 1983, Richard Mallery Papers, Snell & Wilmer, Phoenix, Ariz.

[22]Richard Mallery, letter to Selden Kent.

[23]Richard Mallery, letter to Selden Kent.

Chapter Seven: Prince of the City

[1]Terry Goddard, interview by author, Phoenix, Ariz., October 23, 1996.

[2]First elected mayor in 1983, and subsequently reelected three times, Terry Goddard led the city of Phoenix from 1984 through 1990. *American City and County* magazine named him "Municipal Leader of the Year" in 1989. After an unsuccessful run for governor in 1990, he served as state director of the U.S. Department of Housing and Urban Development from 1995 to 2002. Elected Arizona attorney general in 2002, Goddard was reelected in 2006.

[3]*Phoenix Magazine,* May 1983.

[4]See *Arizona Republic,* November 8, 10, 1984; *Arizona Republic,* December 12, 15, 1984; *Phoenix Gazette,* January 18, 24, 1985; and *Phoenix Magazine,* December 1984.

[5]Few people knew that Terry Goddard was actually Samuel Goddard III, an appellation he never used. His father, former Governor Samuel Goddard Jr., was a classical languages buff; he adapted *teritus,* Latin for "third," into Terry, a more suitable name for his outgoing son.

[6]Goddard attended Phillips Exeter Academy in New Hampshire and graduated from Harvard in 1969 before attending and graduating from Arizona State University College of Law in 1976. See *Arizona Republic,* November 1, 2, 4, 5, 1990.

[7]Jack Tevlin, interview by author, Phoenix, Ariz., March 28, 1996.

[8]Gary Herberger also was president of Herberger Enterprises, Incorporated, a land-acquisition firm involved in planning and development of commercial, industrial, and residential property, created by his father, Bob Herberger.

[9]Gary Herberger, interview by author, Scottsdale, Ariz., February 15, 1996.

[10]Bradley Morison, interview by author, Minneapolis, Minn., November 9, 2002.

[11]Gary Herberger, interview.

[12]Terry Goddard, letter to Richard Mallery and Gary Herberger, June 28, 1984, Herberger Theater Center Collection, Herberger Family Papers, file 4, Scottsdale, Ariz.

[13]Minutes, Board of Directors Meeting, June 6, 1984, Phoenix Performing Arts Center, Arizona. Herberger Theater Center Collection, Herberger Family Papers, file 4, Scottsdale, Ariz.

[14]Darrow "Duke" Tully recently replaced his wife, Patricia, on the Phoenix Performing Arts Center board of directors.

[15]Gary Herberger, interview. Herberger originally had suggested David Hawkanson for the selection committee, but agreed on Deborah Whitehurst as a suitable member because she could speak for all the possible user groups.

[16]Julie Dalgleish, interview by author, St. Paul, Minn., April 28, 2009.

[17]Minutes, Board of Directors Meeting, June 6, 1984. These eight semifinalist architectural firms were to use Morison's updated feasibility study, as well as a recent site survey. Unsuccessful firms that did not make it to the last round would be compensated with payments of $3,000 to $5,000. Mayor Goddard approved of the process.

[18]Gary Herberger, interview.

[19]Gary Herberger, interview.

[20]Keith Turley was born in Mesa, Arizona, the youngest of four children of Ora and Zella Turley. Like Mallery, he possessed an entrepreneurial spirit as a youngster and sold vegetables

door-to-door to supplement his father's income as a mail carrier. Turley attended Arizona State University, where he studied journalism and education. He started his career with the Arizona Public Service in 1948 as assistant editor of the employee newspaper, *Spark and Flame*. Turley worked his way up to general manager by 1972 and to president and chief executive officer by 1973. When he retired in 1990, he was president, chief executive officer, and board chair of Pinnacle West Capital Corporation, the parent company of Arizona Public Service, and board chair of Arizona Public Service. He was a director of the Central Arizona Project and president of the Heard Museum board of trustees. Turley served on the boards of many educational institutions, including the Arizona State University Foundation and the American Graduate School of International Management. He received a Doctor of Humane Letters degree from Arizona State University and Northern Arizona University, the Anti-Defamation League's Torch of Liberty Award in 1979, the National Conference of Christians and Jews Brotherhood Award in 1983, and was named Phoenix Man of the Year in 1986. He died on December 13, 1999. Keith Turley, interview by author, Phoenix, Ariz., February 12, 1997. Also see *Arizona Republic*, December 14, 1999.

[21]*Phoenix Gazette*, January 25, 1984.

[22]*Arizona Republic*, April 17, 1984.

[23]Darrow "Duke" Tully hosted the meeting of the Phoenix Performing Arts Center board of directors at the University Club, just north of downtown Phoenix.

[24]Minutes, Board of Directors Meeting, May 10, 1984, Phoenix Performing Arts Center, Arizona. Herberger Theater Center Collection, Herberger Family Papers, file 3, Scottsdale, Ariz.

[25]*Arizona Republic*, May 7, 1984.

[26]Proposition 15 sought $32.5 million for downtown development, which included $2.5 million for the purchase and restoration of the Palace West property. Proposition 8 sought $13.5 million for the purchase of the twenty-seven-acre campus of the Phoenix Union High School, with the intention of converting it for recreational and cultural use, including the restoration of the auditorium.

[27]*Arizona Republic*, May 7, 1984.

[28]Mayor Goddard changed the name of the Central Phoenix Redevelopment Agency, which was under the previous mayor, to the Downtown Phoenix Redevelopment Agency.

[29]*Arizona Republic*, May 7, 1984.

[30]Dino DeConcini, interview by author, Washington, D.C., October 29, 1998.

[31]A consultant for a feasibility committee representing Phoenix, the Rio Salado District, and the Arizona Coliseum and Exposition Center was evaluating eight sites for a stadium. See *Arizona Republic*, March 24, 1984.

[32]See *Arizona Republic*, May 12, 14, 15, 20, 1984; *Arizona Republic*, June 4, 8, 13, 15, 1984; *Phoenix Gazette*, May 15, 16, 17, 20, 21, 28, 1984; and *Phoenix Gazette*, June 14, 15, 16, 1984. Even though many people came to Mallery's defense, including Frank Snell and Mark Wilmer, cofounders of Snell & Wilmer, Mallery resigned from the Phoenix Community Alliance.

[33]The house was the oldest brick structure in Phoenix and all that remained of the Francis Marion Mognett Ranch, circa 1881. After moving the house to Heritage Square, the city renamed it the Burgess Carriage House.

[34]*Arizona Republic*, June 14, 1984.

[35]Morison worked on the updated feasibility study with Peter VanDine, who possessed expertise in capital cost estimates and had worked on the original feasibility study. It had become common to refer to the proposed building as the Herberger Theater by this time; even Morison had adopted this vernacular. It proved easier than fumbling with the full name, Phoenix Performing Arts Center, and better than using an unpalatable acronym like PPAC.

[36]Bradley Morison, letter to Phoenix Performing Arts Center board, September 12, 1984. Herberger Theater Center Collection, Herberger Family Papers, file 3, Scottsdale, Ariz.

Chapter Eight: The Architect

[1]Harriet Babbitt, interview by author, Washington, D.C., January 13, 2003. Several stakeholders made up the architect selection committee. From the Phoenix Performing Arts Center board of directors were Hattie Babbitt, Dino DeConcini, Gary Herberger, Richard Mallery, Darrow "Duke" Tully, and Keith Turley. From the city of Phoenix were Ed Korrick, city councilman; Barry Starr, city councilman; Marvin Andrews, city manager; and Richard Counts, city planning director. Others on the committee included Newton Rosenzweig, president of the Civic Plaza Building Corporation; Denny Maus, director of the Phoenix Civic Plaza; Gerald McSheffrey, dean of Arizona State University College of Architecture; Bradley Morison, president of Arts

Development Associates, Minneapolis, and advisor to the Phoenix Performing Arts Center board and the selection committee; and Deborah Whitehurst, museum and special projects director for the Arizona Commission on the Arts.

[2]Public discussion about the need for and the design of the proposed theater appeared with greater frequency in the summer of 1984. See *Phoenix Gazette*, June 6, 1984; *Arizona Republic*, June 26, 1984; and *Arizona Capitol Times* (Phoenix), June 27, 1984.

[3]In some cases, particularly in the United States today, the use of greenrooms to entertain donors has become the primary use for these spaces; thus, they no longer necessarily are located backstage. A fee or donation is often a requirement to be invited to these spaces.

[4]William Tyrone Guthrie (1900–1971) was an Anglo-Irish, Tony award-winning theatrical director who was instrumental in the founding of the Stratford Festival of Canada; the Guthrie Theater in Minneapolis, Minnesota; and the Tyrone Guthrie Centre at his family's home, Annaghmakerrig, in County Monaghan, Ireland. See Tyrone Guthrie, *A Life in the Theater: The Autobiography of Tyrone Guthrie* (London: Hamish Hamilton, 1959). Also, Bradley Morison, letter to the Phoenix Performing Arts Center board, September 12, 1984, Herberger Theater Center Collection, Herberger Family Papers, file 2, Scottsdale, Ariz. Morison emphasized that practicality was woven throughout the design decisions to meet multiple requirements, yet stay within a reasonable budget.

[5]Mallery held great admiration for environments that combined space and use effectively, while at the same time avoiding showiness. His home in Bartlett Estates reflected this ethic; its somewhat nondescript exterior ultimately revealed an interior of great beauty. The home encouraged a robust family life, yet it easily was adaptable for small- and large-group entertaining.

[6]Gary Herberger, letter to Richard Mallery, August 16, 1984, Herberger Theater Center Collection, Herberger Family Papers, file 2, Scottsdale, Ariz.

[7]Bradley Morison, interview by author, Minneapolis, Minn., December 1, 1997.

[8]Gary Herberger, interview by author, Scottsdale, Ariz., February 15, 1996.

[9]Long revered as an Arizona architectural gem, French pastors founded St. Mary's Basilica, a downtown Phoenix landmark, in the nineteenth century. It features glorious stained glass, remarkable acoustics, distinctive statuary, and an uplifting and unrivaled mix of native and traditional arts. See Gary Weiand, *An Historical Guide to the Sacred Art of St. Mary's Basilica* (Phoenix: St. Mary's Altar Society, 1998).

[10]Harriet Babbitt, interview.

[11]Bradley Morison, letter.

[12]Bradley Morison, letter.

[13]Bradley Morison, letter.

[14]Deborah Whitehurst, interview by author, Phoenix, Ariz., April 24, 2003.

[15]Richard Mallery, interviews by author, Phoenix, Ariz., April 17, 2003 and July 17, 2008; Gary Herberger, interviews by author, Scottsdale, Ariz., February 15, 1996 and August 2, 2008. Also, Gary Herberger, list of team firms to Architecture One, August 8, 1984, Herberger Theater Center Collection, Herberger Family Papers, file 2, Scottsdale, Ariz.

[16]Richard Mallery, interview.

[17]Richard Mallery, letter to Gary Herberger, October 31, 1984, Richard Mallery Papers, Snell & Wilmer, Phoenix, Ariz.

[18]Gary Herberger, memo to design team finalists, October 11, 1984, Herberger Theater Center Collection, Herberger Family Papers, file 4, Scottsdale, Ariz.

[19]Unfortunately, Bob Herberger's health at the time did not allow him to travel. Katherine Herberger, interview by author, Scottsdale, Ariz., October 24, 1996.

[20]ELS Design Group had provided full working drawings and models for both theaters.

[21]Eugene's population in 1985 hovered around 105,000.

[22]Gary Herberger, interview.

[23]The Hults gave $2.5 million for a permanent endowment to help finance programming, operation, and maintenance, and $500,000 toward construction. The small hall in the center was named the Soreng Theater in honor of a $750,000 gift from John and Betty Soreng; and the Silva Concert Hall was named after Julio and Elizabeth Silva in honor of a $1.5 million contribution from their daughter, Carolyn Silva Chambers.

[24]Black-box theaters are easily built and maintained. They usually are used for plays or other performances that require only very basic technical arrangements, such as a limited set and simple lighting effects. There is an intimate focus on the story, the writing, and the performances, rather than on the technical elements. The seating is typically composed of loose chairs on platforms, which easily can be moved or removed to allow the space to be adapted to the artistic elements of a production. Common floor plans include a thrust stage, a modified thrust stage, and an arena.

[25]Richard Mallery, interview.

[26]Richard Mallery, interview.

[27]Bradley G. Morison and Peter VanDine, "A Current Program and Projections Supplement to the Report on the 1981 Central Phoenix Study Project," 4, October 10, 1984, Herberger Theater Center Collection, Herberger Family Papers, file 5, Scottsdale, Ariz.

[28]Morison and VanDine, "A Current Program and Projections Supplement to the Report on the 1981 Central Phoenix Study Project," 2.

[29]Morison and VanDine, "A Current Program and Projections Supplement to the Report on the 1981 Central Phoenix Study Project," 3.

[30]Morison and VanDine, "A Current Program and Projections Supplement to the Report on the 1981 Central Phoenix Study Project," 14.

[31]Morison and VanDine, "A Current Program and Projections Supplement to the Report on the 1981 Central Phoenix Study Project," 14.

Chapter Nine: Expansion

[1]At this time, the Civic Plaza Building Corporation board recently had expended $55 million to expand the convention center, which added 300,000 square feet of meeting space and a 28,000 square foot ballroom. It reopened in June 1985.

[2]The Phoenix Symphony had experienced a budget shortfall since it had undertaken an ambitious fund-raising campaign in 1982 to raise $6.5 million, which was the largest goal set by a nonprofit organization in Arizona at that time. The purpose was to elevate the orchestra to major status over a three-year period. The musicians would become full-time employees, able to devote their energy to becoming the finest symphony possible. By attaining major status, the orchestra would be ranked in thirty-first place on the country's list of major orchestras, edging out much smaller cities, such as Colorado Springs. The financial consequences were staggering, and the board raised only $900,000 of their first benchmark goal of $1.5 million. Mark DeMichele, president of Arizona Public Service and newly elected board president of the Phoenix Symphony, negotiated a loan from a consortium of banks for a credit line of $1.4 million, but it was insufficient. Closing down appeared imminent until Mayor Goddard used his political capital to convince the Civic Plaza Building Corporation board to help. Goddard remained angry with the symphony board and said, "Never again." See *Phoenix Magazine*, April 1984; *Phoenix Magazine*, August 1984.

[3]Mark DeMichele succeeded Keith Turley as president of Arizona Public Service when Turley became board chair, president, and chief executive officer of the parent company, AZP Group Incorporated. Turley also was serving as board chair of Arizona Public Service. AZP Group Incorporated had formed in 1985 to hold Arizona Public Service. The company changed its name to Pinnacle West Capital Corporation in 1987.

[4]*Phoenix Magazine*, April 1984.

[5]*Arizona Republic*, December 12, 17, 22, 1984; *Phoenix Magazine*, January 1985.

[6]Dino DeConcini won the Governor's Arts Award in 1984 for his significant contribution to the arts in Arizona. He received a six-by-three-foot work titled *Former Landmark*, by Gary Greenberg. Previous award winners included Lewis Ruskin, 1981; Louise Tester Pollard, 1982; and Edward "Bud" Jacobson, 1983.

[7]Mallery and Herberger also eliminated the Robert R. Frankenberger/ELS Design Group team at this time, although the team had demonstrated considerable strength.

[8]Bradley Morison, memo to the Phoenix Performing Arts Center board, April 7, 1985, Herberger Theater Center Collection, Herberger Family Papers, file 5, Scottsdale, Ariz.

[9]Bradley Morison, memo.

[10]Bradley Morison, memo.

[11]Both Mallery and Herberger sought their wives input; according to those close to the process, Mallery relied greatly on his wife Francie's views.

[12]Gerald Nash, *The American West in the Twentieth Century: A Short History of an Urban Oasis* (Albuquerque: University of New Mexico Press, 1977), 125–127, 256. The innovations of western architects—Richard Neutra, Pietro Belluschi, William W. Wurster, Edridge T. Spencer, Ronald R. Campbell, Donn Emmons, Welton D. Becket, and William L. Pereira—were widely imitated throughout the United States, and the Phoenix Civic Plaza's environs clearly reflected an adaptive watering down of these architects' styles.

[13]*Arizona Republic*, April 20, 1985; *Phoenix Magazine*, April 1985.

[14]Born in Chicago on March 18, 1922, Edward "Bud" Jacobson, like Richard Mallery, was a partner at Phoenix's largest and most influential law firm, Snell & Wilmer. He was a leading supporter of the arts community, serving on numerous cultural development boards, as well as

supporting artists and photographers during the second-half of the twentieth century. He was a graduate of Harvard Business School and the University of Arizona Law School and focused his professional life on tax law. He died in Phoenix on March 4, 2005.

[15]Mayor Goddard wanted to create a city agency to support the arts. To achieve this, and other related goals, he appointed Edward "Bud" Jacobson to chair the ad hoc Advisory Committee on the Arts, with ten people appointed to serve on the committee. Goddard challenged the committee to take a comprehensive look at the arts in Phoenix and to assess the needs and identify what role the city could play in stimulating the growth of the arts. "Everybody wanted to be on the committee," said Goddard, "so Bud established 'permanent guests.' It grew to include over 100 people. Through this committee, Jacobson expanded the idea of a city agency to include the One Percent for Art Program." Terry Goddard, interview by author, Phoenix, Ariz., August 15, 2009.

[16]*Phoenix Magazine*, May 1985.

[17]*Arizona Republic*, April 17, 18, 1985. Deborah Whitehurst became the Phoenix Arts Commission's executive director one year after the creation of the commission.

[18]Minutes, Board of Directors Meeting, May 22, 1985, Phoenix Civic Plaza Building Corporation, Arizona. Phoenix Civic Plaza Building Corporation Collection, box 14, folder 10. Mayor Goddard's assistant, Jim Binns, started the meeting with a briefing on downtown development, stating that it was the mayor's wish to work more closely with the Civic Plaza Building Corporation board and not come to them for support only in times of emergency or for last minute decisions on projects. Next, Ron Engelen, chair of the mayor's ad hoc Advisory Committee on Downtown, described their master plan for expanding Heritage Square, adding a science museum and a history museum and renaming the project Heritage and Science Park. There also was a desire to develop a retail space, such as a Mercado, in the area. Although the mayor's committee was not requesting funds from the Civic Plaza Building Corporation board, Engelen expressed his philosophical view that certain projects might be appropriate for Civic Plaza Building Corporation support sometime in the future.

[19]Minutes, Board of Directors Meeting, May 22, 1985. Also see *Phoenix Gazette*, May 23, 1985; *Phoenix Gazette*, July 3, 1985.

[20]Minutes, Board of Directors Meeting, May 22, 1985. The May 22 meeting ended with one board member asking that the others review a list of future or potential projects for downtown development that might require Civic Plaza Building Corporation funding.

[21]Minutes, Board of Directors Meeting, May 30, 1985, Phoenix Civic Plaza Building Corporation, Arizona. Phoenix Civic Plaza Building Corporation Collection, box 14, folder 10. The auditorium was on a five-year lease to the city of Phoenix, with an option to extend the lease for ninety-nine years. *Arizona Republic*, July 3, 1985.

[22]The Phoenix Symphony board disdained the idea when they heard about Maus's suggestion.

[23]Minutes, Board of Directors Meeting, May 30, 1985. Also see *Arizona Republic*, May 31, 1985; *Arizona Republic*, June 1, 1985; and *Phoenix Gazette*, May 31, 1985. Rosenzweig deferred taking a vote until Stephen Dragos and James Forsberg presented their comments on downtown development. Dragos, representing the Phoenix Community Alliance, spoke of plans for Square One, the proposed new science museum, Heritage Square expansion to include a Mercado nearby, and downtown housing. Forsberg, director of the Downtown Phoenix Redevelopment Agency, spoke about the urgency for a third hotel downtown, which led to a wide-ranging discussion.

[24]Minutes, Board of Directors Meeting, May 30, 1985.

[25]Minutes, Board of Directors Meeting, May 30, 1985. See *Phoenix Gazette*, July 3, 1985.

[26]See *Arizona Republic*, July 3, 1985; *Arizona Republic*, July 4, 1985; and *Phoenix Gazette*, July 3, 1985.

[27]Richard Mallery, interview by author, Phoenix, Ariz., April 17, 2003. Both Gary and Kax Herberger declined to broach the subject of an additional $1 million gift with Bob Herberger; they told Mallery that he was the person to approach him on the matter.

[28]Richard Mallery, interviews by author, Phoenix, Ariz., April 17, 2003 and January 2, 2008.

[29]*Arizona Republic*, October 16, 1985; *Phoenix Gazette*, October 15, 1985. Also, Mayor Terry Goddard, press release, October 15, 1985, Herberger Theater Center Collection, Herberger Family Papers, file 5, Scottsdale Ariz.

[30]With the additional $1 million gift from Bob Herberger, the Phoenix Performing Arts Center board began using the name Herberger Theater for both the project and the board name, even though the name did not formally change in the articles of incorporation.

[31]*Arizona Republic*, October 16, 1985; *Phoenix Gazette*, October 15, 1985.

[32]Xicanindio Artists Coalition, founded by Carmen de Novias, was a group of musicians who

played authentic and sophisticated Central and South American music. Carmen's husband, Zarco Guerrera, was an artist who made masks and performed with the group as a dancer. The group developed a significant following in Phoenix. They often played at nightclubs, particularly at the Acapulco Bay Beach Club in a discount shopping center on Thomas Road in Phoenix between Thirty-sixth and Fortieth Streets.

Chapter Ten: The Design

[1]Dennis DeConcini and Jack L. August, *Senator Dennis DeConcini: From the Center of the Aisle* (Tucson: University of Arizona Press, 2006), 202.

[2]Stephen Pizzo, Mary Fricker, and Paul Muolo, *Inside Job: The Looting of America's Savings and Loans* (New York: McGraw Hill, 1989), 1–2. Also see James R. Adams, *The Big Fix, Inside the S&L Scandal: How an Unholy Alliance of Politics and Money Destroyed America's Banking System* (New York: John Wiley and Sons, 1990); Michael Binstein and Charles Bowden, *Trust Me: Charles Keating and the Missing Billions* (New York: Random House, 1993); Kathy Calavita, Henry N. Pontell, and Robert H. Tillman, *Big Money Crime: Fraud and Politics in the S&L Crisis* (Berkeley: University of California Press, 1997); Kathleen Day, *S&L Hell: The People and Politics Behind the $1 Trillion Savings and Loan Scandal* (New York: W. W. Norton, 1993); Martin Mayer, *The Greatest-Ever Bank Robbery: The Collapse of the Savings and Loan Industry* (New York: Charles Scribner and Sons, 1990).

[3]*Arizona Republic*, February 3, 2002.

[4]*Arizona Republic*, December 26, 27, 28, 1985; *Arizona Republic*, March 1, 2007; *Phoenix Gazette*, December 27, 28, 1985; *Los Angeles Times*, December 27, 28, 1985; *Daily Dispatch* (Casa Grande, Arizona), December 28, 1985; and *New York Times*, February 1, 2000.

[5]The actions taken in 1985 triggered a revolution in transportation taxes and policy. The Arizona state legislature passed a law enabling the citizens of Maricopa County to vote on a sales tax increase to fund regional freeway improvements and to provide for the creation of the Regional Public Transportation Authority. In October of that year, Maricopa County voters approved the passage of a proposition for a half-cent sales tax to fund freeway construction. A portion of the funds collected, $5 million per year (inflated annually), was to be used as seed money for regional transit service expansion. The Regional Public Transportation Authority received this funding through 2005 and was charged with developing a regional transit plan, finding a dedicated funding source for transit, and developing and operating a regional transit system. In 1988 Scottsdale residents passed a similar transportation tax. In 1993 the Regional Public Transportation Authority board of directors adopted Valley Metro as the identity for the regional transit system. In 1996 Tempe residents passed a half-cent sales tax dedicated for transit. In 1998 Mesa residents passed a quality-of-life half-cent sales tax, which dedicated a small portion for transit. In 2000 Phoenix residents passed a four-tenths of a percent sales tax for improvements to local bus service, Bus Rapid Transit (began in 2003), Light Rail (beginning in 2008), Neighborhood Minibus service, and more. In 2004 Maricopa County residents extended the half-cent countywide sales tax originally authorized in 1985. The tax allocates over one-third of tax revenues, or $5.8 billion (before inflation), for transit, including light rail. Members of Valley Metro must spend Local Transportation Assistance Fund revenues from the Arizona state lottery on public transportation. A city with a population of 300,000 or more must spend all of its Local Transportation Assistance Funds on transit services. Local Transportation Assistance Funds II revenues are obtained from the national powerball lottery, and Regional Public Transportation Authority acts as a pass-through for jurisdictions receiving this funding for public transportation.

[6]Bradley Morison, letter to Gary Herberger, August 20, 1985; Michael Hallmark, letter to Gary Herberger, August 15, 1985; Michael Hallmark, letter to Gary Herberger, August 16, 1985, Herberger Theater Center Collection, Herberger Family Papers, file 5, Scottsdale, Ariz.

[7]Bradley Morison and Julie Dalgleish, letter to Richard Mallery and Gary Herberger, March 12, 1986, Herberger Theater Center Collection, Herberger Family Papers, file 4, Scottsdale, Ariz. Also, Bradley Morrison, letter to Gary Herberger, August 20, 1985, Herberger Theater Center Collection, Herberger Family Papers, file 4, Scottsdale, Ariz. Morison dug deeper into Arcop Associates and reported, "In anticipation of your probable desire to try to determine exactly what Fred's death might have on Arcop, I took the liberty of calling my friend David Midland in Tampa, Florida, yesterday. David is the executive director of the Tampa Bay Center for the Performing Arts, which is a three-hall complex now under construction and scheduled for official opening in December of 1986. Arcop is the architectural firm for that project and David has been working very closely with them for several years now. Art Nichol, Fred's partner, has been

David's primary contact with Arcop, although Fred was involved in a major way at the beginning and David knew him well.... David's feeling is that Fred has not been very actively involved in the actual design work of the firm for several years now, but has concentrated on being the visible, public contact for the company. Art Nichol is much quieter and less flamboyant, according to David, and is an extremely talented and effective designer, although less the inspirational leader. Fred has really provided the creative spark for the organization and been its soul, so to speak.... David feels that Arcop will probably be just as capable and effective a firm of architects in the short run as they were when Fred was alive."

[8]Bradley Morison, letter to Gary Herberger, September 13, 1985, Herberger Theater Center Collection, Herberger Family Papers, file 5, Scottsdale, Ariz.

[9]Morison arranged two sets of meetings between potential users and the architectural team in late September and October 1985. With the aid of his associate, Julie Dalgleish, who knew the arts community well from her experience as director of audience development and public relations for the Tucson Symphony, Morison brought this important group of stakeholders into the planning process. Enthusiasm ran high in the initial meetings of the first phase, as the arts groups articulated their requirements for an excellent theater design. Their input improved the technical aspects of the design and ensured that the off-street loading dock was big enough for two trucks, and they pointed out the problem that trucks would have to turn a corner once inside the loading area. They were instrumental in an improved dressing-room area circulation. The arts groups insisted on additional toilets and sinks; that the actors' lounge area be moved closer to the stage door; that there was a wooden spring floor in the large rehearsal room, as well as mirrors so that it was usable by dancers; and numerous other details.

[10]Richard Mallery, interview by author, Phoenix, Ariz., March 23, 1996.

[11]In designing the campus in the late nineteenth century, Leland Stanford Jr. engaged famed landscape architect Frederick Law Olmsted who, among numerous other monumental projects, created New York's Central Park and pioneered the urban parks movement in the United States. The collaboration was contentious, but Olmsted designed the physical plan for the university, which resulted in an organization of quadrangles on an east–west axis. The literature on Olmsted and his life's work is extensive. For the best one-volume study that captures his essence, see Witold Rybczynski, *A Clearing in the Distance: Frederick Law Olmsted and America in the Nineteenth Century* (New York: Scribner, 2000). Olmsted mused on his notion of beauty in the natural world: "What artist so noble... as he who, with far-reaching conception of beauty, in designing power, sketches the outlines, writes the colors, and directs the shadows of a picture so great that Nature shall be employed upon it for generations, before the work he arranged for her shall realize his intentions."

[12]Richard Mallery, interviews by author, Phoenix, Ariz., March 23, 1996 and April 3, 2009.

[13]Howard, Needles, Tammen, and Bergendoff, memorandum to Herberger Theater board of directors, January 22, 1986. Herberger Theater Center Collection, Herberger Family Papers, file 6, Scottsdale, Ariz.

[14]Howard, Needles, Tammen, and Bergendoff, meeting notes to Herberger Theater board of directors, March 3, 1986, Herberger Theater Center Collection, Herberger Family Papers, file 6, Scottsdale, Ariz. Connection to the Superblock, the site of the future Arizona Center, also came under consideration for the corner of Third Street and Van Buren. Developer Jerry Smalley from Rouse Corporation attended a design meeting to discuss this connection. Discussion ensued, and the board asked Rouse to consider developing the retail and restaurant component of the complex.

[15]Brian Hall, memorandum to the Herberger Design Team, May 21,1986, Herberger Theater Center Collection, Herberger Family Papers, file 6, Scottsdale, Ariz. Hall quoted W. H. Auden. "When I was a child, the streets were full of street vendors and street entertainers of every kind." Also, Bradley Morison, letter to Herberger Theater board; Howard, Needles, Tammen, and Bergendoff; and Arcop Associates, November 13, 1985, Herberger Theater Center Collection, Herberger Family Papers, file 6, Scottsdale, Ariz. Morison argued strongly for an inviting exterior, "...the design of performing arts buildings in their public spaces, their exterior appearance and their environs can have enormous effect...on the cultivation of audience."

[16]Gary Herberger, press release, October 15, 1985, Herberger Theater Center Collection, Herberger Family Papers, file 4, Scottsdale, Ariz.; Minutes, Board of Directors Meeting, May 6, 1986, Howard, Needles, Tammen, and Bergendoff; Phoenix, Arizona. Herberger Theater Center Collection, Herberger Family Papers, file 6, Scottsdale, Ariz.

[17]The reference Stage West indicated that the theater was west of the Center Stage theater.

[18]Morison tried to broker a solution to this dilemma by having the architects create a relatively large-scale model so that all concerned could get a better feeling for the space. Morison was correct about the design; although a greatly admired theater space, Stage West has never been used in the arena configuration.

[19]Michael Hallmark, letter to Richard Mallery and Gary Herberger, October 8, 1985, Herberger Theater Center Collection, Herberger Family Papers, file 5, Scottsdale, Ariz.

[20]Brian Hall, meeting notes to Richard Mallery and Gary Herberger, November 8, 1985, Herberger Theater Center Collection, Herberger Family Papers, file 5, Scottsdale, Ariz.

[21]Brian Hall, meeting notes.

[22]Morison's estimate of $12 million for the theater in the feasibility study included construction only and had not included architectural and engineering fees. These fees are figured as a percentage of the construction costs. In addition, his estimates were based on 1980 construction costs, and inflation added significantly to the escalation of the numbers.

[23]Bradley Morison, letter to Joseph Zeigler, November 4, 1985, Herberger Theater Center Collection, Herberger Family Papers, file 5, Scottsdale, Ariz.

[24]Bradley Morison, letter to Gary Herberger, October 22, 1985, Herberger Theater Center Collection, Herberger Family Papers, file 5, Scottsdale, Ariz.

[25]Richard Mallery, press release, May 20, 1986, Herberger Theater Center Collection, Herberger Family Papers, file 6, Scottsdale, Ariz. Also see *Arizona Republic*, May 21, 1986; *Phoenix Gazette*, April 29, 1986; and *New Times* (Phoenix), June 4, 1986.

[26]Gary Moore, letter and résumé to Herberger Theater board, May 1, 1985, Herberger Theater Center Collection, Herberger Family Papers, file 4, Scottsdale, Ariz.

[27]Gary Moore, letter and résumé.

[28]At the request of the board, Morison held a meeting with arts organizations who were potential users of the theater to describe the theater's broad mission to be more than just a landlord, but also to be a catalyst and a creative force to help the arts organizations that used the facility with technical production assistance and audience development. The arts organizations responded positively and suggested that there might be a council formed of user groups to advise the board. They also discussed the idea that some qualitative judgment be made on who could use the facility so that the theater would always stand for excellence in the minds of the audience, suggesting that perhaps a peer panel similar to those used by the National Endowment for the Arts could make these discernments. Nothing came of these ideas, however, when they were relayed to the Herberger Theater board.

[29]*Arizona Republic*, March 16, 1986.

[30]*Arizona Republic*, March 16, 1986.

[31]*Arizona Republic*, March 16, 1986.

[32]*Arizona Republic*, March 16, 1986.

[33]*Arizona Republic*, March 16, 1986.

Chapter Eleven: Tucson's Temple of Music and Art

[1]A common joke in Tucson at the time was that the difference between Phoenix and yogurt was that yogurt had culture.

[2]As noted in chapter 1, Sandy Rosenthal and about twenty civic leaders founded the Arizona Civic Theatre in Tucson in 1966. It reached professional status in 1972 when it began hiring Actors' Equity performers on a modified League of Resident Theater contract. The company began presenting a portion of its season in Phoenix in 1978, and one year later, the name was changed to Arizona Theatre Company. Governor Rose Mofford designated the company the State Theatre of Arizona in 1990.

[3]"Return of the Muse: Temple of Music and Art," (Tucson: The Tucson Weekly in collaboration with Arizona Theatre Company, 1990).

[4]*Tucson Weekly*, November 21, 1984.

[5]The National Historic Preservation Act of 1966 triggered several federal, state, and local initiatives that encouraged the preservation of the nation's historically significant built environment. Tax credits and other economic incentives were a consequence of these developments. See *National Historic Preservation Act, U.S. Code*, vol. 16, sec. 470 (1966). Also consult Christopher Duerken, ed. *A Handbook on Historic Preservation Law* (Washington, D.C.: Conservation Foundation for Preservation Law, 1986); Thomas F. King, *Cultural Resource: Law and Practice*, 2nd ed. (New York: Altamira Press, 2004); and Mitchell Schwarzer, "Myth of Permanence and Transience in the Discussion of Historic Preservation in the United States," *Journal of Architectural Education*, 48 (September 1994): 3–4.

[6]The stage house is the area behind, around, and above the stage.

[7]*Tucson Daily Citizen*, April 29, 1944; *Tucson Daily Citizen*, September 27, 1965; and *Tucson Daily Citizen*, July 15, 1976. Unfortunately, the local banks would not lend the club any money for the building's construction, so the women had to seek other sources. Also see "Return of the Muse: Temple of Music and Arts."

[8]Alexander Berger was referred to as a wealthy philanthropist from either Virginia, or Philadelphia, or both.

[9]Alexander's wife was Mary Sholes Berger.

[10]*Tucson Daily Citizen*, April 29, 1944; *Tucson Daily Citizen*, July 15, 1976.

[11]"Return of the Muse: Temple of Music and Art."

[12]*Arizona Daily Star*, December 12, 1926. Also see Lanfranco Rasponi, *The Last Prima Donnas* (New York: Alfred A. Knopf, 1982).

[13]Rufus von Kleinschmid's wife also was a member of the Saturday Morning Musical Club.

[14]*Tucson Daily Citizen*, April 29, 1944; *Tucson Daily Citizen*, September 27, 1965; *Tucson Daily Citizen*, July 15, 1976. Initial estimates claimed that the Temple of Music and Art could seat 923 to 950 people.

[15]Arthur Hawes had previously worked at the California studio of Elmer Grey during the time that Grey designed the Pasadena Playhouse.

[16]*Tucson Daily Citizen*, December 5, 2008.

[17]The Hutchinsons previously had turned the Copper Queen Hotel in Bisbee, Arizona, into a showcase. They had hoped for a similar success with the Temple of Music and Art in Tucson, but failed.

[18]"Return of the Muse: Temple of Music and Art."

[19]John Hudak, interview by author, Tucson, Ariz., October 19, 2007.

[20]Hudak would be the first to say that he was not the only person who was actively involved in forming the Tucson Artists Coalition. Painter Judith D'Agostino and realtor Margaret Keenan, among others, assisted him. Hudak came to Arizona from Pittsburgh after high school and obtained two degrees from the University of Arizona in journalism and creative writing, where he also created a literary magazine. He was instrumental in the creation of the Tucson Poetry Festival and served as its first executive director. Hudak also served as editor of a small press, San Gemini. He was a cofounder of the Tucson Artists Coalition and the Downtown Arts District Partnership. Hudak was appointed by the governor twice to serve as commissioner for the Arizona Commission on the Arts. He joined Madden Media in 1987 and is now a partner and the publisher. John Hudak, interview.

[21]Hudak raised $6,500 and secured a $20,000 challenge grant from the Tucson/Pima Arts Council.

[22]*Arizona Daily Star* (Tucson), December 12, 1984; *Tucson Daily Citizen*, December 12, 1984.

[23]"Return of the Muse: Temple of Music and Art."

[24]When asked if members of the Tucson Artists Coalition had tipped off the inspectors, John Hudak hedged and then said, "We might have looked young, but we weren't stupid.... Sending an inspector by when we see something that might be a little out of mix was fair game as far as we were concerned.... It was just a matter of finding ways to muddy the water and slow things down and get some time to get all of our ducks in a row." John Hudak, interview.

[25]The city offered the owners $425,000 for the Temple of Music and Art. In turn, the owners sued the city. On April 23, 1987, a jury awarded the investors $842,800.

[26]Playing a significant role in the negotiations for the Temple of Music and Art were Arizona Theatre Company board members George Miraben, Clague and Sally Van Slyke, and George Rosenberg. John Hudak, interview; Jessica Andrews, interview by author, Tucson, Ariz., February 5, 2008.

[27]The Tucson Artists Coalition received some money for its projects, including low-income housing for artists at the Shane House on South Fourth Avenue. The Tucson Children's Museum was able to renovate and move into the historic Carnegie Library; it opened in its new home in 1991. Small theater groups also enjoyed the renovation of All Saint's Church for a few years, until the city shuttered it because of structural problems. It remains empty today, although many small arts groups would like to be able to use it again, including the Invisible Theater, the Mariachi Festival, and the Borderlands Theater. John Hudak, interview.

[28]On February 2, 1988, Arizona Theatre Company accepted the final management agreement. See *Arizona Daily Star*, February 3, 1988; *Tucson Daily Citizen*, November 22, 1988.

[29]Hawkanson had brought Mark Lamos to Arizona in 1978 to direct the company's highly successful production of *Equus*. Lamos remained with Arizona Theatre Company as acting artistic director during Sandy Rosenthal's yearlong sabbatical. He then went to Hartford Stage Company. Hawkanson served for eight years with Lamos as managing director. Before becoming executive director of the Steppenwolf Theater Company in Chicago in 2004, he was the managing director of the Guthrie Theater, under the artistic leadership of Joe Dowling. Hawkanson was a senior staff member at the National Endowment for the Arts, and he subsequently was chair of its theater program. He also had an active career as an arts consultant and board member for

such organizations as the Kennedy Center Fund for New American Plays, the Ford Foundation's Working Capital Fund, the National Arts Stabilization Fund, the Alliance for Arts Advocates, the League of Resident Theaters, Theatre Trustees of America, Theatre Communications Group, New York Stage and Film, the American Arts Alliance, and Door County's Peninsula Players, where he is an honorary board member. In Chicago, he is a board member of the Illinois Arts Alliance and the League of Chicago Theatres.

[30]Jessica Andrews, interview; Barbara Levy, interview by author, Tucson, Ariz., April 22, 2009.

[31]John Hudak also received a copper letter of commendation from Mayor Tom Volge. The Tucson/Pima Arts Council subsequently honored Hudak with a prestigious Lummie Award in 2008, and Arizona Theatre Company also honored him with the 2008 Georgy Award.

[32]"Return of the Muse: Temple of Music and Art."

Chapter Twelve: The Groundbreaking

[1]The model for the Herberger Theater complex also included additional low-rise buildings on the east side, which would hold offices for arts organizations, classrooms, restaurants, and other retail space to provide a festive atmosphere.

[2]*Phoenix Gazette*, November 8, 1986. Moore issued his interview from offices generously donated by Valley National Bank.

[3]Minutes, Board of Directors Meeting, October 15, 1986, Civic Plaza Building Corporation, Phoenix. Newton Rosenzweig Collection, Arizona Historical Foundation, Hayden Library, Arizona State University, box 5, file 1, Tempe, Ariz. Also see *Arizona Republic*, October 16, 1986; *Arizona Republic*, November 5, 1986.

[4]*Arizona Republic*, March 27, 1987.

[5]*New Times* (Phoenix), April 22, 1987.

[6]*New Times* (Phoenix), April 22, 1987.

[7]*New Times* (Phoenix), April 22, 1987.

[8]Valley National Bank, proposed terms for the line of credit to the Phoenix Performing Arts Center board of directors, May 13, 1987, Herberger Theater Center Collection, Herberger Family Papers, file 6, Scottsdale, Ariz.

[9]Minutes, Board of Directors Meeting, April 22, 1987, Civic Plaza Building Corporation, Phoenix. Newton Rosenzweig Collection, Arizona Historical Foundation, Hayden Library, Arizona State University, box 5, file 1, Tempe, Ariz. The additional $60,000 in the budget increase was from the expense for the One Percent for Art program.

[10]Minutes, Board of Directors Meeting, April 22, 1987. Also see *Arizona Republic*, April 23, 1987.

[11]The locally based Kitchell CEM served as the construction management firm of the Herberger Theater project.

[12]Minutes, Board of Directors Meeting, April 22, 1987. Also, Ray Bladine, city community and economic development manager, city council report to Denny Maus, April 21, 1987 and April 23, 1987, authors' files. Also see *Arizona Republic*, April 23, 1987; *Arizona Republic*, May 6, 1987. The agreement with the city also clarified that once the theater opened, the Phoenix Performing Arts Center (also known as the Herberger Theater) would retain all revenues from rentals of the theaters to offset their operating expenses. Revenues from the retail and commercial development section, when completed, would be divided with the city on the 51 percent to 49 percent formula. Projects desired by the Herberger Theater board included first-class restaurants, office space for performing arts organizations, and retail spaces. Mallery reiterated that an estimated $4 million had been taken out of the project costs, including the $475,000 ornamental ceiling; however, he noted that many of these items could be added back after completion, in the same way that Symphony Hall benefited from gifts after completion of the construction.

[13]Minutes, Board of Directors Meeting, July 9, 1987, Civic Plaza Building Corporation, Phoenix. Newton Rosenzweig Collection, Arizona Historical Foundation, Hayden Library, Arizona State University, box 5, file 1, Tempe, Ariz. Also see *Arizona Republic*, July 9, 10, 1987.

[14]*Phoenix Business Journal*, August 3, 18, 1987; *Arizona Republic*, August 12, 1987. There were seven bidders for the project. Before the Nielsen Construction Company could receive the contract for the Herberger Theater project, it had to stave off a bid dispute by the Westbrook Construction Company, which had appealed the decision. Westbrook Construction Company's bid differed from the Nielsen Construction Company's bid by only $42,441; they claimed they were entitled to a 5 percent preference because they had done previous public works projects and had paid qualified taxes for two consecutive years prior to their bid. Nielsen Construction

Company countered that in-state bidders are by law to be given preference, and Westbrook Construction Company was based in Colorado and a subsidiary of a Canadian company. In addition, the Nielsen Construction Company hired within the state, while Westbrook Construction Company typically brought in people from outside Arizona. Nielsen Construction Company also had experience building theaters, which Westbrook Construction Company did not. On August 11, 1987, after attorneys from both companies presented their respective arguments, the board called an executive session and affirmed its award of the Herberger Theater project to the Nielsen Construction Company.

[15]Minutes, Board of Directors Meeting, July 9, 1987. Also see *Arizona Republic,* July 9, 10, 1987.

[16]Minutes, Board of Directors Meeting, July 9, 1987. Also see *Arizona Republic,* July 9, 10, 1987.

[17]*Arizona Republic,* July 24, 1987.

[18]*Arizona Republic,* July 24, 1987.

[19]*Arizona Republic,* July 24, 1987; *Phoenix Gazette,* July 23, 24, 1987. Also, G. Robert Herberger, interview by author, Scottsdale, Ariz., December 15, 1995; Gary Herberger, interview by author, Scottsdale, Ariz., February 15, 1996.

[20]Terry Goddard, interview by author, Phoenix, Ariz., October 23, 1996.

[21]Terry Goddard, interview. C. A. Howlett echoed Goddard's evaluation of the Herberger project's effect on convincing the Rouse Corporation to invest in Phoenix. C. A. Howlett, interview by author, Tempe, Ariz., February 13, 1996; Jack Tevlin, interview by author, Phoenix, Ariz., March 28, 1996; and Gary Herberger, interview. Mark DeMichele was somewhat skeptical, saying the key factor was the tax incentive offered by the city. Mark DeMichele, interview by author, Phoenix, Ariz., March 27, 1996.

[22]*Phoenix Magazine,* June 1986; *Phoenix Magazine,* July 1986. Arizona Public Service needed 400,000 square feet for its headquarters.

[23]*Phoenix Magazine,* July 1986. St. Mary's High School, founded in 1917, had been a downtown landmark for fifty years. In July 1986 school officials announced that it would relocate because their gymnasium was in the Superblock area. Earlier, school officials had moved the girls' high school because it was in the area where the Phoenix Civic Plaza was built.

[24]Phoenix had the worst carbon monoxide pollution in the nation at this time.

[25]*Phoenix Magazine,* June 1986; *Phoenix Magazine*, March 1987. The Fantus Consulting report quoted a high-tech consortium leader that chose to locate in Texas rather than Arizona as saying, "Arizona is a wonderful state in many ways. You have magnificent climate, recreational activities, and honest government, but it is a cultural wasteland."

[26]See for example, Jack L. August Jr. "Old Arizona and the New Conservative Agenda: The Hayden versus Mecham Senate Campaign of 1962." *Journal of Arizona History* (Winter 2001); *Arizona Republic,* November 10, 11, 12, 1986; *Phoenix Gazette,* November 5, 7, 9, 1986; and *Arizona Daily Star* (Tucson), November 5, 6, 7, 8, 1986.

[27]The cost for the purchase of the northern section of the block was taken out of the 51 percent to 49 percent calculation.

[28]Mark DeMichele, interview.

[29]*Phoenix Magazine,* June 1988.

[30]Jill Pearns, Mountain West director of marketing, letter to Gary Moore, June 26, 1987, Herberger Theater Center Collection, Herberger Family Papers, file 6, Scottsdale, Ariz.

Chapter Thirteen: Stabilization and Meltdown

[1]Flinn Foundation, "National Arts Stabilization in Arizona: A Report to the Community," (Phoenix: Flinn Foundation, 1998). The Ford Foundation pioneered the program from 1971 to 1982, with W. MacNeil Lowry shepherding the program. It was so successful that it was spun off into its own organization, with support from multiple foundations. This thorough report describes the nine Arizona organizations that participated in the National Arts Stabilization Fund program. Other communities who have worked with the National Arts Stabilization Fund on comparable projects include Baltimore, Boston, Columbus, Kansas City, New York City, and Seattle. Arizona's was the only statewide effort.

[2]Mark DeMichele succeeded Howard McCrady in this role in 1991.

[3]Because of escalating operating budgets and the growth of several arts organizations, they later increased the $4.5 million to $5.7 million. This required an additional $400,000 each from the National Arts Stabilization Fund, the Flinn Foundation, and the Arizona Arts Stabilization Committee. Sam Kathryn Campana, executive director of Arizonans for Cultural Development,

later renamed Arizona Citizens/Action for the Arts, and future mayor of the city of Scottsdale, spearheaded the effort to raise the additional $1.2 million.

[4]See Flinn Foundation, "National Arts Stabilization in Arizona: A Report to the Community." While endowments increased, the state still lagged behind other areas in the country, reflecting the relative immaturity of Arizona's cultural environment. The Arizona stabilization process also led to the establishment of ArtShare, a public- and private-sector endowment enacted by the Arizona state legislature in 1996, which made $20 million available to the arts from existing amusement taxes over the next ten years, with an equal amount to be raised from the private sector. The idea was to continue the stabilization process, this time for medium-sized arts organizations in Arizona. ArtShare began with twelve organizations.

[5]Charles Bowden and Michael Binstein, *Trust Me: Charles Keating and the Missing Billions* (New York: Random House, 1993), 365.

[6]Kathleen Day, *S&L Hell: The People and the Politics behind the $1 Trillion Savings and Loan Scandal* (New York: W. W. Norton, 1993), 88.

[7]The starting salary for a savings and loan examiner in 1982 was $14,000 per year.

[8]Day, *S&L Hell*, 193.

[9]Day, *S&L Hell*, 270.

[10]James R. Adams, *The Big Fix, Inside the S&L Scandal: How an Unholy Alliance of Politics and Money Destroyed America's Banking System* (New York: John Wiley & Sons, 1989), 41.

[11]Adams, *The Big Fix, Inside the S&L Scandal*, 51.

[12]Jon Talton, letter to Jack August Jr., December 15, 2008.

[13]Dennis DeConcini and Jack L. August, *Senator Dennis DeConcini: From the Center of the Aisle* (Tucson: University of Arizona Press, 2006), chap. 8. Also, Bowden and Binstein, *Trust Me*, 6.

[14]Bowden and Binstein, *Trust Me*, 184.

[15]Bowden and Binstein, *Trust Me*, 5, 9, 365.

[16]Bowden and Binstein, *Trust Me*, 200.

[17]Bowden and Binstein, *Trust Me*, 18.

[18]Bowden and Binstein, *Trust Me*, 7.

[19]See *Arizona Republic*, October 8, 1989; *Arizona Republic*, March 1, 2007.

[20]John Kenneth Galbraith, *The Culture of Contentment* (New York: Houghton Mifflin, 1992).

Chapter Fourteen: The Opening

[1]*Arizona Republic*, October 22, 24, 1988; *Arizona Republic*, November 7, 10, 1988; and *Arizona Daily Star* (Tucson), November 17, 1988.

[2]*Arizona Republic*, April 5, 6, 7, 1988.

[3]The Solar Oasis was an out-of-the-box solution to the two-acre cement plaza—or heat island—between Symphony Hall and the Herberger Theater. Dr. Carl Hodges, director of the University of Arizona Environmental Research Laboratory, convinced Mayor Terry Goddard and the Phoenix City Council to rip out most of the cement and replace it with an oasis of plants, shade structures, and changing environmental demonstrations. A passive 200-foot-high evaporative cooling tower was designed to cool the area, with virtually no energy consumption, as well as to become a symbol of the city, much like the Gateway Arch is for St. Louis. Dino DeConcini supervised the competitive design process, with Arizona State University Dean of Architecture John Meunier; and he cobbled together funding from city, county, and corporate contributions. However, the project failed for various reasons, mostly financial. The new mayor, Paul Johnson, diverted the city funds earmarked for the project to pay for exhibits for the four-year-old, but almost empty, Arizona Museum of Science and Technology. Then, citizens voted down a huge parks and recreation county bond issue, which included funding for the Solar Oasis. Finally, according to *New Times*, the new Civic Plaza Building Corporation board chair Tracy Thomas voiced his opposition to the project, saying, "The Oasis will go in over my dead body." Thomas and other opponents effectively killed the Solar Oasis. See *New Times* (Phoenix), April 19, 1989. DeConcini returned all the private money collected, over $500,000, noting, "The donors were quite surprised, and very pleasantly so, at getting their money back." Dino DeConcini, interview by author, Washington, D.C., June 3, 2009.

[4]*Horizon: A Magazine for the Arts*, July/August, 1988.

[5]In the nonprofit performing arts field, there are two types of organizations, broadly speaking: arts-producing organizations and arts-presenting organizations. The Herberger Theater was not an arts-producing organization; it did not create the art of theater, dance, or music. Performing arts organizations, such as Arizona Theatre Company, did that by hiring actors and directors, building sets, managing rehearsals, and producing plays for a full season of drama, encompassing

all aspects of production. The Herberger Theater role, instead, was to present these performances, providing a place to show the performing arts that had been created by others. Thus, in the arts field, the Herberger Theater is defined as a presenting organization.

[6]*Arizona Republic,* September 18, 1988.

[7]Carol MacLeod founded the Actors Theatre in March 1986. The theater company employed local Actors' Equity artists, with a mission to develop and nurture Valley talent and to create professional theater with a social conscience.

[8]Frances Smith Cohen and Marvin Cohen, interview by author, Phoenix, Ariz., March 29, 1996.

[9]At the time, the company used an unusual punctuation and lowercase spelling for its name, a Ludwig company: dance theatre.

[10]Glynn Ross was a high-profile opera impresario who gained notice as the founding general director of the Seattle Opera in 1963, where he produced the *Ring* cycles; this made Seattle the first American company, other than the Metropolitan Opera, to attempt Richard Wagner's masterwork in its entirety. He left Seattle in 1983 to become the general director of Arizona Opera, where he stayed until 1998. Ross expanded the opera company's offerings and restored it to financial health. He was a cofounder of Opera America in 1970, an industry trade association for American opera companies. Born in Omaha, Nebraska, as Glynn W. Aus to a Norwegian immigrant father and a mother of Swedish descent, he retired in 1998. Glynn Ross died of a stroke on July 21, 2005.

[11]Dr. Smith had led the Phoenix Boys Choir for twenty-seven years.

[12]*Arizona Republic,* April 26, 1989.

[13]*Arizona Republic,* April 29, 1989; *Arizona Republic,* May 2, 4, 7, 15, 20, 21, 29, 1989; and *Arizona Republic,* June 2, 13, 22, 1989.

[14]*Phoenix Magazine,* June 1989.

[15]*Phoenix Magazine,* June 1989.

[16]*Phoenix Magazine,* June 1989.

[17]*Arizona Republic,* March 10, 1989.

[18]Musical Theater of Arizona originally began in the Valley under the auspices of Arizona State University, which had assumed 50 percent of their costs for the first three years. *Arizona Republic,* July 25, 1989.

[19]*Arizona Republic,* July 21, 1989.

[20]*Phoenix Gazette,* July 19, 1989.

[21]*Arizona Republic,* July 23, 1989.

[22]*Arizona Business Gazette,* June 30, 1989.

[23]*Arizona Business Gazette,* June 30, 1989. The reporter asked the Herbergers what they wanted people to think about them for having built the theater. Their response, in essence, was that they hoped their example was something people would emulate.

[24]*Arizona Republic,* October 5, 7, 10, 1989; *Phoenix Gazette,* October 6, 7, 8, 10, 1989.

[25]*Arizona Woman,* October 1989. Moore envisioned the Herberger Theater operating in the same way by providing an environment that would nurture artists, thereby helping them do their best work.

[26]*Arizona Woman,* October 1989.

[27]*Arizona Republic,* November 17, 1989.

[28]*Arizona Republic,* November 17, 1989.

Chapter Fifteen: The Work Out

[1]*Arizona Business Gazette,* June 30, 1989. Pinnacle West Capital Corporation was also the parent company of Arizona Public Service and one of the major corporations in Arizona. Also see *New Times* (Phoenix), September 6, 1989.

[2]*Arizona Business Gazette,* June 30, 1989.

[3]*Arizona Business Gazette,* June 30, 1989.

[4]*Arizona Business Gazette,* June 30, 1989.

[5]*Arizona Business Gazette,* June 30, 1989.

[6]*Arizona Business Gazette,* June 30, 1989.

[7]Minutes, Board of Directors Meeting, January 24, 1990, Phoenix Performing Arts Center, Arizona. Herberger Theater Center Collection, Herberger Family Papers, file 6, Scottsdale, Ariz. Pamela Grant, a native of Grosse Point, Michigan, and a graduate of the University of Utah, joined Goldwater's department store in 1963 as a buyer. She rose through her merchandising position and became vice president in 1978, president and chief executive officer in late 1978,

and board chair in 1981. She was the first woman invited to join Phoenix 40. Grant also served on the board of Arizona Public Service and First Interstate Bank of Arizona. She was a member of the Council of 100 for Arizona State University, as well as a member of the Committee of 200, a select group of the nation's 200 top professional businesswomen.

[8]Minutes, Board of Directors Meeting, January 24, 1990. Mark DeMichele was still fund-raising committee chair of the Herberger Theater board. The board elected him as vice president.

[9]Minutes, Board of Directors Meeting, March 28, 1990, Phoenix Performing Arts Center, Arizona. Herberger Theater Center Collection, Herberger Family Papers, file 6, Scottsdale, Ariz. Also, David Sprenthall, interview by author, Phoenix, Ariz., March 30, 1998.

[10]Steven Kolesar ultimately was somewhat successful; however, the seat-underwriting campaign never caught on in Phoenix, although other new theaters around the country had used this strategy more successfully.

[11]Minutes, Board of Directors Meeting, May 30, 1990, Phoenix Performing Arts Center, Arizona. Herberger Theater Center Collection, Herberger Family Papers, file 6, Scottsdale, Ariz.

[12]Minutes, Board of Directors Meeting, May 30, 1990.

[13]Mark DeMichele, interview by author, Phoenix, Ariz., March 4, 1996.

[14]Mark DeMichele, interview.

[15]Mark DeMichele, interview.

[16]The comfort letter only required the city of Phoenix to explore all legal avenues available to assure payment and noted that the city would support private fund-raising efforts for such purpose.

[17]Mark DeMichele, interview.

[18]Minutes, Board of Directors Meeting, September 24, 1990, Phoenix Performing Arts Center, Arizona. Herberger Theater Center Collection, Herberger Family Papers, file 6, Scottsdale, Ariz.

[19]The chair of the Horace C. Steele Foundation was prominent attorney Dan Cracchiolo, husband of Pamela Grant.

[20]Richard Mallery, Gary Herberger, and Pamela Grant also loaned personal funds, all of which eventually were repaid.

[21]Phoenix City Council Arts, Culture, and Sports Subcommittee Report, November 8, 1990. Herberger Theater Center Collection, Herberger Family Papers, file 7, Scottsdale, Ariz.

[22]*Arizona Republic*, May 6, 1990.

Chapter Sixteen: A Sense of Place

[1]Arizona State College became Arizona State University in 1958. Arizona State University's name changed several times since being established in 1885 by the territorial legislature as the Normal School of Arizona. Subsequent names included Tempe State Teachers College, Arizona State Teachers College, then Arizona State College. In 1994 Arizona State University reached Research I university status and has become international in scope. In 2002 Michael Crow became the sixteenth president of Arizona State University, and he began the university's transformation into a prototype for what he calls the "New American University."

[2]Born in Des Moines, Iowa, in 1921, John Henry Waddell was the son of William Wilder Waddell and Isabel McGee. The family moved to Evanston, Illinois, in 1931. The senior Waddell was an executive at Fireman's Fund Insurance Company. See Michel F. Sarda, *John Henry Waddell: The Art and the Artist* (Phoenix: Bridgewood Press, 1996); John Henry Waddell and Ann R. Mealy, *The Beauty of Individual Differences* (Flagstaff: Northland Press, 1985); Select Art Gallery, *John Henry Waddell: An American Master Artist of Our Time* (Phoenix: Bridgewood Press, 1996).

[3]Unfortunately, the Mercado failed as a retail center and ceased operations in 1992; it is now owned by Arizona State University, as part of its downtown campus. The Arizona Center has not been a financial success either, nor the entertainment and shopping mecca its planners envisioned, even though it added immeasurably and beautifully to a sense of place downtown.

[4]In time, an outside institution, Bank One, even purchased Valley National Bank. J. P. Morgan Chase later purchased Bank One.

[5]As the resident company with anchor tenant status, Arizona Theatre Company had first choice of dates, but the scheduling situation required them to make decisions about dates far in advance, up to two years. They often had little or no flexibility for changes.

[6]Landlord–tenant relations with the resident companies proved problematic in the incipient stages of the Herberger Theater's opening season and for years thereafter. Yearly contract negotiations turned testy, and rental increases and heated discussion surrounding those increases, soured attitudes. Depending on personalities and the degree of strained relations, these landlord–tenant relationships sometimes devolved into frosty standoffs. In fact, in 1999 Arizona Theatre

Company gave serious thought to leaving the Herberger Theater. *Arizona Republic*, April 4, 1999.

[7]Although the city of Tucson owned the building, Arizona Theatre Company's agreement with the city placed them more in the position of sole operator.

[8]Todd London, *The Artistic Home: Discussions with Artistic Directors of America's Institutional Theatres* (New York: Theater Communications Group, 1993).

[9]Pamela Grant, interview by author, Phoenix, Ariz., November 18, 1997.

[10]Being a tenant at the Herberger Theater also complicated Arizona Theatre Company's efforts to establish its identity in Phoenix. For example, Arizona Theatre Company's name was not anywhere on the building. At times, the performers knew the audience was unaware that they were witnessing an Arizona Theatre Company performance. The ushers were employees of the Herberger Theater and until recently they said, "Welcome to the Herberger Theater" not "Welcome to the Arizona Theatre Company."

[11]*Arizona Republic*, July 26, 1989; August 1, 1989.

[12]Kim Sterling, interview by author, Scottsdale, Ariz., December 19, 1995.

[13]Everett King, interview by author, Phoenix, Ariz., October 13, 1996.

[14]Childsplay now has its home at the new Tempe Center for the Arts, as does A Ludwig Dance Theatre and the Desert Dance Theatre. Black Theatre Troupe performs occasionally at the Herberger Theater, but like many small organizations, they find the rents beyond their reach.

[15]Actors Theatre of Phoenix is the only resident company that uses the rehearsal hall. Thus, the space is generally available for bookings as the Performance Outreach Theater.

[16]Richard Bowers, interview by author, Phoenix, Ariz., March 5, 2009; Mark Mettes, interview by author, Phoenix, Ariz., March 5, 2009.

[17]*Phoenix Magazine*, February 2003.

[18]The corridor is closed. If one looks closely through the glass doors from inside the convention center toward Monroe Street, when the light is just right and exhibits are not in the way, the octagonal Steele Pavilion of the Herberger Theater can be seen perfectly in alignment with the convention center doors on Monroe Street. Unfortunately, it is impossible to see the entrance of Symphony Hall from the plaza of the Herberger Theater.

[19]*Phoenix Magazine*, February 2003. Also, Richard Bowers, letter to Civic Plaza Expansion Advisory Committee chair Don Keuth, August 22, 2003.

[20]Sheryl Sculley, assistant city manager under then-Mayor Skip Rimsza, was the city's point person on the Phoenix Civic Plaza expansion into what was renamed the Phoenix Convention Center. "What could be uglier than the Symphony Hall building?" Scully said. *Phoenix Magazine*, February 2003.

[21]Richard Bowers, interview.

[22]The founders of the Herberger Theater came very close to getting the Bass family of Texas to create something similar to the now-defunct Caravan of Dreams in Fort Worth on the block that housed the Herberger Theater. Terry Goddard, Richard Mallery, and a few other individuals flew to Texas to spend a day with the Bass family to discuss the effort; however, the project did not happen. Richard Mallery, interview by author, Phoenix, Ariz., October 27, 2007.

[23]Richard Bowers, interview.

[24]City of Phoenix, "Downtown Phoenix: A Strategic Vision and Blueprint for the Future," (December 14, 2004), 19–22.

[25]See Edward Glaeser, *Cities, Agglomeration, and Spatial Equilibrium* (New York: Oxford University Press, 2008); Edward Glaeser, "The Economics of Cities," *National Bureau of Economic Research* (December 1997); and Edward Glaeser, "The Economics of Place-making Policies," *Brookings Paper on Economic Activity* (Washington, D.C.: Brookings Institution Press, 2008). Also see Richard Florida, *Cities and the Creative Class* (New York: Routledge, 2004); Richard Florida, *The Rise of the Creative Class...and How It's Transforming Work, Leisure, Community, and Everyday Life* (New York: Basic Books, 2003); Richard Florida, *What's Your City: How the Creative Economy Is Making Where to Live the Most Important Decision of Your Life* (New York: Basic Books, 2008); and Richard Florida, *The Flight of the Creative Class: The New Global Competition for Talent* (New York: Collins Business, 2007).

[26]See, for example, Morrison Institute for Public Policy, "Five Shoes Waiting to Drop on Arizona's Future," Tempe, Ariz., Morrison Institute for Public Policy, School of Public Affairs, Arizona State University, 2001; AEA Consulting, "The Arts in Arizona: A Discussion Document," 2002; Battelle Memorial Institute, "Maricopa Region Arts and Culture Benchmarking Study," 2003; Morrison Institute for Public Policy, "A Place for Arts and Culture: A Maricopa County Overview," 2003; Battelle Memorial Institute and Morrison Institute for Public Policy, "Vibrant Cultures—Thriving Economy: Art, Culture, and Prosperity in Arizona's Valley of the Sun," 2004;

Morrison Institute for Public Policy, "Perfect Pitch: Considerations for a Dedicated Funding Source for Arts and Culture," 2005; Maricopa Partnership for Arts and Culture, "Creative Connections: Arts, Ideas, and Economic Progress in Greater Phoenix," 2006; Morrison Institute for Public Policy, "Sustainability for Arizona: The Issue of Our Age," 2007; Metro Phoenix Partnership for Arts and Culture, "Cultural Participation Study for Maricopa County," 2007; Metro Phoenix Partnership for Arts and Culture and Greater Phoenix Economic Council, "Perceptions Matter: Attracting and Retaining Talented Workers to the Greater Phoenix Region," 2007; Metro Phoenix Partnership for Arts and Culture, Arizona Needs Arts and Culture: Economic Diversity," 2009.

[27]The nine new growth cities that compete with Phoenix for bioscience, biotechnology, and other new growth industries include: Atlanta, Austin, Charlotte, Denver, Indianapolis, Portland, Salt Lake City, San Diego, and Seattle. Metro Phoenix Partnership for Arts and Culture, Battelle Memorial Institute and Morrison Institute for Public Policy, "Vibrant Cultures—Thriving Economy: Art, Culture, and Prosperity in Arizona's Valley of the Sun," 2004.

[28]Battelle Memorial Institute, "Maricopa Region Arts and Culture Benchmarking Study."

[29]Battelle Memorial Institute and Morrison Institute for Public Policy, "Vibrant Cultures—Thriving Economy," vi.

[30]Battelle Memorial Institute and Morrison Institute for Public Policy, "Vibrant Cultures—Thriving Economy," xiv.

[31]*Arizona Republic*, April 23, 2003; *Arizona Republic*, March 13, 2007.

[32]Richard Mallery, interview.

[33]Although the Flinn Foundation was not new to Arizona, it also played a pivotal role in supporting the bioscience effort.

[34]Tracy Benson, press release, April 29, 2003, Arizona State University Foundation, April 29, 2003. Also, *Arizona Republic*, April 4, 1999.

Selected Bibliography

Books

Abbott, Carl. *The New Urban America: Growth and Politics in Sunbelt Cities.* Chapel Hill: University of North Carolina Press, 1982.

Adams, James R. *The Big Fix, Inside the S&L Scandal: How an Unholy Alliance of Politics and Money Destroyed America's Banking System.* New York: John Wiley and Sons, 1990.

Alexander, Jane. *Command Performance: Actress in the Theater of Politics.* New York: Perseus Books, 2000.

August, Jack L., Jr. *Vision in the Desert: Carl Hayden and Hydropolitics in the American Southwest.* Fort Worth: Texas Christian University Press, 1999.

____________. *Dividing Western Waters: Mark Wilmer and Arizona v California.* Fort Worth: Texas Christian University Press, 2007.

Beeson, William, ed. *Thresholds: The Story of Nina Vance's Alley Theatre.* Houston: Alley Theatre, 1968.

Biddle, Livingston L. *Our Government and the Arts: A Perspective from the Inside.* Lancaster, Penn.: Reed Books, 1988.

Binkiewicz, Donna M. *Federalizing the Muse: United States Arts Policy and the National Endowment for the Arts, 1965–1980.* Chapel Hill: University of North Carolina Press, 2004.

Binstein, Michael, and Charles Bowden. *Trust Me: Charles Keating and the Missing Billions.* New York: Random House, 1993.

Blau, Herbert. *The Impossible Theater: A Manifesto.* New York: Collier, 1965.

Edward Booth-Clibborn, ed. *Phoenix: Twenty-First Century City.* United Kingdom: Booth-Clibborn Editions, 2006.

Calavita, Kathy, Henry N. Pontell, and Robert Tillman. *Big Money Crime: Fraud and Politics in the S&L Crisis.* Berkeley: University of California Press, 1997.

Carson, Donald W., and James W. Johnson. *Mo: The Life and Times of Morris K. Udall.* Tucson: University of Arizona Press, 2004.

Crowe, Rosalie, and Diane Tod. *Arizona Women's Hall of Fame.* Phoenix: Arizona Historical Society, 1990.

Day, Kathleen. *S&L Hell: The People and Politics behind the $1 Trillion Savings and Loan Scandal.* New York: W. W. Norton, 1993.

DeConcini, Dennis, and Jack L. August, *Senator Dennis DeConcini: From the Center of the Aisle.* Tucson: University of Arizona Press, 2006.

Duerken, Christopher, ed. *A Handbook on Historic Preservation Law.* Washington, D.C.: Conservation Foundation for Preservation Law, 1986.

Durham, Weldon B. *American Theatre Companies: 1931–1986.* Westport, Conn.: Greenwood Press, 1989.

Farish, Thomas Edwin. *Arizona History.* Phoenix: Phoenix Manufacturing Company, 1920.

Fichandler, Zelda, Peter Zeisler, and Arvin Brown. *TCG Oral History Project: Voices of the American Theater,* Preserving the Legacy series, *Zelda Fichandler, Peter Zeisler, Arvin Brown.* New York: Theater Communication Group Oral History Project, 2003.

Galbraith, John Kenneth. *The Culture of Contentment.* New York: Houghton Mifflin, 1992.

Garreau, Joel. *Edge City: Life on the New Frontier.* New York: Doubleday, 1990.

Glaeser, Edward. *Cities, Agglomeration, and Spatial Equilibrium.* New York: Oxford University Press, 2008.

Goldberg, Robert Alan. *Barry Goldwater.* New Haven: Yale University Press, 1995.

Guilfoyle, Peg. *The Guthrie Theater: Images, History, and Inside Stories.* Minneapolis: Nodin Press, 2006.

Guthrie, Tyrone. *A Life in the Theater: The Autobiography of Tyrone Guthrie.* London: Hamish Hamilton, 1959.

Guthrie, Tyrone. *A New Theatre.* Minneapolis: University of Minnesota Press, 1964; expanded edition, 2008.

Hyde, Lewis. *The Gift: Creativity and the Artist in the Modern World.* New York: Vintage Books, 2007.

Irving, Jules. *Beyond Broadway: The Quest for Permanent Theatres*. New York: Hill and Wang, 1968.
Jones, Margo. *Theatre-in-the-Round*. New York: McGraw-Hill, 1965.
King, Thomas F. *Cultural Resource: Law and Practice*, 2nd ed. New York: Altamira Press, 2004.
Lamar, Howard R. *The Far Southwest, A Territorial History: 1846–1912*. New Haven: Yale University Press, 1963.
London, Todd. *The Artistic Home: Discussions with Artistic Directors of America's Institutional Theatres* (New York: Theatre Communications Group, 1993).
Luckingham, Bradford. *Phoenix: The History of a Southwestern Metropolis*. Tucson: University of Arizona Press, 1989.
____________. *The Urban Southwest: A Profile History of Albuquerque, El Paso, Phoenix, and Tucson*. El Paso: Texas Western Press, 1982.
Mayer, Martin. *The Greatest-Ever Bank Robbery: The Collapse of the Savings and Loan Industry*. New York: Charles Scribner and Sons, 1990.
Morison, Bradley G., and Kay Fliehr. *In Search of an Audience: How an Audience Was Found for the Tyrone Guthrie Theater*. New York: Pitman Publishing, 1968.
Nash, Gerald. *The American West in the Twentieth Century: A Short History of an Urban Oasis*. Albuquerque: University of New Mexico Press, 1977.
____________. *The American West Transformed: The Impact of World War Two*. Bloomington: Indian University Press, 1985.
____________. *World War II and the West: Reshaping the Economy*. Lincoln: University of Nebraska Press, 1990.
Nugent, Walter. *Into the West: A Story of Its People*. New York: Vintage Books, 1999.
Pizzo, Stephen, Mary Fricker, and Paul Muolo. *Inside Job: The Looting of America's Savings and Loans*. New York: McGraw-Hill, 1989.
Pulliam, Russell. *Publisher Gene Pulliam: Last of the Newspaper Titans*. Ottawa, Ill.: Jameson Books, 1984.
Rybczynski, Witold. *A Clearing in the Distance: Frederick Law Olmsted and America in the Nineteenth Century*. New York: Scribner, 2000.
Sarda, Michel F. *John Henry Waddell: The Art and the Artist*. Phoenix: Bridgewood Press, 1996.
Schweikert, Larry. *A History of Banking in Arizona*. Tucson: University of Arizona Press, 1982.
Sheridan, Thomas. *Arizona: A History*. Tucson: University of Arizona Press, 1995.
Smith, Jim. *The Bob Herberger Story*. Phoenix: Jim Smith, 1990.
Taubman, Howard. *The Making of the American Theatre*. New York: Coward-McCann, 1965.
Vaughan, Stuart. *A Possible Theatre*. New York: McGraw-Hill, 1969.
Waddell, John Henry, and Ann R. Mealy. *The Beauty of Individual Differences*. Flagstaff: Northland Press, 1985.
Watkins, Ronald J. *High Crimes and Misdemeanors: The Term and Trial of Former Governor Evan Mecham*. New York: William Morrow and Company, 1990.
Weber, David J. *The Spanish Frontier in North America*. New Haven: Yale University Press, 1994.
____________. *The Mexican Frontier, 1821–1846: The American Southwest Under Mexico*. Albuquerque: University of New Mexico Press, 1982.
White, Richard. *It's Your Misfortune and None of My Own: A New History of the American West*. Norman: University of Oklahoma Press, 1993.
Wiley, Peter, and Robert Gottlieb. *Empires in the Sun: The Rise of the New American West*. New York: Putnam and Sons, 1982.
Zeigler, Joseph Wesley. *Regional Theater: The Revolutionary Stage*. Minneapolis: University of Minnesota Press, 1973.

Journal Articles

August, Jack L., Jr. "Old Arizona and the New Conservative Agenda: The Hayden versus Mecham Senate Campaign of 1962." *Journal of Arizona History* 41 (winter 2000).
Glaeser, Edward. "The Economics of Cities." *National Bureau of Economic Research* (December 1997).
____________. "The Economics of Place-making Policies," *Brookings Paper on Economic Activity*. Brookings Institution: Washington, D.C., 2008.
Konig, Michael. "Phoenix in the 1950s: Urban Growth in the 'Sunbelt.'" *Arizona and the West* 24 (1982).

Lamar, Howard R. "Persistent Frontier: The West in the Twentieth Century." *Western Historical Quarterly* 4 (January 1973).
Luckingham, Bradford. "Urban Development in Arizona: The Rise of Phoenix." *Journal of Arizona History* 22 (summer 1981).
Ridge, Martin. "Ray Allen Billington, Western History, and American Exceptionalism." *Pacific Historical Review* 56 (November 1987).
Robbins, William G. "The 'Plundered Province' Thesis and Recent Historiography of the American West." *Pacific Historical Review* 55 (November 1986).
Schwarzer, Mitchell. "Myth of Permanence and Transience in the Discussion of Historic Preservation in the United States," *Journal of Architectural Education*, 48, no. 1 (September 1994).
Worster, Donald. "New West, True West: Interpreting the Region's History." *Western Historical Quarterly* 18 (April 1987).

Archive and Manuscript Collections

Arizona Republic, Photo Archives, Phoenix, Arizona.
Arizona Theatre Company, Photo Archive Collection, Arizona Theatre Company, Tucson, Arizona.
Dennis DeConcini Congressional Papers Collection, Special Collections, University of Arizona Library, Tuscon.
Herberger Theater Center Collection, Herberger Family Papers, Scottsdale, Arizona.
Herberger Theater Photo Archive Collection, Herberger Theater Center, Phoenix, Arizona.
Margaret Taylor Hance Papers, 1971–1990, Department of Archives and Special Collections, Arizona State University, Tempe.
Newton Rosenzweig Collection, Arizona Historical Foundation, Hayden Library, Arizona State University, Tempe.
Richard Mallery Papers, Snell & Wilmer, Phoenix, Arizona.
The Personal and Political Papers of Barry M. Goldwater, Arizona Historical Foundation, Hayden Library, Arizona State University, Tempe.

Newspapers and Periodicals

Arizona Business Gazette
Arizona Capitol Times (Phoenix)
Arizona Daily Star (Tucson)
Arizona Daily Sun (Flagstaff)
Arizona Republic (Phoenix)
Daily Dispatch (Casa Grande, Arizona)
Los Angeles Times
Metro Phoenix Magazine
New Times (Phoenix)
New York Times
Phoenix Business Journal
Phoenix Gazette
Phoenix Magazine
Saturday Evening Post
Scottsdale Progress
The Daily Courier (Prescott)
Tucson Daily Citizen
Tucson Weekly

Interviews

Jessica Andrews
Harriet Babbitt
Ray Bladine
Richard Bowers

Brent Brown*
Frances Cohen
Marvin Cohen*
Shelly Cohn
Andrew Conlin
Julie Dalgleish
Dino DeConcini
Mark DeMichele
Terry Goddard
Pamela Grant
John Hall
G. Robert Herberger*
Gary Herberger
Jeanne Herberger
Katherine Herberger*
Adrienne Hirsch
C. A. Howlett
John Hudak
Edward "Bud" Jacobson*
Scott Jacobson
Selden Kent
Kevin Keogh
Everett King*
Peter Lesnik
Barbara Levy
Bradford Luckingham
Frances Mallery*
Kathleen Mallery
Richard Mallery
Mark Mettes
Myra Millinger
Kevin Moore
Bradley Morison*
Cindy Myers
Cecilia Parkston
A. J. "Jack" Pfister*
Henry Sargent
Karen Scates
Leon Scioscia
Maurice Sevigny
William Shover
David Sprenthall
Jack Tevlin
Keith Turley*
Harold "Chip" Ulrich
Deborah Whitehurst
**Now deceased*

Unpublished Manuscripts

Mallery, Kathleen. "In the Arena." Author's files, n.d. Photocopy.
Shover, William. "No Good Deed Shall Go Unpunished: The Story of Greater Phoenix Metropolitan Goals to Phoenix 40 to Greater Phoenix Leadership, 1974–1993." Author's files, n.d. Photocopy.

Index

Page numbers in *italics* indicate photographs.

B

C

D

G

H

I

J

K

L

M

R

U

V